Early Praise for *Programming Phoenix 1.4*

Programming Phoenix offers a very engaging hands-on approach without compromising depth in content, making it a balanced source of knowledge for beginners and hackers alike. The authors' credibility comes not only from the fact that they are creators of Elixir and Phoenix, but for their experience in the field designing, building, and scaling big apps—and that completely shows in this book.

➤ **João Augusto B.C. Alves**
   Software Consultant, Plataformatec

Programming Phoenix will provide you with the most in-depth, cutting-edge insights into how to harness the full power of the Phoenix framework. If you want to be the best, learn from the best.

➤ **Tetiana Dushenkivska**
   Creator of ElixirCards, Clever Bunny

I write Elixir for a living, and *Programming Phoenix* was exactly what I needed. It filled in the sticky details, like how to tie authentication into web applications and channels. It also showed me how to layer services with OTP. The experience of Chris and José makes all of the difference in the world.

➤ **Eric Meadows-Jönsson**
   Elixir Core Team

Phoenix gives you all the tools needed to handle very complex problems in a very elegant way. *Programming Phoenix* gives you all the tips you need to solve such problems. It's a must have.

➤ **Marcos Ramos**
   Senior Elixir Developer, Plataformatec

Even if you have no current plans to write a Phoenix web app, you need to read *Programming Phoenix*. The insights this book gives into Elixir, Erlang, and OTP—their strengths, and the corresponding thoughtful design patterns that went into the Phoenix framework—are invaluable to any developer in the Elixir/Erlang ecosystem.

➤ **Mike Binns**
   Senior Software Engineer, Dockyard

Programming Phoenix ≥ 1.4

Productive |> Reliable |> Fast

Chris McCord

Bruce Tate

José Valim

The Pragmatic Bookshelf

Raleigh, North Carolina

Many of the designations used by manufacturers and sellers to distinguish their products are claimed as trademarks. Where those designations appear in this book, and The Pragmatic Programmers, LLC was aware of a trademark claim, the designations have been printed in initial capital letters or in all capitals. The Pragmatic Starter Kit, The Pragmatic Programmer, Pragmatic Programming, Pragmatic Bookshelf, PragProg and the linking *g* device are trademarks of The Pragmatic Programmers, LLC.

Every precaution was taken in the preparation of this book. However, the publisher assumes no responsibility for errors or omissions, or for damages that may result from the use of information (including program listings) contained herein.

Our Pragmatic books, screencasts, and audio books can help you and your team create better software and have more fun. Visit us at *https://pragprog.com*.

The team that produced this book includes:

Publisher: Andy Hunt
VP of Operations: Janet Furlow
Managing Editor: Susan Conant
Development Editor: Jacquelyn Carter
Copy Editor: Jasmine Kwityn
Indexing: Potomac Indexing, LLC
Layout: Gilson Graphics

For sales, volume licensing, and support, please contact *support@pragprog.com*.

For international rights, please contact *rights@pragprog.com*.

ISBN-13: 978-1-68050-226-8
Book version: P1.0—October 2019

Contents

Part I — Building with Functional MVC

Part II — Writing Interactive and Maintainable Applications

Acknowledgments

Most of this book is written in a collective voice, but acknowledgments are deep and personal things. We'll speak a little here as a team before expressing some individual gratitude. You'll notice that of the three of us Chris has the most to say, which is fitting since he is the creator of Phoenix and has been invested in it from the very beginning.

The endeavor of writing a book touches each author in their own way. Writing a beta book means this process often happens in the public eye so each author's job is made simultaneously more difficult. Criticisms are levied against an unfinished product, but adjustments can be made in real time resulting in a better book and surprising interactions with readers. Thanks to all of our beta readers who waited with patience as Chris released two versions of Phoenix and LiveView.

As a team, we'd like to thank this production crew. It's been the finest any of us have ever worked with. Potomac Indexing, LLC, handled our indexing, Jasmine Kwityn did our copyedit, and Janet Furlow managed the endless production details.

These contributions were invaluable, but we'd also like to single one out for deeper praise. Jackie Carter is more than an editor. After working with us year after year, the relationship has transcended mere editorial advice. She's a friend and mentor. This book was trying but your voice shaped it reliably and skillfully.

Our reviewers worked hard to provide excellent feedback, even though the code serving as the foundation for this book was constantly shifting. Of course, we had our formal technical reviews. We'd like to thank Lance Halvorsen, Doug Yun, Marcos Ramos, Elaine Watanabe, Luke Imhoff, Mike Binns, and João Britto for providing excellent feedback.

This book spent a long time in beta; perhaps too long. You will ultimately benefit from that with a better book. The advice and care our beta readers took to fill in errors and make suggestions was fantastic. Finally, thanks to all of the folks who have supported us with reviews, kind words, and meaningful conversations.

José Valim

Elixir has been a labor of love and a project that has exceeded my wildest expectations. Elixir wouldn't exist without the support of my partners at Plataformatec. They were the first to believe Elixir could make a dent in the world, and their investments in the community have helped Elixir grow with strength and grace.

Getting this far wouldn't have been possible without the unconditional support of my wife, Małgosia. Most of Elixir was written on a small desk placed in the corner of our bedroom. Of all the corners in the world, I can't imagine a better one.

Bruce Tate

A completed book fills a hole on many bookshelves but leaves other holes behind. Thanks to Maggie, my joy and inspiration, for sharing me with a smile. Introducing a new language to the world is demanding. Sharing our home with this metaphorical guest (which led to more than a few corporal guests) is going above and beyond. What can I say besides thank you? Julia and Kayla, it's been a joy raising you and knowing that you are growing from the two wide-eyed does watching the world change to two tigresses doing the changing. Get ready, world!

Thanks to José and Chris for taking this journey with me; to Francesco for your friendship and companionship; to Brett Wise who has become an extension of me for the great things we want to do in the world. Thanks to JEG2 and Chris K. for being contrarian voices in a world of sameness.

To my mentees, especially Doc, Grace, and Ram (Richard to those who might not know him well), thanks for believing in me and working to be the best people you can. You inspire me.

Chris McCord

First, I would like to thank José Valim for creating Elixir, for his contributions to Phoenix, and for building a community that has been such a pleasure to be a part of. It goes without saying that Phoenix wouldn't be possible without his work on Elixir, but it goes deeper than that. He has my deepest gratitude for setting in motion my dream career, sharing his wisdom on running large open source projects, and being a helpful friend in between hectic releases.

He has shared with the world a true gift, and I can't wait to see where his creativity leads.

Thanks also go to Bruce Tate for contributing his superb writing skills, helping to form the abstractions behind Phoenix, and encouraging me to seek out José's help with the project. His craftsmanship in this book really shows, and it's been a pleasure having him on the team.

I extend my warmest thanks to Brian Cardarella and DockYard, for making early bets on Phoenix, supporting the project's development to get to where we are today, and giving me the chance to work with some of the finest folks in the industry.

Behind many of the open source projects or books you reference day to day is an understanding spouse who bears late nights and all too much laptop time. My deepest love and appreciation goes out to my lovely wife, Jaclyn, for all her support and encouragement throughout the years along the path to Phoenix and writing this book. A life with you is a truly happy one.

And finally, to the community for this great project, I extend both heartfelt appreciation and bright hope that we might continue to build something special, together.

Preface

It doesn't seem possible, but it's been three years since we released the first edition of this book. Indeed, the Phoenix team has been busy. The additions of Channel Presence and LiveView are changing the way all programmers think about web development. The underlying directories have changed, having a rippling impact on all of the code in this book. Ecto has also produced a major release.

Through it all, one thing remains constant. Phoenix is still positioned as one of the most productive and scalable web development platforms available anywhere. From cryptocurrencies to media companies to commerce, Elixir developers are using Phoenix to push the boundaries of what's possible. In this book, the same folks who built Elixir and Phoenix will show you how you can do the same.

Is This Book for You?

If you've followed Phoenix for any period of time, you already know that this book is the definitive resource for Phoenix programming. If you're using Phoenix or are seriously considering doing professional Elixir development, you're going to want this book. It's packed with insights from the team that created it. Find just one tip in these pages, and the book will pay for itself many times over. This section seeks to answer a different question, though. Beyond folks who've already decided to make an investment in Phoenix, who should buy this book?

Programmers Embracing the Functional Paradigm

Every twenty years or so, new programming paradigms emerge. The industry is currently in the midst of a shift from object-oriented programming to functional programming. If you've noticed this trend, you know that a half dozen or so functional languages are competing for mindshare. The best way to understand a programming language is to go beyond basic online tutorials to see how to approach nontrivial programs.

With *Programming Phoenix*, we don't shy away from difficult problems such as customizing authentication, designing for scale, or creating interactive web pages. As you explore the language, you'll learn how the pieces fit together to solve difficult problems and how functional programming helps us do it elegantly. When you're done, you might not choose Phoenix, but you'll at least understand the critical pieces that make it popular and if those pieces are likely to work for you.

Developers Seeking to Modernize

Developers from many web frameworks written in many languages can find something here. Phoenix measures response times in microseconds, and it has been shown to handle millions of concurrent WebSocket connections on a single machine without sacrificing the productivity we've come to appreciate. If you're pushing your favorite framework to be more scalable or more interactive, you're not alone. You're going to find Phoenix powerful and interesting. And if you are trying to build single page apps or provide a more consistent or interactive experience for your user, you'll find Elixir one of the best available languages for solving that problem, period.

Dynamic Programmers Looking for a Mature Environment

Like the authors of this book, you may be a fan of dynamic languages like JavaScript, Python, and Ruby. You may have used them in production or even contributed to those ecosystems. Many developers like us are looking for similar flexibility but with a more robust runtime experience. We may love the programming experience in those languages, but we often find ourselves worn out by the many compromises we have to make for performance, concurrency, and maintainability. Phoenix resonates with us because many of the creators of this ecosystem built it to solve these problems.

Elixir is a modern dynamic language built on the three-decades-old, battle-tested Erlang runtime. Elixir macros bring a lot of the flexibility that Ruby, Python, and JavaScript developers came to love, but those dynamic features are quarantined to compile time. With Elixir, during runtime, you have a consistent system with great type support that's generally unseen in other dynamic languages.

Mix these features with the concurrency power, and you'll see why Phoenix provides such excellent performance for everything on the web, and beyond.

Java Developers Seeking More

When Java emerged twenty years ago, it had everything a frustrated C++ community was missing. It was object-oriented, secure, ready for the Internet, and simple, especially when compared to other C++ alternatives at the time. As the Java community flourished and consolidated, the tools and support came. Just about everyone supported Java, and that ubiquity led to a language dominance that we'd never seen before.

As Java has aged, it's lost some of that luster. As the committees that shaped Java compromised, Java lost some of the edge and leadership that the small leadership team provided in early versions. Backward compatibility means that the language evolves slowly as new solutions emerge. You might find that all of that early ubiquity has led to an experience that's more fragmented or bloated than you like it. You may enjoy the extra punch of emerging languages like Elixir. The Java concurrency story *does* place plenty of burden on the developer, leaving libraries that may or may not be safe for production systems to cope with increasingly parallel designs.

If you're a Java developer looking for where to go next, or a JVM-language developer looking for a better concurrency story, Phoenix would mean leaving the JVM behind. Maybe that's a good thing. You'll find a unified, integrated story in Phoenix with sound abstractions on top. The choice is up to you.

Erlang Developers Doing Integrated Web Development

As time goes on, the number of Erlang developers who also gain proficiency in Elixir is growing. The toolchain for Phoenix is spectacular, and many of the tools that exist for Erlang can work in this ecosystem as well. If you're an Erlang developer, you may want to take advantage of Mix's excellent scripting for the development, build, and testing workflow. You may like the package management in Hex, or the neat composition of concerns in the Plug library. You may want to use macros to extend the language for your business, or test with greater leverage. You'll have new programming features like protocols or structs.

If you do decide to embrace Elixir, that doesn't mean you need to leave Erlang behind. You'll still be able to use the Erlang libraries you enjoy today, including the Erlang process model and full OTP integration. You'll be able to access your OTP 'GenServer's directly from the Elixir environment, and directly call libraries without the need for extra complex syntax. If these terms aren't familiar to you, don't worry. We'll explore each of them over the course of the book.

Heat Seekers

As web demands grow, an increasing number of developers require infrastructure that will serve more users reliably. If you need raw power supported by a rich language, we have a solution and the numbers to back it up. You'll have to work for it, but you'll get much better speed and reliability when you're done. We've run a single chat room on one box supporting two million users. That means that each new message had to go out two million times. Phoenix performs well out of the box and our numbers improve as more cores are added. If you need speed, we have the tonic for what ails you.

Others

Certainly, this book isn't for everyone. We do think that if you're in one of these groups, you'll find something you like here. We're equally confident that folks that we haven't described will pick up this book and find something valuable. If you're one of those types, let us know your story.

About this Book

This book is about building web applications with the primary web framework for the Elixir language, Phoenix. In its pages we will walk you through building a web application, piece by piece.

In Part I, we will show you how to build a traditional model-view-controller (MVC) application. We'll guide you through the Phoenix landscape, showing you in intimate detail how things are stitched together. We will show you how to build a controller and how to organize your business logic into modules called contexts. Along the way, we'll build our own authentication and build database-backed code with a database library called Ecto.

In Part II, we will explore channels and presence, Phoenix features that allow a highly interactive experience. Then we'll learn to tie those interactive features into Elixir's extensive OTP, a framework for building concurrent, self-healing projects. We will focus on techniques for productively writing code that will be easier to maintain in the future.

To illustrate both parts of this book fully, we will build a web application together. The application will let users take videos and annotate them with real-time events.

Online Resources

The apps and examples shown in this book can be found at the Pragmatic Programmers website for this book.[1] You'll also find the errata-submission form, where you can report problems with the text or make suggestions for future versions.

When you're ready, turn the page and we'll get started. Let's build something together!

---

1. http://pragprog.com/book/phoenix14/

## CHAPTER 1

Introducing Phoenix

The web has gone real time. The days of clicking links to load full pages are over. Websites are as interactive as desktop applications these days, if not more so. Servers manipulate widgets on a page with small data exchanges. Pages ship form data up piece by piece as it becomes available instead of waiting for one massive update. Today's web developers need a framework designed from the ground up around a real-time architecture, and Phoenix is that framework.

Ironically, most of the individual pieces from Phoenix can also be found in other places. You'll find metaprogramming capabilities that remind you of Lisp and domain-specific languages (DSLs) that remind you at times of Ruby. Our method of composing services with a series of functional transformations is reminiscent of Clojure's Ring. We achieved high throughput and reliability by climbing onto the shoulders of Erlang. Similarly, some of the groundbreaking features like channels and reactive-friendly APIs combine the best features of some of the best JavaScript frameworks but Phoenix makes it work at scale. This precise cocktail of features, where each feature multiplies the impact of the next, can't be found elsewhere and that's what makes Phoenix stand out. *Phoenix just feels right.*

After using (and writing about) frameworks spanning a half dozen languages across a couple of decades, we think the precise bundle of goodness that we'll share is powerful enough for the most serious problems you throw at it, beautiful enough to be maintainable for years to come, and—most important—fun to code. Give us a couple of pages and you'll find that the framework represents a great philosophy, one that leverages the reliability and grace of Elixir. You'll have a front-row seat to understand how we made the decisions that define Phoenix and how best to use them to your advantage.

Simply put, Phoenix is about productive, concurrent, beautiful, interactive, and reliable applications. Let's break each of these claims down.

Productive

Phoenix makes programmers productive. Right out of the box, Phoenix gives you everything you'd expect from a web framework:

- A base architecture for your application
- A database access and management library for connecting to databases
- A routing layer for connecting web requests to your code
- A templating language and helpers for you to write HTML
- Flexible and performant JSON encoding and decoding for external APIs
- Internationalization strategies for taking your application to the world
- All the breadth and power behind Erlang and Elixir so you can grow

Like all web frameworks, Phoenix provides a good cross section of features as functions so users don't have to code their own. However, features are not enough.

Productivity vs. Maintainability

All framework designers must walk a tightrope. Frameworks must anticipate change by allowing customization, but presenting customization options introduces complexity. Each new feature simply makes the high wire act more treacherous. Let's call one side of the line *productivity* and the other *maintainability*.

When developers have to learn too much too soon, they must slow down to absorb information. One way to keep developers productive early on is hiding details. When a framework designer leans too far this way, developers must pay a price because at some point, the framework will hide information their users need to solve a critical problem. Unusual customizations lead to hours of tedious searching for some mystery incantation to make things work.

Use such a framework long enough and you'll inevitably make changes that cause your application to drift away from the designers' intentions, setting yourself up for an eternal upstream battle against the framework. Whether it's a conflicting upgrade or an optimization that isn't compatible with your change doesn't matter. The framework developer's desire for short-term productivity has cost users long-term maintainability. You can find plenty of stale issues inside the issue trackers for both private and commercial web frameworks, telling this tale with stark clarity.

Sometimes, understanding this limitation, framework designers lean too far in the opposite direction. Too many options in too many places can also have rippling consequences. Options presented in the wrong way force users to make early uninformed decisions. Crippling detail work slowly starves users of the time they need at the beginning of a project, when productivity is the most important.

Phoenix takes a slightly different approach as it walks this tightrope. Phoenix is an opinionated framework that favors convention over configuration. But rather than *hiding complexity*, it *layers complexity*, providing details piece by piece.

Phoenix lets users see exactly what's happening by providing an explicit list of every bit of code a specific route will invoke, one after another. Phoenix hides details in layers by breaking its functionality into small functions and modules and naming them well so they can tell the story. Every application using Phoenix has an endpoint that looks like this:

```
defmodule MyApp.Endpoint do
  use Phoenix.Endpoint, otp_app: :my_app

  plug Plug.Static, ...
  plug Plug.RequestId
  plug Plug.Telemetry, ...
  plug Plug.Parsers, ...
  plug Plug.MethodOverride
  plug Plug.Head
  plug Plug.Session, ...
  plug MyApp.Router
end
```

We are going to dive deep into the mechanics later in the book. For now, what matters is that we have an overview of what our web application provides at a high level.

Rather than forcing users to configure the server with thousands of tiny decisions, Phoenix provides a default outline. If all you want to do is peek under the hood, you can open up a file. You don't need to modify this base outline at all, but when it's time to make that obscure change, you can edit this outline to your heart's content.

So often, productivity means avoiding blocks, and that means developers must have adequate information. Couple the layered architecture with Elixir's fantastic tools for documentation and you have the tools to be quite productive. For example, you can learn more about any of the components above by simply typing h Plug.Session in your Elixir terminal, or by accessing the documentation online[1] or directly in your favorite editor.

At the end of the day, Phoenix wants to optimize both productivity and maintainability. After all, maintainability means productivity over time.

Functional Programming 101: Immutability

One of the secrets for Phoenix's long-term productivity comes from a trait shared across many functional programming languages: immutability.

Imagine the following code:

```
list = [1, 2, 3]
do_something(list)
list
```

In most programming languages, you cannot assert with a 100% guarantee the list will still be [1, 2, 3] after calling do_something. That's because do_something can change the list in place. In Elixir, that's simply not possible. Our data structures are immutable, so instead of changing the list, we can only build new lists. Therefore our code is written as a series of small functions that receive everything they have to work with as input and return everything they have changed.

This plays a very important role in code readability and maintainability. You will spend much less time and brain cycles trying to figure out what object changed what or what is the current state of a certain component.

While this is a small example, you will find working with Elixir and functional programming to be full of small changes and improvements that make your code easier to understand, both for your teammates and your future self.

Concurrent

Over the last decade, we have been hearing more and more about concurrency. If you have never used a language with first-class concurrency support before, you may be wondering what all the fuss is about. In this section, we will cover why concurrency matters in the context of web applications and how Phoenix developers leverage it to build fast, performant applications. First let's talk about the different types of concurrency.

---

1. https://hexdocs.pm/plug/Plug.Session.html

Types of Concurrency

For our purposes, let's think of concurrency as a web application's ability to process two or more web requests at the same time. The simplest way to handle multiple requests is by executing them one right after the other, but that strategy isn't very efficient. To process a request, most web apps need to perform I/O such as making database requests or communicating with an external API. While you're waiting for those external services to complete, you could start working on the next request. This is I/O concurrency. Most programming languages provide I/O concurrency out of the box or via libraries. Sometimes, however, the I/O concurrency abstraction ends up leaking to the developer, who must write code in a confusing way, with callbacks of some form.

Another type of concurrency is multi-core concurrency, which focuses on the CPU. If your machine has more than one core, one core processes one request while a second core processes another one. For the rest of this discussion, we will consider machines with four cores in our examples, which is commonplace, as even smart watches have multiple cores today.

There are two main ways to leverage multi-core concurrency:

- With an operating system process per core: If your machine has four cores, you will start four different instances of your web application.

- With user space routines: If your machine has four cores, you start a single instance of your web application that is capable of using all cores efficiently.

The downside of using operating system processes is that those four instances cannot share memory. This solution typically leads to higher resource usage and more complex solutions.

Thanks to the Erlang VM, Elixir provides I/O concurrency without callbacks, with user-space multi-core concurrency. In a nutshell, this means Elixir developers write code in the simplest and most straightforward fashion and the virtual machine takes care of using all of the resources, both CPU and I/O, for you. The result is a better application. Let's talk about why.

Simpler Solutions

One issue with concurrency via operating system processes is the poor resource usage. Each core needs a separate instance of your application. If you have 16 cores, you need 16 instances, each on its own memory space.

With user space concurrency, you always start a single instance of your application. As you receive new requests, they are naturally spread throughout all cores. Furthermore, they all share the same memory. This small drawback might seem a little vague, so let's make it more explicit by looking at one specific problem, a common dashboard.

Imagine each user in your application has a dashboard. The data in this dashboard takes around 200ms to load and it takes about 100kB in memory. Since we want to provide good experience to users, we decide to cache this data. Let's say your web application supports only operating system process concurrency. That means each application instance needs to keep its own cache. For ten thousand (10,000) active users, that's a 1GB data cache for all of the dashboards *per instance*. For 16 cores with 16 instances, that's 16GB of cache, and it's only for the dashboard data. Furthermore, since each instance has its own cache shared across all users, each cache will be less effective at startup time because cache hit rates will be lower, leading to poor startup times.

To save memory and improve the hit rates, you may decide to put the data in an external caching system, such as Redis or memcached. This external cache increases your complexity for both development and deployment concerns because you now have a new external dependency. Your application is much faster than it would be if you were simply querying the database, but every time users access the dashboard, your application still needs to go over the network, load the cache data, and deserialize it.

In Elixir, since we start a single web application instance across all cores, we have a single cache of 1GB, shared across all cores, regardless of whether the machine has 1, 4, or 16 cores. We don't need to add external dependencies and we can serve the dashboard as quickly as possible because we don't need to go over the network.

Does this mean Elixir eliminates the need for caching systems? Surely not. For example, if you have a high number of machines running in production, you may still want an external caching system as a fallback to the local one. We just don't need external cache systems nearly as often. Elixir developers typically get a lot of mileage from their servers, without a need to resort to external caching. For example, Bleacher Report was able to replace 150 instances running Ruby on Rails with 5 Phoenix instances, which has been proven to handle eight times their average load at a fraction of the cost.[2]

---

2. https://www.techworld.com/apps-wearables/how-elixir-helped-bleacher-report-handle-8x-more-traffic-3653957/

And while this is just one example, we have the option to make similar trade-offs at different times in our stacks. For simple asynchronous processing, you don't need a background job framework. For real-time messaging across nodes, you don't need an external queue system. We may still use those tools, but Elixir developers don't need to reach for them as often as other developers might. We can avoid or delay buying into complex solutions, spending more time on domain and business logic.

Performance for Developers

Developers are users too. Elixir's concurrency can have a dramatic impact on our experience as we write software. When we compile software, run tests, or even fetch dependencies, Elixir is using all cores in your machine, and these shorter cycles over the course of a day can stack up.

Here is a fun story. In its first versions, Elixir used to start as many tests concurrently as the number of cores in your machine. For instance, if your machine has four cores, it would run at most four tests at the same time. This is a great choice if your tests are mostly using the CPU.

However, for web applications, it is most likely that your tests are also waiting on I/O, due to the database or external systems. Based on this insight, the Elixir team bumped the default number of concurrent tests to double the number of cores. The result? Users reported their test suites became 20%-30% faster. Overall, it is not uncommon for us to hear about web applications running thousands of tests in under 10 seconds.

But Concurrency Is Hard

You may have heard that concurrency is hard and we don't dispute that. We *do* claim that traditional languages make concurrency considerably harder than it should be. Many of the issues with concurrency in traditional programming languages come from in-memory race conditions, caused by mutability.

Let's take an example. If you have two user space routines trying to remove an element from the same list, you can have a segmentation fault or similarly scary error, as those routines may change the same address in memory at the same time. This means developers need to track where all of the state is and how it is changing across multiple routines.

In functional programming languages, such as Elixir, the data is immutable. If you want to remove an element from a list, you don't change that list in memory. You create a new list instead. That means as a functional developer, you don't need to be concerned with bugs that are caused by concurrent access to memory. You'll deal only with concurrency issues that are natural to your domain.

For example, what is the issue with this code sample?

```
product = get_product_from_the_database(id)
product = set_product_pageviews(get_product_pageviews(product) + 1)
update_product_in_the_database(product)
```

Consider a product with 100 pageviews. Now imagine two requests are happening at the same time. Each request reads the product from the database, sees that the counter is 100, increments the counter to 101, and updates the product in the database. When both requests are done, the end result *could* be 101 in the database while we expected it to be 102. This is a race condition that will happen regardless of the programming language you are using. Different databases will have different solutions to the problem. The simplest one is to perform the increment atomically in the database.

Therefore, when talking about web applications, concurrency issues are natural. Using a language like Elixir and a framework such as Phoenix makes all of the difference in the world. When your chosen environment is equipped with excellent tools to reason about concurrency, you'll have all of the tools you need to grow as a developer and improve your reasoning about concurrency in the wild.

In Elixir, our user-space abstraction for concurrency is also called *processes*, but do not confuse them with operating system processes. Elixir processes are abstractions inside the Erlang VM that are very cheap and very lightweight. Here is how you can start 100,000 of them in a couple of seconds:

```
for i <- 1..100_000 do
  spawn(fn -> Process.sleep(:infinity) end)
end
```

From now on, when you read the word *process*, you should think about Elixir's lightweight processes rather than operating system processes. That's enough about concurrency for now but we will be sure to revisit this topic later.

Beautiful Code

Elixir is perhaps the first functional language to support Lisp-style macros with a more natural syntax. This feature, like a *template for code*, is not always the right tool for everyday users, but macros are invaluable for extending the Elixir language to add the common features all web servers need to support.

For example, web servers need to map routes onto functions that do the job:

```
pipeline :browser do
  plug :accepts, ["html"]
  plug :fetch_session
  plug :protect_from_forgery
end

pipeline :api do
  plug :accepts, ["json"]
end

scope "/", MyApp do
  pipe_through :browser

  get "/users", UserController, :index
  ...
end

scope "/api/", MyApp do
  pipe_through :api

  ...
end
```

You'll see this code a little later. You don't have to understand exactly what it does. For now, know that the first group of functions will run for all browser-based applications, and the second group of functions will run for all JSON-based applications. The third and fourth blocks define which URLs will go to which controller.

You've likely seen code like this before. Here's the point. You don't have to sacrifice beautiful code to use a functional language. Your code organization can be even better. In Phoenix, you won't have to read through inheritance chains to know how your code works. You'll just build a pipeline for each group of routes that work the same way.

You can find an embarrassing number of frameworks that break this kind of code down into something that is horribly inefficient. Consultancies have made millions on performance tuning by doing nothing more than tuning route tables. This Phoenix example reduces your router to pattern matching that's further optimized by the virtual machine, becoming extremely fast. We've built a layer that ties together Elixir's pattern matching with the macro syntax to provide an excellent routing layer, and one that fits the Phoenix framework well.

You'll find many more examples like this one, such as Ecto's elegant query syntax or how we express requests as a pipeline of functions that compose well and run quickly. In each case, you're left with code that's easier to read, write, and understand.

We're not here to tell you that macros are the solution to all problems, or that you should use a DSL when a function call should do. We'll use macros when they can dramatically simplify your daily tasks, making them easier to understand and produce. When we do build a DSL, you can bet that we've done our best to make it fast and intelligent.

Effortlessly Extensible Architecture

The Phoenix framework gives you the right set of abstractions for extension. Your applications will break down into individual functions. Rather than rely on other mechanisms like inheritance that hide intentions, you'll roll up your functions into *pipelines*, where each function feeds into the next. It's like building a shopping list for your requests.

In this book, you'll write your own authentication code, based on secure open standards. You'll see how easy it is to tune behavior to your needs and extend it when you need to.

The Phoenix abstractions, in their current incarnation, are new, but each has withstood the test of time. When it's time to extend Phoenix—whether you're plugging in your own session store or doing something as comprehensive as attaching third-party applications like a Twitter wrapper—you'll have the right abstractions available to ensure that the ideas can scale as well as they did when you wrote the first line of code.

Interactive

By this point, you may be noticing that each concept builds on the previous one. Elixir makes productive, explicit layers available to programmers who can use them to build concurrent applications. Phoenix introduces beautiful, concurrent abstractions for use in beautiful APIs.

For the first four years, the Phoenix team worked at building this infrastructure, and this past year we've seen the culmination of this investment in new, exciting APIs for building interactive applications. The best example is Phoenix LiveView, a library for building applications without custom JavaScript. Until the right infrastructure was in place, LiveView could be only a dream.

Building interactive applications does require APIs that shield many different concerns from an end user, but APIs are just the tip of the iceberg. Underneath that tip is a tremendous amount of infrastructure. Let's take a peak beneath the surface.

Scaling by Forgetting

Traditional web servers scale by treating each tiny user interaction as an identical stateless request. The application doesn't save state between requests at all. It simply looks up the user and simultaneously looks up the context of the conversation in a user session. Presto. All scalability problems go away because there's only one type of connection.

But there's a cost. The developer must keep track of the state for each request, and that burden can be particularly arduous for newer, more interactive applications with intimate, long-running rich interactions. As a developer, until now, you've been forced to make a choice between applications that intentionally forget important details to scale and applications that try to remember too much and break under load.

Processes and Channels

With Elixir, you can create hundreds of thousands of *lightweight processes* without breaking a sweat. Lightweight processes also mean lightweight connections, and that matters because *connections can be conversations*. Whether you're building a chat on a game channel or a map to the grocery store, you won't have to juggle the details by hand anymore. This application style is called *channels*, and Phoenix makes it easy. Here's what a typical channels feature might look like:

```
def handle_in("new_annotation", params, socket) do
  broadcast! socket, "new_annotation", %{
    user: %{username: "anon"},
    body: params["body"],
    at: params["at"]
  }

  {:reply, :ok, socket}
end
```

You don't have to understand the details. Just understand that when your application needs to connect your users and broadcast information in real time, your code can get much simpler and faster.

Even now, you'll see many different types of frameworks begin to support channel-style features, from Java to JavaScript and even Ruby. Here's the problem. None of them comes with the simple guarantees that Phoenix has: isolation and concurrency. Isolation guarantees that if a bug affects one channel, all other channels continue running. Breaking one feature won't bleed into other site functionality. Concurrency means one channel can never block another one, whether code is waiting on the database or crunching data. This key advantage means that the UI never becomes unresponsive because the user started a heavy action. Without those guarantees, the development bogs down into a quagmire of low-level concurrency details.

You may also be wondering whether keeping an open connection per user can scale. The Phoenix team decided to benchmark their channels abstraction and they were able to reach two million connections on a single node.[3] And while that proves Phoenix Channels scale vertically (i.e., on powerful machines), it also scales horizontally. If you need to run a cluster of Phoenix instances, Phoenix will broadcast messages across all nodes out of the box, without a need for external dependencies.

It's true, you can build these kinds of applications without Phoenix, but building them without the guarantees of isolation and concurrency is never pleasant. The results will almost universally be infected with reliability and scalability problems, and your users will never be as satisfied as you'd like to make them.

Presence and LiveView

As Phoenix grows and matures, the team continues to provide tools developers can use to build interactive applications. The first addition was support for tracking presence. Tracking which users are connected to a cluster of machines is a notoriously difficult problem. But in Phoenix, it takes as little as ten lines of code to track which users, fridges, cars, doors, or houses are connected to your application. In a world that is getting more and more connected, this feature is essential.

The best part about presence is that it doesn't require any external dependencies. Regardless of whether you are running two Phoenix nodes or twenty, those nodes will communicate with each other, making sure to track connections regardless of where they happen in the cluster. You get a fantastic feature set right out of the box.

The most recent interactive development tool is LiveView. LiveView allows developers to build rich, interactive real-time applications without writing custom JavaScript.[4] For the JavaScript developers out there, it can be summarized as "server-side React". Here is a simple counter built with LiveView:

---

3. https://phoenixframework.org/blog/the-road-to-2-million-websocket-connections
4. https://dockyard.com/blog/2018/12/12/phoenix-liveview-interactive-real-time-apps-no-need-to-write-javascript

```elixir
defmodule DemoWeb.CounterLive do
  use Phoenix.LiveView

  def render(assigns) do
    ~L"""
    <span><%= @val %></span>
    <button phx-click="inc">+</button>
    """
  end

  def mount(_session, socket) do
    {:ok, assign(socket, val: 0)}
  end

  def handle_event("inc", _, socket) do
    {:noreply, update(socket, :val, &(&1 + 1))}
  end
end
```

When Phoenix renders the page the first time, it works just like any other static page. That means browsers get a fast first-page view and search engines have something to index. Once rendered, Phoenix connects to the LiveView on the server, using WebSockets and Channels. LiveView applications are breathtakingly simple:

- A function renders a web page.
- That function accepts state as an input and returns a web page as output.
- Events can change that state, bit by bit.

State is a simple data structure that can hold whatever you want it to. Events that change your state can come from a button or a form on a web page. Other events can come from your application, like a low-battery sensor elsewhere in your application.

The best part is that LiveView is smart enough to send only what changes, and only when it changes. And once again, all you need to make this work is Phoenix.

Combine LiveView with Phoenix's ability to broadcast changes and track users in a cluster and you have the most complete tooling for building rich and interactive applications out of the box.

Reliable

As Chris followed José into the Elixir community, he learned to appreciate the frameworks that Erlang programmers have used to make the most reliable applications in the world. Before Elixir, the language of linked and supervised processes wasn't part of his vocabulary. After spending some time with Elixir, he found the missing pieces he'd been seeking.

You see, you might have interactive applications built from beautiful, concurrent, responsive code, but it doesn't matter unless your code is reliable. Erlang applications have always been more reliable than others in the industry. The secret is the process linking structure and the process communication, which allow effective supervision. You can start concurrent tasks and services that are fully supervised. When one crashes, Elixir can restart it in the last known good state, along with any tainted related service. Erlang's supervisors can have supervisors too, so your whole application will have a tree of supervisors.

The nice thing is that you won't have to write that supervision code yourself. By default, Phoenix has set up most of the supervision structure for you. For example, if you want to talk to the database, you need to keep a pool of database connections, and Phoenix provides one out of the box. As you'll see later on, we can monitor and introspect this pool. It's straightforward to study bottlenecks and even emulate failures by crashing database connections on purpose, only to see supervisors establishing new connections in their place. As a programmer, these abstractions will give you the freedom of a carpenter building on a fresh clean slab, *but your foundation solves many of your hardest problems before you even start.* As an administrator, you'll thank us every day of the week because of the support calls that don't come in.

In the next chapter, you'll dive right in. From the beginning, you'll build a quick application, and we'll walk you through each layer of Phoenix. The water is fine. Come on in!

Part I

Building with Functional MVC

In Part I, we'll talk about traditional request/response web applications. We'll walk through the basic layers of Phoenix in great detail. You'll learn how to structure your application into small functions, with each one transforming the results of the previous ones. This pipeline of small functions will lead to the controller, from where we call your model domain and views, but splitting the responsibilities slightly differently from what you've seen elsewhere. You'll also learn to integrate databases through the Ecto persistence layer and even build your own authentication API. Then, you'll learn to test what you've built so far. In short, you'll learn to build traditional applications that are faster, more reliable, and easier to understand.

## CHAPTER 2

The Lay of the Land

Welcome to Phoenix. In this chapter, we're not going to try to sell you too hard. We think that once you begin the work of learning this framework, the benefits will quickly become evident.

You can think of any web server as a function. Each time you type a URL, think of it as a function call to some remote server. That function takes your request and generates some response. As we will see, *a web server is a natural problem for a functional language to solve.*

When all is said and done, each Phoenix application is made of functions. In this chapter, we're going to break down a typical web request, and we'll talk about what happens from the moment the user types the URL to the moment Phoenix returns some result.

Simple Functions

Phoenix is built on Elixir, which is a beautiful language, so we're going to use Elixir to talk about the way the layers of Phoenix fit together. In Elixir, we might have a couple of functions like these:

```
def inc(x), do: x + 1
def dec(x), do: x - 1
```

We can chain together several different function calls like this:

```
2 |> inc |> inc |> dec
```

The |>, or *pipe operator*, takes the value on the left and passes it as the first argument to the function on the right. We call these compositions *pipes* or *pipelines*, and we call each individual function a *segment* or *pipe segment*.

There's a side benefit, though. Pipelines are also functions. That means you can make pipelines of pipelines. This idea will help you understand how the various layers fit together. Let's take a look at what a Phoenix program might look like, using pipes:

```
connection |> phoenix
```

Most of the time, you'd write phoenix(connection), but bear with us for a moment. We're going to expand that phoenix function in a bit. We don't care how the request gets to Phoenix. At some point, we know that a browser establishes a connection with an end user, and then there's this big hairy function called phoenix. We pipe the connection into phoenix, it does its magic, and we're done.

In Phoenix, that connection is the whole universe of things we need to know about a user's request. It is a *struct*, which is a map with a known set of fields. The connection comes in with information about the *request*: whether it's HTTP or HTTPS, what the URL is, what the parameters look like. Then, each layer of Phoenix makes a little change to that connection. When Phoenix is done, that connection will have the response in it.

Where Are All of the Diagrams?

In this book, we're going to try something a little different. We're going to use an experimental alternative to architectural diagrams.

For example, let's say we're showing you how to bake a cake. We could have a little diagram with boxes representing process steps that have beautiful bevels or drop shadows or other embellishments. Such a diagram would give you a quick mental picture of what's happening. Then, you could mentally translate that diagram into code.

We can do better, though. Instead, we could choose to express the same idea with an Elixir pipe, like this:

```
ingredients
|> mix()
|> bake()
```

That code isn't as beautiful as a blinking diagram with fountain fills, but it's tremendously exciting. That ugly text shows you exactly what the layers are, and also how the functions work together. It also helps you build a mental picture of what's happening, because in Phoenix it *is what's happening*. When you understand *that* diagram, you understand Phoenix. You'll actually see code like that throughout the Phoenix framework, so we think it's an excellent way to show how the parts fit together.

Now you know what the API of *every layer of Phoenix looks like.* Functions call other functions, and the first argument for each of those other functions is the connection.

The Layers of Phoenix

Let's take our simplified version of Phoenix and break it down a bit. Let's say that the request is a classic HTTP-style request. (The book will cover the more interactive channels API a little later, but the basic premise will be the same.) As we drill down to the next layer of detail, here's what you see:

```
connection
|> endpoint()
|> router()
|> pipelines()
|> controller()
```

Each request comes in through an endpoint, the first point of contact. It's literally the end, or the beginning, of the Phoenix world. A request comes into an endpoint. From there, requests go into our router layer, which directs a request into the appropriate controller, after passing it through a series of pipelines. As you might expect, a pipeline groups functions together to handle common tasks. You might have a pipeline for browser requests, and another for JSON requests.

Inside Controllers

Web frameworks have been around for a long time. The main pattern we use has been around even longer. The Smalltalk language introduced a pattern called *model-view-controller* (MVC). Models access data, views present data, and controllers coordinate between the two. In a sense, the purpose of a web server is to get requests to functions that perform the right task. In most web frameworks, including Phoenix, that task is called an *action*, and we group like functions together in controllers.

To give you a little more perspective, the controller is also a pipeline of functions, one that looks like this:

```
connection
|> controller()
|> common_services()
|> action()
```

This view of the world may look much like what you'd expect from a typical web framework. The connection flows into the controller and calls common services. In Phoenix, those common services are implemented with Plug. You'll get more details as we go. For now, think of Plug as a strategy for building web applications and a library with a few simple tools to enable that strategy.

In this book our actions will do many different things, from accessing other websites to authenticating a user. Most often, our actions will access a database and render a view. Here's what an action to show a user might look like:

```
connection
|> find_user()
|> view()
|> template()
```

In Phoenix, we like to encapsulate all business logic in simple modules called *contexts*. If you're using a database in Phoenix, you'll probably use Ecto, the persistence layer. If you want to talk to another web application, there are many HTTP clients to choose from. Whether that code interacts with another web server or a database, you will want to keep the controllers clean and skinny.

There you have it. You don't have to memorize all of these layers now, but you've seen the major pieces, and you know how they fit together. After a few pages of theory, you're probably eager to roll up your sleeves and get started.

Installing Your Development Environment

Like many great programming projects, Phoenix builds on some of the best open source projects available. You'll install all of those dependencies now, using the best resources you can find for your own environment.

Elixir Needs Erlang

Erlang provides the base programming virtual machine. It supports our base programming model for concurrency, failover, and distribution. It also provides an exhaustive programming library that's the foundation of the Elixir language. Go download Erlang,[1] choosing the best installation for your environment. You'll want version 20.0 or greater.

Phoenix Needs Elixir

The Elixir programming language powers Phoenix. You can find installation instructions on the Elixir[2] site. You'll want version 1.6 or greater. Before you

---

1. http://www.erlang.org
2. http://elixir-lang.org

work through this book, it would be helpful to know Elixir. Good online resources[3] exist, but we recommend the excellent book *Programming Elixir [Tho16]*, by Dave Thomas, which will get you all of the way through concurrency concepts and OTP. For now, think of OTP as the layer for managing concurrent, distributed services. Rest assured that you'll get more details on OTP later.

You can check to see that Elixir and Erlang are working correctly, like this:

```
$ elixir -v
Elixir 1.8.0
```

Let's also install Hex, Elixir's package manager:

```
$ mix local.hex
* creating ~/.mix/archives/hex-0.19.0
```

Elixir is working, and if you were building strictly a JSON API or a very simple application it would be enough. For this application, since you'll be building both frontend and backend with Phoenix, you need to install a database and the code that will help you manage assets. That means you'll have to install PostgreSQL and Node.js.

Ecto Needs PostgreSQL

Ecto uses the PostgreSQL[4] database adapter by default, and Phoenix adopts this default. It's the database engine we'll be using throughout the book, so you'll need version 9.5 or greater. You can check your local version like this:

```
$ psql --version
psql (PostgreSQL) 9.5.1
```

Node.js for Assets

Web development often requires web assets to be processed for deployment. Rather than reinvent the wheel, developers can optionally use Node.js tools for those services. Phoenix will use webpack.js.org to compile static assets such as JavaScript and CSS by default, and webpack uses npm, the Node.js package manager, to install its dependencies. Once it's installed, Phoenix will rely on them for asset management. Follow the directions on the Node.js[5] site and make sure you have version 5.3.0 or greater. Test your installation like this:

```
$ node --version
v5.3.0
```

---

3. http://elixir-lang.org/getting-started/introduction.html
4. http://www.postgresql.org/download/
5. http://nodejs.org

Phoenix has a feature called *live reloading*, which automatically reloads web pages as our assets and templates change. If you're running Linux, you're also going to need to install inotify[6] to support live reloading. Other operating systems are covered.

We're finally ready for Phoenix.

Phoenix

You're going to work in the Elixir language to write your code, so you'll use the Mix utility to run development tasks. Let's use Mix to install the Phoenix archive, and then to install Phoenix itself:

```
$  mix archive.install hex phx_new

* creating ~/.mix/archives/phx_new
```

In case you already had Phoenix installed, make sure you have version v1.4.7 or later:

```
$  mix phx.new -v
Phoenix v1.4.7
```

Now you're ready to roll!

Creating a Throwaway Project

Since C programmers wrote the first "Hello, World" examples in 1978, it's traditionally been the first program you write when learning almost any language. So we don't break with tradition, we're going to create a "Hello, World" application as our first project. It will help you get your feet wet. When you're done, you'll get to see all of those layers we talked about in practice.

You now have a shiny new Phoenix installation. It's time to build a project. You're in a functional language, so you're going to spend all of your time writing functions. This common project structure will help you organize things so you don't have to reimagine it for each project.

In Elixir, repetitive tasks that manage the programming cycle will run in Mix. Each time you call this utility, you specify a *task*—an Elixir script—to run. Let's use a task now to create our first Phoenix project, like this:

```
$ mix phx.new hello
* creating hello/config/config.exs
...
```

---

6.   https://hexdocs.pm/phoenix/installation.html#inotify-tools-for-linux-users

```
Fetch and install dependencies? [Yn] y
* running mix deps.get
* running mix deps.compile
...
$ cd hello
$ cd assets
$ npm install
...
$ cd ..
```

We're all set! We created a new project and built our static assets. At the bottom of the mix phx.new output, you can see a few sentences that tell you what to do next. Change into the hello directory and run the mix tasks to create the database and boot up the Phoenix web server, which will start looking for requests on port 4000.

Run your Phoenix application like this:

```
$ mix ecto.create
$ mix phx.server
```

Database errors

 If you receive database errors when running mix ecto.create, double-check your Hello.Repo username and password values in config/dev.exs and match your system settings where necessary.

You can see that the server started on port 4000. The [info] blocks tell you exactly where this server is running. Point your browser to http://localhost:4000/. You can see a simple Phoenix welcome page on page 24.

And we're live! There's no way we're going to get a million-dollar valuation with this product, though. Let's begin to change that by building our first feature.

Building a Feature

Our first feature won't be complicated. It'll print a string when you load a specific URL. To build that feature, we're going to use a small fraction of the files that mix phx.new created. Don't worry. You'll get a tour of the whole tree a little later. For now, everything we need is in the lib/hello_web subdirectory. We'll edit router.ex to point a URL to our code. We'll also add a controller to the lib/hello_web/controllers subdirectory, a view to lib/hello_web/views, and a template to lib/hello_web/templates.

First things first. We want to map requests coming in to a specific URL to the code that satisfies our request. We'll tie a URL to a function on a controller,

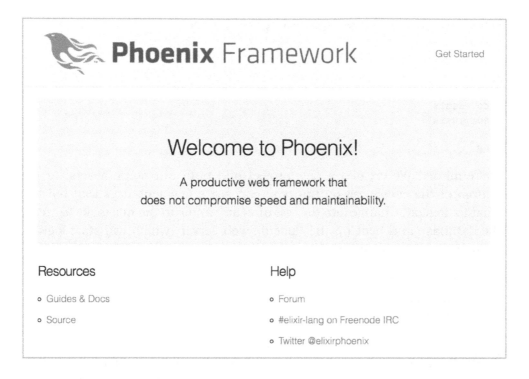

and that function to a view. You'll do so in the routing layer, as you would for other web frameworks. Routes in Phoenix go in lib/hello_web/router.ex by default. The .ex extension is for compiled Elixir files. Take a look at that file now. Scroll to the bottom, and you'll find a block that looks like this:

```
getting_started/listings/hello/lib/hello_web/router.ex
scope "/", HelloWeb do
  pipe_through :browser # Use the default browser stack

  get "/", PageController, :index
end
```

You can see a block of requests, scoped to /. That means that this group of routes will attempt to match all routes beginning with /. The pipe_through :browser macro handles some housekeeping for all common browser-style requests. You can see one route that takes requests that look like / and sends them to the :index action on the PageController. This looks like the right place to add our route. Add the following route *above the existing route*:

```
get "/hello", HelloController, :world
get "/", PageController, :index
```

This new code will match routes starting with /hello and send them to the :world function on the HelloController module. If you'd like, you can point your browser to localhost:4000/hello, but you'll get an error page because our controller module doesn't exist yet:

Before moving forward, let's briefly review the error page. At the top of the page we get the exception name: UndefinedFunctionError. Next, we see the error message. It seems HelloWeb.HelloController.init, which expects one argument, is undefined because the module does not exist. That's a good start and you can also see the detailed code related to the error.

The lefthand pane will usually show the relevant code snippets. Because the module in this case does not exist, there is no code snippet loaded by default, but you can populate this pane by clicking any of the stacktrace entries on the righthand side. In the stack trace, orange dots denote calls within the application and gray ones identify dependency code. Finally the bottom of the page has general request information, such as request headers, cookies, session, and the like.

Let's fix that error now. All controllers in Phoenix are in lib/hello_web/controllers. Create a lib/hello_web/controllers/hello_controller.ex file that looks like this:

getting_started/listings/hello/lib/hello_web/controllers/hello_controller.ex
```
defmodule HelloWeb.HelloController do
  use HelloWeb, :controller

  def world(conn, _params) do
    render(conn, "world.html")
  end
end
```

This controller is simple. If you're new to Elixir, you'll often see use SomeModule to introduce specific functionality to a module. The use HelloWeb, :controller call prepares us to use the Phoenix Controller API, including making some functions available that we'll want to use later. The router will call the world action on our controller, passing all of the information we need. We call the functions invoked by the router on our controller's actions, but don't get confused. They're just functions.

Once again, you might point your browser to localhost:4000/hello, but you'd find that it's still not working. We have yet to create our view, so Phoenix reports:

```
undefined function: HelloWeb.HelloView.render/2
    (module HelloWeb.HelloView is not available)
```

That makes sense. Let's easily fix that problem by creating a view called lib/hello_web/views/hello_view.ex with the following contents:

```
getting_started/listings/hello/lib/hello_web/views/hello_view.ex
defmodule HelloWeb.HelloView do
  use HelloWeb, :view
end
```

That file doesn't actually do any work beyond tying the view for world with some code to render a template. We'll rely on the defaults to render a template, which doesn't yet exist. One more time, you see an error when you point your browser to localhost:4000/hello:

```
Could not render "world.html" for HelloWeb.HelloView, please define a matching
clause for render/2 or define a template at "lib/hello_web/templates/hello".
  No templates were compiled for this module.
```

We are getting closer. Create the following template at lib/hello_web/templates/hello/world.html.eex, and we're done:

```
getting_started/listings/hello/lib/hello_web/templates/hello/world.html.eex
<h1>From template: Hello world!</h1>
```

As soon as you save your code, notice that the web page reloads! We have live reloading enabled, so whenever we touch templates or template assets, you'll see an automatic page reload.

The .eex extension denotes a template, which Phoenix will compile into a function. If you look closely, you can see the page we loaded has a header. We're implicitly using the layout defined in the lib/hello_web/views/layout_view.ex view and the template defined in lib/hello_web/templates/layout/app.html.eex. We'll work more with views a little later. For now, it's enough for you to know it's there.

Enjoy the results. It's not a fully operational death star, but you're well on your way.

Using Routes and Params

Right now, there's no dynamic information in our route, and we don't need any *yet*, but later we'll need to grab dynamic data from the URL to look up data from our database. Let's use our sandbox to see how that works. We'll use dynamic routes closely with Elixir's pattern matching. First, let's revise our route. Replace the first route in lib/hello_web/router.ex with this one:

```
get "/hello/:name", HelloController, :world
```

Notice that we're matching a URL pattern—/hello, as before—but we also add /:name to the route. The : tells Phoenix to create a parameter called :name in our route and pass that name as a parameter to the controller. Change the world function on lib/hello_web/controllers/hello_controller.ex to look like this:

```
def world(conn, %{"name" => name}) do
  render(conn, "world.html", name: name)
end
```

Since it's the first time we're using the shorthand hash notation, we'll give it a brief introduction. The code name: name is shorthand for :name => name. They are both shorthand notations for representing key-value pairs. [name: name] is shorthand for [{:name, name}]. Finally, since name: name is the last argument, of a function, we can omit the brackets. That means render(conn, "world.html", name: name) is shorthand for render(conn, "world.html", [name: name]). Whew. Now, on to the code.

Our new action uses the second argument, which is a map of inbound parameters. We match to capture the name key in the name variable, and pass the result to render in a keyword list. If you're new to Elixir, that function header looks a little different from what you might have seen before. Something special is happening, so let's look at it in a little more detail. If you already understand pattern matching, you can skip to the next section.

Pattern Matching in Functions

The Elixir language has an excellent feature called *pattern matching*. When Elixir encounters a = operator, it means "make the thing on the left match the thing on the right." You can use this feature in two different ways: to take data structures apart, or to test. Let's look at an example. Open up interactive Elixir by typing iex in your OS shell and follow this script:

```
iex> {first, second, third} = {:lions, :tigers, :bears}
{:lions, :tigers, :bears}

iex> first
:lions

iex> {first, second, :bears} = {:lions, :tigers, :bears}
{:lions, :tigers, :bears}

iex> {first, second, :armadillos} = {:lions, :tigers, :bears}
** (MatchError) no match of right hand side value: {:lions, :tigers, :bears}
```

In the first statement, we're matching a 3-tuple to {:lions, :tigers, :bears}. Elixir tries to make the expression on the left match, and it can do so by assigning first to :lions, and second to :tigers. In this case, we're using the pattern match to pick off pieces of the inside of the data structure.

In the third or fourth statement, we're doing something different. We're matching to do a test. When the interpreter tries to match the two, it succeeds and passes on, or fails and throws an exception.

You can also use pattern-matching syntax within your function heads in both of these ways. Type the following into your console:

```
iex> austin = %{city: "Austin", state: "Tx"}
%{city: "Austin", state: "Tx"}

iex> defmodule Place do
...>   def city(%{city: city}), do: city
...>   def texas?(%{state: "Tx"}), do: true
...>   def texas?(_), do: false
...> end
```

This module uses pattern matching in two different ways. The first function uses pattern matching to destructure the data, or take it apart. We use it to extract the city. It grabs the value for the :city key from any map. Although this bit of destructuring is trivial, sometimes the data structures can be deep, and you can reach in and grab the attributes you need with a surgeon's precision.

The second function, texas?, is using a pattern match as a test. If the inbound map has a :state keyword that's set to Tx, it'll match. Otherwise, it'll fall through to the next function, returning false. If we wanted to, we could:

- Match all maps with a given key, as in has_state?(%{state: _}), where the underscore _ will match anything

- Use strings as keys instead of atoms, as in has_state?(%{"state" => "Tx"})

- Match a state, and assign the whole map to a variable, as in has_state?(%{"state" => "Tx"} = place)

The point is, pattern matching is a huge part of Elixir and Phoenix programming. We'll use it to grab only certain types of connections, and also to grab individual pieces of the connection, conveniently within the function heading.

With all of that in mind, let's look at our controller action again:

```
def world(conn, %{"name" => name}) do
  render(conn, "world.html", name: name)
end
```

That makes more sense now. We're grabbing the name field from the second argument, which contains the inbound parameters. Our controller then renders the world.html template, passing in the local data. The local data prepares a map of variables for use by the templates. Now our views can access the name variable we've specified.

Chris says:
Atom Keys vs. String Keys?

In the world action in our controllers, the external parameters have string keys, "name" => name, while internally we use name: name. That's a convention followed throughout Phoenix. External data can't safely be converted to atoms, because the atom table isn't garbage-collected. Instead, we explicitly match on the string keys, and then our application boundaries like controllers and channels will convert them into atom keys, which we'll rely on everywhere else inside Phoenix.

Using Assigns in Templates

Now, all that remains is to tweak our template in lib/hello_web/templates/hello/world.html.eex to make use of the value. You can access the name specified in the world action as @name, like this:

```
<h1>Hello <%= String.capitalize(@name) %>!</h1>
```

The <%= %> brackets surround the code we want to substitute into the rendered page. @name will have the value of the :name option that we passed to render. We've worked for this reward, so point your browser to localhost:4000/hello/phoenix. It's ALIVE!

We've done a lot in a short time. Some of this plumbing might seem like magic to you, but you'll find that Phoenix is marvelously explicit, so it's easy to understand exactly what's happening, when, for each request. It's time to make this magic more tangible.

Going Deeper: The Request Pipeline

When we created the hello project, Mix created a bunch of directories and files. It's time to take a more detailed look at what all of those files do and, by extension, how Phoenix helps you organize applications.

When you think about it, typical web applications are just big functions. Each web request is a function call taking a single formatted string—the URL—as an argument. That function returns a response that's nothing more than a formatted string. If you look at your application in this way, your goal is to understand how functions are composed to make the one big function call that handles each request. In some web frameworks, that task is easier said than done. Most frameworks have hidden functions that are only exposed to those with deep, intimate internal knowledge.

The Phoenix experience is different because it encourages breaking big functions down into smaller ones. Then, it provides a place to explicitly register each smaller function in a way that's easy to understand and replace. We'll tie all of these functions together with the Plug library.

Think of the Plug library as a specification for building applications that connect to the web. Each plug consumes and produces a common data structure called Plug.Conn. Remember, that struct represents *the whole universe for a given request*, because it has things that web applications need: the inbound request, the protocol, the parsed parameters, and so on.

Think of each individual plug as a function that takes a conn, does something small, and returns a slightly changed conn. The web server provides the initial data for our request, and then Phoenix calls one plug after another. Each plug can transform the conn in some small way until you eventually send a response back to the user.

Even responses are just transformations on the connection. When you hear words like *request* and *response*, you might be tempted to think that a request is a plug function call, and a response is the return value. That's not what happens. A response is just one more action on the connection, like this:

```
conn
|> ...
|> render_response()
```

The whole Phoenix framework is made up of organizing functions that do something small to connections, *even rendering the result*. Said another way…

Plugs are functions.

Your web applications are pipelines of plugs.

Phoenix File Structure

If web applications in Phoenix are functions, the next logical step is to learn where to find those individual functions and how they fit together to build a coherent application. Let's work through the project directory structure, focusing on only the most important ones for now. Here's what your directories look like now:

```
...
├── assets
├── config
├── lib
├──── hello
├──── hello_web
├── test
...
```

Browser files like JavaScript and CSS go into assets and the Phoenix configuration goes into config. Your supervision trees (we'll explore those more in chapters to come), long-running processes, and application business logic go into lib/hello. Your web-related code—including controllers, views, and templates—goes in lib/hello_web. Predictably, you'll put tests in test.

In this section, you will walk through each of these pieces, including the pieces you created and many other ones that Phoenix generated. To sleuth out the entire pipeline of functions for a full web request, you need to start at the beginning. You will start with the basic code that Elixir and Erlang depend on.

Elixir Configuration

Since Phoenix projects are Elixir applications, they have the same structure as other Mix projects. Let's look at the basic files in the project:

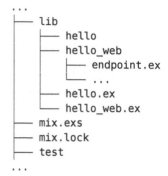

```
...
├── lib
│   ├── hello
│   ├── hello_web
│   │   ├── endpoint.ex
│   │   └── ...
│   ├── hello.ex
│   └── hello_web.ex
├── mix.exs
├── mix.lock
├── test
...
```

We've already encountered the .ex files. These contain Elixir code which you'll compile to the .beam files that run on the Erlang virtual machine. The .exs files are Elixir scripts. They're not compiled to .beam files. The compilation happens in memory, each time they are run. They're excellent for quick-changing scripts or standalone development-time tasks.

The project we created is a Mix project, named after the build tool that nearly all Elixir projects use. All Mix projects have a common structure. Each project has a configuration file, mix.exs, containing basic information about the project that supports tasks like compiling files, starting the server, and managing dependencies. When we add dependencies to our project, we'll need to make sure they show up here. Also, after we compile the project, mix.lock will include the specific versions of the libraries we depend on, so we guarantee that our production machines use exactly the same versions that we used during development and in our build servers.

Each Mix project also has a lib directory. Support for starting, stopping, and supervising each application is in lib/hello/application.ex.

Also, each Mix project has a test directory that hosts all tests. Phoenix adds some files to this test structure to support testing-specific files like controllers and views. We have not yet written any tests, but when we do, they will live in test.

Environments and Endpoints

Your application will run in an environment. The environment contains specific configuration that your web application needs. You can find that configuration in config:

```
...
├── config
│   ├── config.exs
│   ├── dev.exs
│   ├── prod.exs
│   ├── prod.secret.exs
│   └── test.exs
...
```

Phoenix supports a master configuration file plus an additional file for each environment you plan to run in. The environments supported by default are development (dev.exs), test (test.exs), and production (prod.exs), but you can add any others that you want.

You can see the three environment files, the master config.exs file containing application-wide configuration concerns, and a file called prod.secret.exs, which is responsible to load secrets and other configuration values from environment variables. Those environment variables are usually populated by deployment tasks.

You switch between prod, dev, and test environments via the MIX_ENV environment variable. We'll spend most of our time in this book in dev and test modes. That'll be easy, because your Mix task will have you working in dev by default, and it'll shift to test when you run automated tests with mix.

The master configuration file, config/config.exs, initially contains information about logging, and *endpoints*. Remember when we said that your web applications were just functions? An endpoint is the boundary where the web server hands off the connection to our application code. Now, you'll see that config/config.exs contains a single endpoint called Hello.Endpoint. Open the file called config/config.exs in your editor:

```
use Mix.Config

# Configures the endpoint
config :hello, HelloWeb.Endpoint,
  url: [host: "localhost"],
  secret_key_base: "U8VmJ...hNnTsFFvrhmD",
  render_errors: [view: HelloWeb.ErrorView, accepts: ~w(html json)],
  pubsub: [name: Hello.PubSub,
           adapter: Phoenix.PubSub.PG2]
```

Even though you might not understand this entire block of code, you can see that this code has our endpoint, which is the beginning of our world. The config function call configures the HelloWeb.Endpoint endpoint in our :hello application, giving a keyword list with configuration options. Let's look at that endpoint, which we find in lib/hello_web/endpoint.ex:

```
defmodule HelloWeb.Endpoint do
  use Phoenix.Endpoint, otp_app: :hello

  plug Plug.Static, ...
  plug Plug.RequestId
  plug Plug.Telemetry, ...

  plug Plug.Parsers, ...
  plug Plug.MethodOverride
  plug Plug.Head

  plug Plug.Session, ...
  plug HelloWeb.Router
end
```

You can see that this chain of functions, or plugs, does the typical things that almost all production web servers need to do: deal with static content, log requests, parse parameters, and the like. Remember, you already know how to read this code. It'll translate to a pipeline of functions, like this:

```
connection
|> Plug.Static.call()
|> Plug.RequestId.call()
|> Plug.Telemetry.call()
|> Plug.Parsers.call()
|> Plug.MethodOverride.call()
|> Plug.Head.call()
|> Plug.Session.call()
|> HelloWeb.Router.call()
```

That's an oversimplification, but the basic premise is correct. Endpoints are the chain of functions at the beginning of each request.

Now you can get a better sense of what's going on. Each request that comes in will be piped through this full list of functions. If you want to change the logging layer, you can change logging for all requests by specifying a different logging function here.

Summarizing what we have so far: an endpoint is a plug, one that's made up of other plugs. Your application is a series of plugs, beginning with an endpoint and ending with a controller:

```
connection
|> endpoint()
|> plug()
|> plug()
...
|> router()
|> HelloWebController()
```

We know that the last plug in the endpoint is the router, and we know we can find that file in lib/hello_web/router.ex.

 José says:
Can I Have More Than One Endpoint?

Although applications usually have a single endpoint, Phoenix doesn't limit the number of endpoints your application can have. For example, you could have your main application endpoint running on port 80 (HTTP) and 443 (HTTPS), as well as a specific admin endpoint running on a special port—let's say 8443 (HTTPS)—with specific characteristics and security constraints.

Alternatively, we could break those endpoints into separate applications but still run them side by side. You'll explore this later on when learning about umbrella projects.

The Router Flow

Now that you know what plugs are, let's take a fresh look at our router. Crack open lib/hello_web/router.ex. You can see that it's made up of two parts: pipelines and a route table. Here's the first part:

```
getting_started/listings/hello/lib/hello_web/router.ex
defmodule HelloWeb.Router do
  use HelloWeb, :router

  pipeline :browser do
    plug :accepts, ["html"]
    plug :fetch_session
    plug :fetch_flash
    plug :protect_from_forgery
    plug :put_secure_browser_headers
  end

  pipeline :api do
    plug :accepts, ["json"]
  end
```

Sometimes, you'll want to perform a common set of tasks, or transformations, for some logical group of functions. Not surprisingly, you'll do each transformation step with a plug and group these plugs into pipelines. When you think about it, a pipeline is just a bigger plug that takes a conn struct and returns one too.

In router.ex, you can see two pipelines, both of which do reasonable things for a typical web application. The *browser pipeline* accepts only HTML. It provides some common services such as fetching the session and a user message system called the *flash*, used for brief user notifications. It also provides some security services, such as request forgery protection.

We'd use the second pipeline of functions for a typical JSON API. This stack strictly calls the function that accepts only JSON requests, so if you had the idea of converting the whole API site to accept only XML, you could do so by changing one plug in one place.

Our hello application uses the browser pipeline, like this:

getting_started/listings/hello/lib/hello_web/router.ex

```
scope "/", HelloWeb do
  pipe_through :browser # Use the default browser stack

  get "/", PageController, :index
end
```

Now you can tell exactly what the pipeline does. All the routes after pipe_through :browser—all the routes in our application—go through the browser pipeline. Then, the router triggers the controller.

In general, the router is the last plug in the endpoint. It gets a connection, calls a pipeline, and then calls a controller. When you break it down, every traditional Phoenix application looks like this:

```
connection
|> endpoint()
|> router()
|> pipeline()
|> controller()
```

- The endpoint has functions that happen for every request.

- The connection goes through a named pipeline, which has common functions for each major type of request.

- The controller invokes the model and renders a template through a view.

Let's look at the final piece of this pipeline, the controller.

Controllers, Views, and Templates

From the previous section, you know that a request comes through an endpoint, through the router, through a pipeline, and into the controller. The controller is the gateway for the bulk of a traditional web application. Like a puppet master, your controller pulls the strings for this application, making data available in the connection for consumption by the view. It potentially fetches database data to stash in the connection and then redirects or renders a view. The view substitutes values for a template.

For Phoenix, your web-related code, including controllers, views, and templates goes into the lib/hello_web/ directory. Right now, that directory looks like:

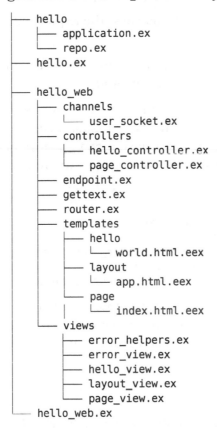

```
── hello
   ── application.ex
   └── repo.ex
── hello.ex

── hello_web
   ── channels
      └── user_socket.ex
   ── controllers
      ── hello_controller.ex
      └── page_controller.ex
   ── endpoint.ex
   ── gettext.ex
   ── router.ex
   ── templates
      ── hello
         └── world.html.eex
      ── layout
         └── app.html.eex
      └── page
         └── index.html.eex
   └── views
      ── error_helpers.ex
      ── error_view.ex
      ── hello_view.ex
      ── layout_view.ex
      └── page_view.ex
└── hello_web.ex
```

You can see two top-level files, hello.ex and hello_web.ex. The Hello module is an empty module which defines the top-level interface and documentation for your application. The HelloWeb module contains some glue code that defines the overall structure to the web-related modules of your application.

The second part of this book will be dedicated to applications that use the channels directory, so let's skip that for now. You've already coded a simple controller, so you know what the basic structure looks like.

As you might expect for the support of old-style MVC applications, you can see that lib/hello_web contains directories for views, and controllers. There's also a directory for templates—because Phoenix separates the views from the templates themselves.

We've created code in the controller, views, and templates/hello directories, and we've added code to router.ex as well. This application is fairly complete. After all, it's handling plenty of production-level concerns for you:

- The Erlang virtual machine and OTP engine will help the application scale.

- The endpoint will filter out static requests and also parse the request into pieces, and trigger the router.

- The browser pipeline will honor Accept headers, fetch the session, and protect from attacks like cross-site request forgery (CSRF).

All of these features are quickly available to you for tailoring, but they're also conveniently stashed out of your way in a structure that's robust, fast, and easy to extend. In fact, there's no magic at all. You have a good picture of exactly which functions Phoenix calls on a request to /hello, and where that code lives within the code base:

```
connection                 # Plug.Conn
|> endpoint()              # lib/hello_web/endpoint.ex
|> browser()               # lib/hello_web/router.ex
|> HelloController.world() # lib/hello_web/controllers/hello_controller.ex
|> HelloView.render(       # lib/hello_web/views/hello_view.ex
       "world.html")       # lib/hello_web/templates/hello/world.html.eex
```

It's easy to gloss over these details and go straight to the hello_web directory, and entrust the rest of the details to Phoenix. We encourage you instead to stop and take a look at exactly what happens for each request, from top to bottom.

Wrapping Up

We've gotten off to a strong start. You've created a first project. Though all of the concepts might still be a bit hazy, you now have a high-level understanding of how Phoenix projects hang together. The core concepts are these:

- We installed Phoenix, which is built using Erlang and OTP for the service layer, Elixir for the language, and Node.js for packaging static assets.

- We used the Elixir build tool mix to create a new project and start our server.

- Web applications in Phoenix are pipelines of plugs.

- The basic flow of traditional applications is endpoint, router, pipeline, controller.

- Routers distribute requests.

- Controllers call services and set up intermediate data for views.

In the next chapter, we're going to build a more hardy controller. You'll see how data flows through Phoenix, from the controller all the way into templates. You'll learn about concepts like layouts along the way. Let's get cracking!

## CHAPTER 3

Controllers

By now, you should have a loose grasp of how Phoenix applications work. You know that a typical request starts at an endpoint, flows through a router, and then flows into a controller. You should be starting to appreciate that web programming is a functional problem, and that it's natural to represent it using a functional language.

The "Hello, World" application we built in the previous chapter was a toy. It was the appropriate way to introduce you to Phoenix and the basics, but we're going to abandon it now so we can grapple with code organization and problem solving. For the rest of the book, we're going to work in a new project, and we'll continue developing it through to the end. Before we get started, though, let's take a deeper look at how controllers work. In addition, we'll introduce all of the things controllers touch, including views, templates, and contexts.

Understanding Controllers

In this chapter, we focus on building the controllers and the pieces of the application they touch. Though Phoenix has generators that could generate much of a simple web app from scratch, we're going to build part of it by hand so we can appreciate how the parts fit together. Before we fire up the generators, let's talk about how the controller hangs together.

Our application will be called rumbl. When we're all done, the application will allow us to take videos (hosted elsewhere), and attach comments to them *in real time* and play them back alongside the comments of other users. Think of it as *Mystery Science Theater 3000* meets Twitter. At scale, this application will be tremendously demanding because each user will record and play back comments that must be saved and served quickly so that the content stays relevant. The figure on page 42 shows what it will look like.

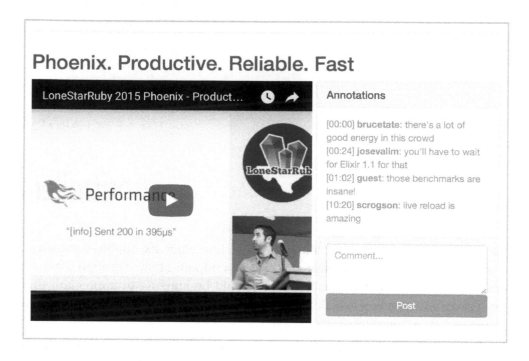

Before we get to the heavy lifting of videos and comments, we're going to handle users so you can get fully grounded in basic concepts first. Initially, we'll focus on a controller that handles our users. Let's talk about what we want to happen when a request for our user controller comes in via a browser:

```
connection
|> endpoint()
|> router()
|> browser_pipeline()
|> UserController.action()
```

A request enters through the endpoint (lib/rumbl_web/endpoint.ex) and then goes into the router (lib/rumbl_web/router.ex). The router matches the URL pattern, dispatches the connection through the browser pipeline, and then calls the UserController action. Let's break that last part down a little further, assuming that the request invokes the index action:

```
connection
|> UserController.index()
|> UserView.render("index.html")
```

We need to build the controller to do the work for our individual request, the view to render our template, and the template.

In order to respond to browser requests, we have to implement our business logic. For example, the UserController.index might be a simple function that returns all users in our application, but where are those users stored? What information does the index view require for each user? Do users have different roles? Is all user information publicly available? Those are business concerns that will vary from application to application.

We could write all of this business logic directly in our controllers but there's a better way. We'll isolate our business logic into a simple API layer called the *context*.

The Context

A context in Phoenix is nothing more than a module that groups functions with a shared purpose. For example, our application will need to read, modify, and delete user accounts. We will strive to keep all of this code in a single module.

Generally speaking, a context *encapsulates all business logic for a common purpose*. This way, we can interact with our business logic from controllers, channels, or remote APIs, without having to duplicate code. In a nutshell, a controller exists to work with context functions. It parses end user requests, calls context functions, and translates those results into something the end user can understand. Each slice of code has an isolated purpose. The context doesn't know about the controller, and the controller doesn't know about the business rules.

As we will see, organizing our code in contexts also does wonders for maintainability. We can add many new features, fixes, or business logic changes by simply changing contexts, without touching the web layer at all. We can also unit test our business logic thoroughly via the context API while focusing our integration tests on the controller.

With a master plan in our pocket, we can start to build our project. Let's get started.

Creating the Project

Let's go ahead and create a new application, called rumbl, with mix phx.new. To save some later heartache, we'll go ahead and create the Ecto configuration so we'll have it down the road:

```
$ mix phx.new rumbl

Fetch and install dependencies? [Yn] y
* running mix deps.get
* running mix deps.compile
* running cd assets && npm install && \
  node node_modules/webpack/bin/webpack.js --mode development

We are all set! Go into your application by running:

    $ cd rumbl

Then configure your database in config/dev.exs and run:

    $ mix ecto.create

Start your Phoenix app with:

    $ mix phx.server

You can also run your app inside IEx (Interactive Elixir) as:

    $ iex -S mix phx.server

$
```

First, run mix ecto.create to prep your database for later use. Next, start the app up with mix phx.server to make sure it's working, and point your browser to http://localhost:4000/. You see the familiar Phoenix home page. That's not exactly what we're looking for. We can steal some of that goodness to build our own messaging.

A Simple Home Page

The default web page is a simple template that has HTML. For now, we can use it to form the foundation of our home page. Let's start to tweak it right now. Make your lib/rumbl_web/templates/page/index.html.eex look like this:

```
controllers_views_templates/listings/rumbl/lib/rumbl_web/templates/page/index.html.eex
<section class="phx-hero">
  <h1><%= gettext "Welcome to %{name}!", name: "Rumbl.io" %></h1>
  <p>Rumbl out loud.</p>
</section>
```

Now we have a home page started. Notice that your browser has already changed as shown in the figure on page 45.

We have a crude home page so we should start to think about what to do about our users. We're not quite ready to integrate a real database, but we *can* start thinking about the way we will make them available to our controller. For that, we'll build a context.

Working with Contexts

All good application programmers must learn how to break down complex ideas into discrete steps. The opposite is also true. To build a beautiful API, you must be able to coalesce discrete functions into ideas by strategically layering and grouping functions.

Every library we use, and even Elixir itself, is structured based on those ideas. For example, any time you call Logger.debug from Elixir's standard library, you are accessing the Logger context. Internally, Logger may be broken into multiple modules, but for us, everything is exposed through a simple, well-defined public API of the Logger module.

Phoenix projects are structured like Elixir libraries and projects. We split our code into contexts. A context will group related functionality, such as posts and comments, often encapsulating patterns such as data access and data validation, all driven by our business needs. By using contexts, we decouple and isolate our systems into manageable, independent parts. Done correctly, these APIs expose critical logical concepts while hiding both complexity and implementation details.

With those goals in mind we'll build a context backed by hardcoded data for the short term. This interface should allow us to rapidly test the application as we build it, and also to test our controllers, views, and templates with simple data-only structs. Later, we can replace our hardcoded implementation with a full database-backed Ecto repository, and our public interface will remain unchanged.

Let's think about where our user functionality should live. User accounts will be a core part of rumbl so let's create a module called Accounts to group those concerns together. As rumbl grows, we can extend that code with other related functions such as authentication or password resets.

Now that we know we need an Accounts context, we can create the bits and pieces we'll need to flesh it out. We'll need a data structure for representing a user, so create a new file in lib/rumbl/accounts/user.ex and key this in:

controllers_views_templates/listings/rumbl/lib/rumbl/accounts/user.ex
```
defmodule Rumbl.Accounts.User do
  defstruct [:id, :name, :username]
end
```

We defined a Rumbl.Accounts.User struct with the fields id, name, and username. A struct is Elixir's main abstraction for working with structured data.

Elixir Structs

Elixir structs are built on top of maps. We could have implemented our User with a simple map. Maps would work just fine, but any developer could misspell a key or make a similar mistake. Let's see that problem play out in action. Run iex -S mix to start an interactive Elixir within our application but without running the Phoenix server:

```
iex> alias Rumbl.Accounts.User
iex> user = %{usernmae: "jose"}
%{usernmae: "jose"}
iex> user.username
** (KeyError) key :username not found in: %{usernmae: "jose"}
```

You may have noticed that we misspelled username as usernmae. A limitation of maps is that they offer protection for bad keys only at runtime, when we effectively access the key. However, many times we'd like to know about such errors as soon as possible, often at compilation time. Structs solve this exact problem. If you know exactly which keys should be in a map, a struct is a better choice. For example, our User has clearly defined keys. Let's try again but this time using our newly defined Rumbl.Accounts.User struct:

```
iex> jose = %User{name: "Jose Valim"}
%Rumbl.Accounts.User{id: nil, name: "Jose Valim", username: nil}

iex> jose.name
"Jose Valim"
```

One of the first things to notice is default values. Even though we specified only the :name field when creating the struct, Elixir conveniently filled in the remaining ones. Now, if we misspell a key, we're protected:

```
iex> chris = %User{nmae: "chris"}
** (KeyError) key :nmae not found in:
%Rumbl.Accounts.User{id: nil, name: nil, username: nil}
```

We misspelled the name: key and got an error. Nice.

Notice that the syntax for structs and maps is nearly identical, except for the name of the struct. There's a good reason for that. A struct *is* a map that has a __struct__ key:

```
iex> jose.__struct__
Rumbl.Accounts.User
```

With our user in place, let's define our Accounts context. We will add a couple of functions which will allow user account fetching. Let's create a new file in lib/rumbl/accounts.ex and key this in:

```
controllers_views_templates/listings/rumbl/lib/rumbl/accounts.ex
Line 1  defmodule Rumbl.Accounts do
   -      @moduledoc """
   -      The Accounts context.
   -      """
   5
   -      alias Rumbl.Accounts.User
   -
   -      def list_users do
   -        [
  10          %User{id: "1", name: "José", username: "josevalim"},
   -          %User{id: "2", name: "Bruce", username: "redrapids"},
   -          %User{id: "3", name: "Chris", username: "chrismccord"}
   -        ]
   -      end
  15
   -      def get_user(id) do
   -        Enum.find(list_users(), fn map -> map.id == id end)
   -      end
   -
  20      def get_user_by(params) do
   -        Enum.find(list_users(), fn map ->
   -          Enum.all?(params, fn {key, val} -> Map.get(map, key) == val end)
   -        end)
   -      end
  25  end
```

In our new module, we defined some of the typical functions you'd expect to find to manage a list of User structs. The list_users() function returns a list of all user structs in our system. Similarly, get_user and get_user_by functions fetch a single user from the system matching an ID or list of attributes.

Now our application has an interface to fetch user accounts in the system. Callers don't know that we're returning hardcoded data instead of talking to the database, and *that's the point*. We can make our data storage more sophisticated later while building out our greater application design.

Let's take the context for a spin. Start the console with iex -S mix. The -S mix option starts IEx in the context of the Mix script, giving us access to all modules in our application directly in IEx:

```
iex> alias Rumbl.Accounts
iex> alias Rumbl.Accounts.User

iex> Accounts.list_users()
[
  %Rumbl.Accounts.User{
    id: "1",
    name: "José",
    username: "josevalim"
  },
  %Rumbl.Accounts.User{
    id: "2",
    name: "Bruce",
    username: "redrapids"
  },
  %Rumbl.Accounts.User{
    id: "3",
    name: "Chris",
    username: "chrismccord"
  }
]
iex> Accounts.get_user("1")
%Rumbl.Accounts.User{
  id: "1",
  name: "José",
  username: "josevalim"
}
iex> Accounts.get_user_by(name: "Bruce")
%Rumbl.Accounts.User{
  id: "2",
  name: "Bruce",
  username: "redrapids"
}
```

And presto, we have a working user account system. Our controller will work fine. In fact, *our tests will work fine as well*. With some minor tweaks, this strategy will serve us well as we take the controller through its paces.

Now that we have user accounts, we can move ahead to the actual code that fetches and renders them.

Building a Controller

You've already built a simple controller, so you know the drill. At this point, we could create all of the routes needed by a user automatically with the resources macro, but we are going to play the teacher and say "Show your work!" If you understand how a single route works, it'll be much easier to explore the powerful shortcuts later. Specifically, we need two routes. UserController.index will show a list of users, and UserController.show will show a single user. As always, create the routes in router.ex:

```
controllers_views_templates/listings/rumbl/lib/rumbl_web/router.ex
scope "/", RumblWeb do
  pipe_through :browser

  get "/users", UserController, :index
  get "/users/:id", UserController, :show
  get "/", PageController, :index
end
```

Notice that we have our two new routes and the default route for /. Our two new routes use the new UserController, which doesn't yet exist, with the :show and :index actions. The names and URLs we've chosen for these actions aren't random. The :show, :index, :new, :create, :edit, :update, and :delete actions are all frequently used in Phoenix. For now, follow along strictly, and you'll learn the shortcuts later.

Let's take a closer look at the :index route:

```
get "/users", UserController, :index
```

You've seen the get macro before. The route matches HTTP GET requests to a URL that looks like /users and sends them to the UserController, calling the index action. That route stores :index—the action we intend to invoke—in the conn and then calls the right pipeline.

Now, restart your server and point your browser to http://localhost:4000/users. You get some debugging information, but you don't have to go beyond the title to find this message:

```
UndefinedFunctionError at GET /users
```

```
function RumblWeb.UserController.init/1 is undefined
(module RumblWeb.UserController is not available)
```

That makes sense; we haven't written the controller yet.

Let's create a controller in lib/rumbl_web/controllers/user_controller.ex. Initially, we'll include one function called index to find the users from our Accounts context:

```
controllers_views_templates/listings/rumbl/lib/rumbl_web/controllers/user_controller.ex
defmodule RumblWeb.UserController do
  use RumblWeb, :controller

  alias Rumbl.Accounts

  def index(conn, _params) do
    users = Accounts.list_users()
    render(conn, "index.html", users: users)
  end
end
```

Let's take that code apart. There's a little bit of ceremony at the top of the file that defines our module and announces that we're going to use the :controller API. Right now, the only action is index.

If you access the users page again, you can see that we're getting an error message, but we've traded up:

```
UndefinedFunctionError at GET /users

undefined function: RumblWeb.UserView.render/2
  (module RumblWeb.UserView is not available)
```

Progress! We have a controller, but we still need to code a view.

Coding Views

This is your second pass through this process. The first time, you built a "Hello, World"-style feature, one with a controller, view, and template. Now it's time for the more detailed explanation that you were promised earlier. In many other web frameworks, the terms *view* and *template* are often used synonymously. It's enough for users to know that when a controller finishes a task, a view is somehow rendered.

In Phoenix, the terminology is a little more explicit. A *view* is a module containing rendering functions that convert data into a format the end user will consume, like HTML or JSON. You can write such functions as you would any other Elixir function. Those rendering functions can also be defined from templates. A *template* is a function on that module, compiled from a file containing a raw markup language and embedded Elixir code to process substitutions and loops. The separation of the view and template concepts makes it easy to render data any way you want, be it with a raw function, an embedded Elixir engine, or any other template engine.

In short, views are modules responsible for rendering. Templates are web pages or fragments that allow both static markup and native code to build response pages, compiled into a function.

Let's build a view in lib/rumbl_web/views/user_view.ex:

```
controllers_views_templates/listings/rumbl/lib/rumbl_web/views/user_view.ex
defmodule RumblWeb.UserView do
  use RumblWeb, :view

  alias Rumbl.Accounts

  def first_name(%Accounts.User{name: name}) do
    name
    |> String.split(" ")
    |> Enum.at(0)
  end
end
```

We added a simple first_name function to parse a user's first name from that user's name field. Next, in lib/rumbl_web/templates, we created a user directory and a new index template in lib/rumbl_web/templates/user/index.html.eex:

```
controllers_views_templates/listings/rumbl/lib/rumbl_web/templates/user/index.html.eex
<h1>Listing Users</h1>

<table>
  <%= for user <- @users do %>
    <tr>
      <td><b><%= first_name(user) %></b> (<%= user.id %>)</td>
      <td><%= link "View", to: Routes.user_path(@conn, :show, user.id) %></td>
    </tr>
  <% end %>
</table>
```

That's mostly HTML markup, with a little Elixir mixed in. This template language is called EEx, which stands for Embedded Elixir, and is part of the Elixir's standard library. At runtime, Phoenix will translate this template to a function using this strategy. EEx executes Elixir code that's within <%= %> tags, injecting the result into the template. EEx evaluates code within <% %> tags without injecting the result, meaning we'll use them for code with side effects. Since we generally try to keep side effects out of views wherever possible, we'll use mostly the <%= %> form. You've seen template code before, but we'll walk through it anyway.

The expression for user <- @users walks through the users, rendering each user using the template code inside the do block, and rolling up the result into the template. Remember, we've already populated @users within our index action.

Each user is a map. We render the name field, the id field, and a link. That link comes from a helper function.

Chris says:
Why Are Templates So Fast in Phoenix?

After compilation, templates are functions. Since Phoenix builds templates using linked lists rather than string concatenation the way many imperative languages do, one of the traditional bottlenecks of many web frameworks goes away. Phoenix doesn't have to make huge copies of giant strings.

Since Elixir has only a single copy of the largest and most frequently used strings in your application, the hardware caching features of most CPUs can come into play. The book's introduction talked about the performance of the routing layer. The performance of the view layer is just as important. For more details, see Elixir RAM and the Template of Doom.[a]

---

a. www.evanmiller.org/elixir-ram-and-the-template-of-doom.html

Using Helpers

That link function packs a surprising amount of punch into a small package. Phoenix helpers provide a convenient way to drop common HTML structures onto your view. There's nothing special about them. Helpers are simply Elixir functions. For example, you can call the functions directly in IEx:

```
$ iex -S mix
```

```
iex> Phoenix.HTML.Link.link("Home", to: "/")
{:safe,  [60, "a", [[32, "href", 61, 34, "/", 34]],
62, "Home", 60,   47, "a", 62]}
```

The return value might look a little odd. We received a tuple with :safe, followed by an unusual looking list of values. This list is known as an *I/O list*. I/O lists are simply lists of values which allow data to be efficiently used for I/O, such as writing values to a socket. Let's convert this result into a human-readable form by calling Phoenix.HTML.safe_to_string/1:

```
iex> Phoenix.HTML.Link.link("Home", to: "/") |> Phoenix.HTML.safe_to_string()
"<a href=\"/\">Home</a>"
```

The second argument to our link function is a keyword list, with the to: argument specifying the target. We use a path that's automatically created for our :show route to specify the link target. Now you can see that our list has the three users we fetched from our repository as shown in the figure on page 53.

Listing Users

José (1)   View

Bruce (2)   View

Chris (3)   View

At this point you may be wondering where the HTML helpers come from. At the top of each view, you can find the following definition: use RumblWeb, :view. This code snippet is the one responsible for setting up our view modules, importing all required functionality. Open up lib/rumbl_web.ex to see exactly what's imported into each view:

```
controllers_views_templates/rumbl/lib/rumbl_web.ex
def view do
  quote do
    use Phoenix.View, root: "lib/rumbl_web/templates",
                      namespace: RumblWeb

    # Import convenience functions from controllers
    import Phoenix.Controller,
           only: [get_flash: 1, get_flash: 2, view_module: 1]

    # Use all HTML functionality (forms, tags, etc)
    use Phoenix.HTML

    import RumblWeb.ErrorHelpers
    import RumblWeb.Gettext
    alias RumblWeb.Router.Helpers, as: Routes
  end
end
```

The view function uses Elixir's quote to inject a chunk of code into each view. Since the contents of each quote are executed for each view, you want to keep it short and sweet, limiting these chunks only to imports, uses, and aliases. In our case, one of those injected statements is use Phoenix.HTML.

Phoenix.HTML is responsible for the HTML functionality in views, from generating links to working with forms. Phoenix.HTML also provides HTML safety: *by default, applications are safe from cross-site scripting (XSS) attacks*, because only the markup generated by Phoenix.HTML functions is considered safe. That's why the link function returns a tuple. The first element of the tuple—the :safe atom—indicates that the content in the second element is known to be safe.

To learn about existing HTML helpers, visit the Phoenix.HTML documentation.[1]

Keep in mind that the rumbl_web.ex file is not a place to attach your own functions. You want to keep this file skinny and easy to understand. For example, the contents of the view function will be macro-expanded *to each and every view*! So remember, in rumbl_web.ex, prefer import statements to defining your own functions.

That's a good amount of progress so far. Let's create one more action, and the corresponding template, to round out our actions.

Showing a User

Now that we've created the code to show a list of users, we can work on showing a single user. To refresh your memory, let's look at the route we created earlier:

```
get "/users/:id", UserController, :show
```

That's easy enough. On a request to /users/:id, where :id is part of the inbound URL, the router will add at least two things we'll need to conn, including the :id that's part of the URL, and the action name, :show. Then, the router will call the plugs in our pipeline, and then the UserController. To show a single user using this request, we need a controller action, which we add to lib/rumbl_web/controllers/user_controller.ex:

```
controllers_views_templates/listings/rumbl/lib/rumbl_web/controllers/user_controller.change1.ex
def show(conn, %{"id" => id}) do
  user = Accounts.get_user(id)
  render(conn, "show.html", user: user)
end
```

Now, you can see why Plug breaks out the params part of the inbound conn. We can use params to extract the individual elements our action needs. In this case, we're matching on the "id" key to populate the id variable. We then use that to ask the Accounts context for the given user, and use that to render the result.

When you point the browser to localhost:4000/users/1, predictably, Phoenix screams at you. You've not yet built the template.

Add this to lib/rumbl_web/templates/user/show.html.eex:

```
controllers_views_templates/listings/rumbl/lib/rumbl_web/templates/user/show.html.eex
<h1>Showing User</h1>
<b><%= first_name(@user) %></b> (<%= @user.id %>)
```

---

1. http://hexdocs.pm/phoenix_html

Point your browser to /users/1. You can see the first user, with the dynamic content piped in as we require.

Naming Conventions

When Phoenix renders templates from a controller, it infers the name of the view module, RumblWeb.UserView, from the name of the controller module, RumblWeb.UserController. The view modules infer their template locations from the view module name. In our example, our RumblWeb.UserView would look for templates in the web/templates/user/ directory. Phoenix uses the explicit names you provide throughout, whether singular or plural. That strategy avoids confusing pluralization rules and naming inconsistencies you might find in other frameworks.

You'll see how to customize these conventions later. For now, know that you can let Phoenix save you some time by letting the good old computer do the work for you. Break the rules if you have to, but if you're smart about it, you'll save some tedious ceremony along the way.

Nesting Templates

Often there's a need to reduce duplication in the templates themselves. For example, both of our templates have common code that renders a user. Take the common code and create a user template in lib/rumbl_web/templates/user/user.html.eex:

```
<strong><%= first_name(@user) %></strong> (<%= @user.id %>)
```

We created another template to render a user. Then, whenever we build tables or listings of users, we can re-use this template. Now, change your show.html.eex template to render it:

```
<h1>Showing User</h1>
<%= render "user.html", user: @user %>
```

Also, change your index.html.eex template to render it:

```
<tr>
  <td><%= render "user.html", user: user %></td>
  <td><%= link "View", to: Routes.user_path(@conn, :show, user.id) %></td>
</tr>
```

At this point, it's worth emphasizing that a view in Phoenix is just a module, and templates are just functions. When we add a template named lib/rumbl_web/templates/user/user.html.eex, the view extracts the template from the filesystem and makes it a function in the view itself. That's why we need the view in the first place. Let's build on this thought inside iex -S mix:

```
iex> user = Rumbl.Accounts.get_user("1")
%Rumbl.Accounts.User{...}

iex> view = RumblWeb.UserView.render("user.html", user: user)
{:safe, [[[[["" | "<strong>"] | "José"] | "</strong> ("] | "1"] | ")\n"]}

iex> Phoenix.HTML.safe_to_string(view)
"<strong>José</strong> (1)\n"
```

We fetch a user from the repository and then render the template directly. Because Phoenix has the notion of HTML safety, we can see that render returns a tuple, tagged as :safe just as we saw with our link helper. Likewise, the contents are also stored in an I/O list for performance.

Each template in our application becomes a render(template_name, assigns) clause in its respective view. So, rendering a template is a combination of pattern matching on the template name and executing the function. The assigns argument is simply a holding hash for user-defined values containing values set by plugs and controller functions. Because the rendering contract is so simple, nothing is stopping developers from defining render clauses directly on the view module, skipping the whole template. For example, in your RumblWeb.ErrorView, you could respond to 404 or 500 status codes with basic error messages by simply implementing the following functions:

```
def render("404.html", _assigns) do
  "Page not found"
end

def render("500.html", _assigns) do
  "Internal server error"
end
```

By default, your generated error view implements the template_not_found/2 callback which renders these basic error messages for you. You can see this in action in your own RumblWeb.ErrorView, which contains:

```
controllers_views_templates/rumbl/lib/rumbl_web/views/error_view.ex
# By default, Phoenix returns the status message from
# the template name. For example, "404.html" becomes
# "Not Found".
def template_not_found(template, _assigns) do
  Phoenix.Controller.status_message_from_template(template)
end
```

The Phoenix.View module—the one used to define the views themselves—also provides functions for rendering views, including a function to render and convert the rendered template into a string in one pass:

```
iex> user = Rumbl.Accounts.get_user("1")
%Rumbl.Accounts.User{...}
```

```
iex> Phoenix.View.render(RumblWeb.UserView, "user.html", user: user)
{:safe, [[[[["" | "<strong>"] | "José"] | "</strong> ("] | "1"] | ")\n"]}
```

```
iex> Phoenix.View.render_to_string(RumblWeb.UserView, "user.html", user: user)
"<strong>José</strong> (1)\n"
```

Behind the scenes, Phoenix.View calls render in the given view and adds some small conveniences, like wrapping our templates in layouts whenever one is available. Let's find out how.

Layouts

When we call render in our controller, instead of rendering the desired view directly, the controller first renders the layout view, which then renders the actual template in a predefined markup. This allows developers to provide a consistent markup across all pages without duplicating it over and over again.

Since layouts are regular views with templates, all the knowledge that you've gained so far applies to them. In particular, each template receives a couple of special assigns when rendering, namely @view_module and @view_template. You can see these in lib/rumbl_web/templates/layout/app.html.eex:

```
controllers_views_templates/rumbl/lib/rumbl_web/templates/layout/app.html.eex
<main role="main" class="container">
  <p class="alert alert-info" role="alert">
    <%= get_flash(@conn, :info) %>
  </p>
  <p class="alert alert-danger" role="alert">
    <%= get_flash(@conn, :error) %>
  </p>
  <%= render @view_module, @view_template, assigns %>
</main>
```

It's just pure HTML with a render call of render @view_module, @view_template, assigns, but it doesn't need to be restricted to HTML. As in any other template, the connection is also available in layouts as @conn, giving you access to any other helper in Phoenix. When you call render in your controller, you're actually rendering with the :layout option set by default. This allows you to render the view and template for your controller action in the layout with a plain render function call. No magic is happening here.

We can tweak the existing layout to be a little more friendly to our application. Rather than slog through a bunch of CSS and HTML here, we'll let you work out your own design. If you choose to do so, replace the layout you find at lib/rumbl_web/templates/layout/app.html.eex with one you like better. As always, you'll see your browser autoupdate.

We're just about done here. By now, our growing company valuation is somewhere north of, well, the tree house you built in the third grade. Don't worry, though; things will pick up in a hurry. You're going to go deeper faster than you thought possible.

Wrapping Up

We packed a ton into this chapter. Let's summarize what you've done:

- We created our first context that encapsulates all of the logic related to account management.

- We created actions, which serve as the main point of control for each request.

- We created views, which exist to render templates.

- We created templates, which generate HTML for our users.

- We employed helpers, which are simple Phoenix functions used in templates.

- We used layouts, which are HTML templates that embed an action's HTML.

In the next chapter, we're going to go back to the context, which we've implemented with a simple in-memory list, with a database backend using Ecto. By the time we're done, we'll be reading our users from the database and entering new users with forms. Along the way, we'll start to see how a little upfront design effort with contexts paves the way for our growing feature set.

Don't stop now! Things are just getting interesting.

## CHAPTER 4

Ecto and Changesets

Up to now, we've been focusing on our application's presentation layer with views and templates, and controlling those views with controllers. Rather than bogging down into technical details, we used an application API to encapsulate all of our business concerns. Our single Accounts context keeps all the data directly in the code instead of using a real database. There's a method to our madness. With very little work, we can now replace our in-memory data structures with a real database and all of our controller code can remain unchanged.

Ecto is the Elixir framework for persisting data. In this chapter, we'll convert our Accounts context to use an Ecto repository backed by a PostgreSQL database. By the time you're done, your accounts context will be able to save users and search for them using an advanced query API.

Understanding Ecto

If you've used data frameworks like LINQ in .NET or persistence frameworks like Active Record in Rails, you'll see some common threads in Ecto but also some significant differences. Ecto is a wrapper that's primarily intended for relational databases, allowing developers to read and persist data to underlying storage such as PostgreSQL. It has an encapsulated query language that you can use to build layered queries that can then be composed into more-sophisticated ones.

Ecto also has a feature called *changesets* that holds all changes you want to perform on the database. It encapsulates the whole process of receiving external data, casting and validating it before writing it to the database.

In this chapter, we'll start with a basic database-backed repository. We'll then move on to creating data and managing updates with changesets, saving most of the query language for later.

When we created our application, Phoenix generated an Ecto repository, called Rumble.Repo:

```
ecto/rumbl/lib/rumbl/repo.ex
defmodule Rumbl.Repo do
  use Ecto.Repo,
    otp_app: :rumbl,
    adapter: Ecto.Adapters.Postgres
end
```

Our repository uses Ecto's default database adapter, PostgreSQL. If you haven't already done so, install PostgreSQL now.

You can configure the repository and the development credentials to access the database in config/dev.exs:

```
ecto/rumbl/config/dev.exs
# Configure your database
config :rumbl, Rumbl.Repo,
  username: "postgres",
  password: "postgres",
  database: "rumbl_dev",
  hostname: "localhost",
  pool_size: 10
```

We specify the username, password, and database parameters. You need to replace those with your own database username and password.

Let's verify our credentials are correct. Type the following command and Ecto will create the underlying database, if it's not already there:

```
$ mix ecto.create
The database for Rumbl.Repo has been created.
```

We haven't yet done the heavy lifting to specify our users. We've only tied Ecto to this PostgreSQL database. Let's create some schemas and tie those tables to code in our Accounts context.

Defining the User Schema and Migration

At its core, Ecto lets you specify a struct that ties individual fields to the fields in database tables through a DSL. Let's use that now. To define our

schema, let's replace our bare user struct in lib/rumbl/accounts/user.ex with the
following:

```
ecto/listings/rumbl/lib/rumbl/accounts/user.change1.ex
defmodule Rumbl.Accounts.User do
  use Ecto.Schema
  import Ecto.Changeset

  schema "users" do
    field :name, :string
    field :username, :string

    timestamps()
  end
end
```

This DSL is built with Elixir macros. The schema and field macros let us specify both the underlying database table and the Elixir struct at the same time.
Each field corresponds to both a field in the database and a field in our local
Accounts.User struct. By default, Ecto defines the primary key called :id automatically. From the schema definition, Ecto automatically defines an Elixir
struct for us, which we can create by calling %Rumbl.Accounts.User{} as we did
before.

Finally, our schema uses use Ecto.Schema at the top and it also imports
Ecto.Changeset functions which will allow us to work more easily with changesets
later on.

We've treated our code with care, and we should give our database *at least*
the same level of respect. Now that we have our Repo and User schema configured, we need to make the database reflect the structure of our application.
Ecto uses *migrations* for that purpose. A migration changes a database to
match the structure our application needs. For our new feature, we need to
add a migration to create our users table with columns matching our User
schema. Let's generate one:

```
$ mix ecto.gen.migration create_users
* creating priv/repo/migrations
* creating priv/repo/migrations/20180315023132_create_users.exs
```

The mix ecto.gen.migration command creates a migration file for us with a special
timestamp to ensure ordering of our database migrations. For this reason,
your migration filename will have a different prefix than ours. Key in these
changes within your empty change function:

ecto/listings/rumbl/priv/repo/migrations/20180315023132_create_users.exs

```
defmodule Rumbl.Repo.Migrations.CreateUsers do
  use Ecto.Migration

  def change do
    create table(:users) do
      add :name, :string
      add :username, :string, null: false
      add :password_hash, :string

      timestamps()
    end

    create unique_index(:users, [:username])
  end
end
```

In the dark days of persistence frameworks, before migrations were common-place, changes to the database weren't versioned with the source code. Often, those changes weren't even automated. That strategy was fine if new code worked the first time, but it opened the door for problems:

- When deploying new code, programmers often introduced errors when changing the database.

- The high stress of code rollbacks led to frequent mistakes when changes were rolled back under pressure.

- Building a fresh development environment was tough because the schema history was too fragmented.

In general, migrating a database, both up for a successful deploy and down for an unsuccessful deploy, should be an automated and repeatable process. The Ecto.Migration API[1] provides several functions to create, remove, and change database tables, fields, and indexes. These functions also have counterparts to do the reverse. Here, we used the create, add, and timestamps macros to build our users table and matched the fields with our User schema. For example, add creates a new field, and timestamps creates a couple of fields for us, inserted_at and updated_at.

Overall, we created a table with six fields: the auto-generated id, the inserted_at and updated_at timestamps, name, username, and password_hash. We added password_hash to the database but we didn't list password_hash as a schema field for now. We will introduce it when it's time to discuss authentication in Chapter 5, Authenticating Users, on page 77. Finally, we add a unique index to guarantee that the username field is unique across the whole table.

---

1.   http://hexdocs.pm/ecto/Ecto.Migration.html

Now all that's left is to migrate up our database:

```
$ mix ecto.migrate
[info] == Running Rumbl.Repo.Migrations.CreateUsers.change/0 forward
[info] create table users
[info] create index users_username_index
[info] == Migrated in 0.0s
```

Be careful. The ecto.migrate task will migrate the database *for your current environment.* So far, we've been running the dev environment. To change the environment, you'd set the MIX_ENV operating-system environment variable.

We've configured our database and created the schema with a migration. We are ready to use our repository through the Accounts context. We just need to make sure our repository services are up and running.

Phoenix is built on top of OTP, a layer for reliably managing services. We can use OTP to start key services like Ecto repositories in a supervised process so that Ecto and Phoenix can do the right thing in case our repository crashes. To do so, we simply need to list the Rumbl.Repo as a child in our supervision tree. Phoenix already did that for us. Open up lib/rumbl/application.ex and you will find this:

```
children = [
  ...
  # Start the Ecto repository
  Rumbl.Repo,
  ...
]
```

Now that our configuration is established, let's take it for a spin.

Using the Repository to Add Data

With our database ready, we can begin to persist our Accounts.User structs. Let's hop into an IEx shell and create the users that we previously hardcoded in our Accounts context.

Spin up your console with iex -S mix, and insert some data:

```
iex> alias Rumbl.Repo
iex> alias Rumbl.Accounts.User

iex> Repo.insert(%User{
...>   name: "José", username: "josevalim"
...> })
[debug] QUERY OK db=5.0ms
INSERT INTO "users" ("name","username","inserted_at",
...
```

```
{:ok,
 %Rumbl.Accounts.User{__meta__: #Ecto.Schema.Metadata<:loaded, "users">,
  id: 1,
  inserted_at: ~N[2017-10-25 19:13:28.878179],
  name: "José",
  updated_at: ~N[2017-10-25 19:13:28.879737],
  username: "josevalim"}}
iex> Repo.insert(%User{
...>   name: "Bruce", username: "redrapids"
...> })
  ...
iex> Repo.insert(%User{
...>   name: "Chris", username: "mccord"
...> })
```

And we're up! You can see that Ecto is creating the id field and populating our timestamps for us. It's great to persist data, but how do we use Ecto to retrieve it? Let's take a look:

```
iex> Repo.all(User)
[debug] QUERY OK source="users" db=3.2ms decode=0.1ms queue=0.1ms
SELECT u0."id", u0."name", u0."username", u0."inserted_at", u0."updated_at"
FROM "users" AS u0 []

[
  %Rumbl.Accounts.User{
    id: 1,
    name: "José",
    username: "josevalim",
    ...
  },
  %Rumbl.Accounts.User{
    id: 2,
    name: "Bruce",
    username: "redrapids",
    ...
  },
  %Rumbl.Accounts.User{
    id: 3,
    name: "Chris",
    username: "mccord",
    ...
  }
]
iex> Repo.get(User, 1)
[debug] QUERY OK source="users" db=3.4ms
SELECT u0."id", u0."name", u0."username",
u0."inserted_at", u0."updated_at"
FROM "users" AS u0 WHERE (u0."id" = $1) [1]
```

```
%Rumbl.Accounts.User{
  id: 1,
  name: "José",
  username: "josevalim",
  ...
}
```

Now that we can persist users to our repo and pull the accounts back out, we're ready to wire up database access to our Accounts context. Make the following changes to your lib/rumbl/accounts.ex file:

```
ecto/listings/rumbl/lib/rumbl/accounts.change1.ex
alias Rumbl.Repo
alias Rumbl.Accounts.User

def get_user(id) do
  Repo.get(User, id)
end

def get_user!(id) do
  Repo.get!(User, id)
end

def get_user_by(params) do
  Repo.get_by(User, params)
end

def list_users do
  Repo.all(User)
end
```

We replaced our get_user, get_user_by, and list_users functions with calls into our Ecto repo. We added a new get_user! which raises an Ecto.NotFoundError when looking up a user that does not exist.

If you've seen plenty of MVC applications in the past, you know how easy it is for that design to get away from you. It's easy to see the concerns about persistence creep into the controller. As controller actions grow, business logic creeps in and the overall separation of concerns devolves, eroding design quality and crippling maintainability.

Contrast that with our context, where there's a logical parking place for all of these concerns. You can already see the benefits of our Accounts context in action. With our repo calls in place, we're ready to try it out even though we haven't touched our controller code at all.

Restart your server and then visit our users page at http://localhost:4000/users and view the logs to see the inserted records:

```
$ mix phx.server
[info] Running RumblWeb.Endpoint with Cowboy on http://localhost:4000
```

Now visit http://localhost:4000/users as before, but watch the logs to see Ecto's SQL statements being executed:

```
[info] GET /users
[debug] Processing with RumblWeb.UserController.index/2
  Parameters: %{}
  Pipelines: [:browser]
[debug] QUERY OK source="users" db=1.0ms
SELECT u0."id", u0."name", u0."username", ...
[info] Sent 200 in 1ms
```

You can see that we're fetching data from the database instead of the in-memory hardcoded data. We're making plenty of progress here, but there's still work to do. Let's build some forms to register new users via a web interface.

Building Forms

Now that we have a database-backed context, let's add the ability to create new users in our system. We're going to use Phoenix's form builders for that purpose. First, open up your controller at lib/rumbl_web/controllers/user_controller.ex and set up a new user account struct for our new template, like this:

```
ecto/listings/rumbl/lib/rumbl_web/controllers/user_controller.change1.ex
alias Rumbl.Accounts.User

def new(conn, _params) do
  changeset = Accounts.change_user(%User{})
  render(conn, "new.html", changeset: changeset)
end
```

Notice the Accounts.change_user function. This function receives a struct, and returns an Ecto.Changeset. Changesets let Ecto manage record changes, cast parameters, and perform validations. We use a changeset to build a customized strategy for dealing with each specific kind of change, such as creating a user or updating sensitive information. Let's add a changeset function to our User struct in lib/rumbl/accounts/user.ex with some essential validations:

```
ecto/listings/rumbl/lib/rumbl/accounts/user.change2.ex
def changeset(user, attrs) do
  user
  |> cast(attrs, [:name, :username])
  |> validate_required([:name, :username])
  |> validate_length(:username, min: 1, max: 20)
end
```

Our changeset accepts an Accounts.User struct and attributes. We then pass the cast function a list of fields to tell Ecto that name and username are allowed to be cast as user input. This casts all allowable user input values to their schema types and rejects everything else. Next, we used validate_required which makes sure we provide all necessary required fields.

We pipe validate_required, which returns an Ecto.Changeset, into validate_length to validate the username length. Ecto.Changeset defines cast, validate_required, and validate_length, which we've imported at the top of our schema module.

Next, we need to expose our new functionality from our public Accounts context. Add a new change_user function which calls our user changeset:

```
ecto/listings/rumbl/lib/rumbl/accounts.change2.ex
def change_user(%User{} = user) do
  User.changeset(user, %{})
end
```

When we're designing the business logic for our accounts, we need to decide what's public and what's private. The Accounts module itself is the only public API our controllers (or any other external components) should touch, but that doesn't mean all logic related to accounts should live there. In this example, we added some private logic to Accounts.User which the context exposes via the Accounts.change_user function.

We're using layers to hide private logic behind a public API. There are many good ways to organize your code inside the context. You'll choose the best one based on how you want to document, structure, and test the context internals.

At this point, you might wonder why Ecto adds this little bit of complexity through changesets. You may have seen other frameworks that add validations directly to the schema. We could simply write a set of one-size-fits-all validations and then pass a set of updated attributes to create or update functions, but that strategy might lead to problems. Here's why.

Handling Update Policies

When conventional persistence frameworks allow one-size-fits-all validations, they're forced to work harder and manage change across multiple concerns. Here's the problem. Say you have an account and your new, simple application saves a simple password, hashed for security sake, along with the record.

Next, imagine that your boss lays down the requirement of logging into your application through Facebook. That update requires a different kind of password validation, and a different kind of enforcement for password rules, so you build a custom validation and tweak your code in clever ways to trigger the right password rules at the right time. That second policy makes your update_account validations more complex, but they're manageable.

Then, your increasingly irritating boss asks for a JSON API, and your API programmers aren't content with the cute "Oops, an error was found" error messages that seemed to work fine for end users. You need to provide more information about what went wrong. You dig deeply into the persistence API and decide that the error reporting no longer works for you. Your stomach sinks as it does for that first rollercoaster drop while you hope against hope that the car will rise again, but you instinctively know that this ride is at its zenith. It's always downhill from here.

Here's the problem. Your code has a *single update mechanism* but *multiple update policies*. Your code will continue to get more complex and difficult to maintain until you separate your update mechanisms. Ecto changesets allow you to do exactly that.

One size does not fit all when it comes to update strategies. Validations, error reporting, security, and the like can change. When they do, if your single update policy is tightly coupled to a schema, it'll *hurt*. The changeset lets Ecto decouple update policy from the schema, and that's a good thing because you can handle each update policy in its own separate changeset function. You'll see a good example of this policy segregation when you learn about authentication.

Building Resource Routes

Now that we've updated our schema, context, and controller to handle new users, we need to add the new action to our router. Replace your main router scope with the following code:

```
ecto/listings/rumbl/lib/rumbl_web/router.change1.ex
scope "/", RumblWeb do
  pipe_through :browser

  get "/", PageController, :index
  resources "/users", UserController, only: [:index, :show, :new, :create]
end
```

resources is a shorthand implementation for a common set of actions that define create, read, update, and delete operations (commonly referred to as CRUD) to access *resources* via simple HTTP verbs. We use the resources macro to add a bunch of common routes that we'd otherwise need to write by hand. Since index and show already followed this convention, we remove the two get macros for the :index and :show actions, and we replace them with the resources macro. Since we don't need the edit or delete actions, we pass the :only option to explicitly list the routes we want generated. The following would be equivalent to a resources "/users", UserController declaration:

```
get "/users", UserController, :index
get "/users/:id/edit", UserController, :edit
get "/users/new", UserController, :new
get "/users/:id", UserController, :show
post "/users", UserController, :create
patch "/users/:id", UserController, :update
put "/users/:id", UserController, :update
delete "/users/:id", UserController, :delete
```

Sure, the resources macro has been known to reduce carpal tunnel syndrome almost as much as an ergonomic workspace, but it's more than a keystroke saver. By keeping to these conventions where you can, you're also communicating in a language that other programmers also understand. Creating these routes also makes additional functions available. You can use routes by name to build links, HTML elements, and the like.

If at any time you want to see all available routes, you can run the phx.routes Mix task, like this:

```
$ mix phx.routes
page_path  GET   /              RumblWeb.PageController :index
user_path  GET   /users         RumblWeb.UserController :index
user_path  GET   /users/new     RumblWeb.UserController :new
user_path  GET   /users/:id     RumblWeb.UserController :show
user_path  POST  /users         RumblWeb.UserController :create
```

With the route behind us, let's move on to the template. Now create a new file named lib/rumbl_web/templates/user/new.html.eex and add this:

```
ecto/listings/rumbl/lib/rumbl_web/templates/user/new.html.eex
<h1>New User</h1>

<%= form_for @changeset, Routes.user_path(@conn, :create), fn f -> %>
  <div>
    <%= text_input f, :name, placeholder: "Name" %>
  </div>
  <div>
    <%= text_input f, :username, placeholder: "Username" %>
  </div>
  <%= submit "Create User" %>
<% end %>
```

We use a function, rather than HTML tags, to build the form, giving it an anonymous function. form_for provides conveniences like security, UTF-8 encoding, and more. The function takes three arguments: a changeset, a path, and an anonymous function. That function takes one argument, the form data we're labeling f. We're asking the template engine to build a function returning everything in the template between fn f -> and end. You can see the additional functions in play as well. These build two input fields and a submit tag. Similar to link, all those functions are documented in the Phoenix.HTML library.[2]

If we visit http://localhost:4000/users/new in our browser to inspect the generated HTML, we see the following markup:

```
<form accept-charset="UTF-8" action="/users" method="post">
  <input name="_csrf_token"
         type="hidden"
         value="MFgTPhAieHUgGzJ2OiRDXXw3Luc7wV7h/reiiA==">
  <input name="_utf8" type="hidden" value="✓">
  <div>
    <input id="user_name"
           name="user[name]"
           placeholder="Name"
           type="text">
  </div>
  <div>
    <input id="user_username"
           name="user[username]"
           placeholder="Username"
           type="text">
  </div>
  <button type="submit" value="Create User"></button>
</form>
```

You can see all of the work the form_for tag and the other functions are doing for you. The special _csrf_token hidden parameter was injected for us, and it makes sure that a user's requests are hard to spoof across sites. Also, though we didn't specify the name user with each of our text fields, the parameter names like user[name] were pulled from our changeset.

You can probably guess where the data will go. The form will send a POST request to "/users", but we haven't yet created the action for it. Let's do that now.

Creating Resources

We have a form that submits the data for a new user. It's time to surface this new feature in our controller. This work should happen in our context. Let's extend Accounts to create users. Open up lib/rumbl/accounts.ex and key this in:

```
ecto/listings/rumbl/lib/rumbl/accounts.change3.ex
def create_user(attrs \\ %{}) do
  %User{}
  |> User.changeset(attrs)
  |> Repo.insert()
end
```

---

2. http://hexdocs.pm/phoenix_html

José says:

How Does Phoenix Know Which Data to Show in the Form?

Our application passes a changeset from Ecto to the form_for function. The Phoenix team had a problem. How should we make the changes in the changeset available to the form? We could have hardcoded form_for to directly use Ecto.Changeset, but we weren't happy with that choice. It would be brittle and hard to extend.

Imagine that your company decides to build an in-house data abstraction for some new technology and you want to integrate it with Phoenix. With forms tightly coupled to changesets, you'd be lost. You'd have to either rewrite forms or fork Phoenix. We needed a contract. Elixir protocols are the perfect solution to this problem.

To solve the form_for coupling problem, we defined a protocol named Phoenix.HTML.Form-Data, which separates the *interface* from the *implementation*. Ecto.Changeset implements this protocol to convert its internal data to the structure required by Phoenix forms, all properly documented in the Phoenix.HTML.FormData contract.

Take a look at the new short create_user function. We save our controller from this tiny bit of complexity. Our function has a short pipeline that starts with an empty user, applies a changeset, and then inserts it into the repository. The controller shouldn't care about these short persistence details, but neither should the schema. We isolate change policy to a single place.

With the context ready, we can plug the changes into the controller. The question is where this work should happen. Recall our changes to the router.ex file, when we added the resources "/users" macro to router.ex to build a set of conventional routes. One new route maps posts to "/users" to the UserController.create action. Add a create function to UserController:

```
ecto/listings/rumbl/lib/rumbl_web/controllers/user_controller.change2.ex
def create(conn, %{"user" => user_params}) do
  {:ok, user} = Accounts.create_user(user_params)

  conn
  |> put_flash(:info, "#{user.name} created!")
  |> redirect(to: Routes.user_path(conn, :index))
end
```

This pattern of code should be getting familiar to you by now. We keep piping functions together until the conn has the final result that we want. Each function does an isolated transform step. We call into our context first, registering our user in the application. Then, we take the connection and transform it twice, adding a flash message with the put_flash function, and then add a redirect instruction with the redirect function. Both of these are simple plug functions that we use to transform the connection, one step at a time.

Let's examine one tiny detail here first. In some places, we're going to need to refer to specific routes in the application. Generally, these get automatically generated, and you can access them from the YourApplication.Router.Helpers module. That's a lot to type each time you need a route. In the auto-generated rumbl_web file, you'll find the following snippet:

```
ecto/rumbl/lib/rumbl_web.ex
def controller do
  quote do
    use Phoenix.Controller, namespace: RumblWeb

    import Plug.Conn
    import RumblWeb.Gettext
    alias RumblWeb.Router.Helpers, as: Routes
  end
end
```

That's the ticket. The line alias RumblWeb.Router.Helpers, as: Routes gives us exactly what we need. Here's why.

Phoenix automatically generates the Helpers inside your router which contains named helpers to help developers generate and keep their routes up to date. Routes is a simple alias for Router.Helpers. That's why you can get any route through Routes.some_path!

Getting back to work, we can try out our shiny new create action. Go visit http://localhost:4000/users/new:

New User

Name

Username

CREATE USER

And when we click Create User, we should be sent back to the users index page to see our inserted user as shown in the figure on page 73.

We still have work to do, though. Type a username that's too long, and you're greeted with Phoenix's debug error page with the error "no match of right hand side value."

We were expecting a result of the shape {:ok, user} but got {:error, %Ecto.Change-set{}}. Our validations failed, throwing an error page. To fix this problem, let's check for both :ok and :error outcomes, showing validation errors upon failure. First we need to update our UserController to react to an invalid changeset:

```
ecto/listings/rumbl/lib/rumbl_web/controllers/user_controller.change3.ex
def create(conn, %{"user" => user_params}) do
  case Accounts.create_user(user_params) do
    {:ok, user} ->
      conn
      |> put_flash(:info, "#{user.name} created!")
      |> redirect(to: Routes.user_path(conn, :index))

    {:error, %Ecto.Changeset{} = changeset} ->
      render(conn, "new.html", changeset: changeset)
  end
end
```

Easy enough. We insert the new user record and then match on the return code. On :ok, we add a flash message to the conn and then redirect to the user_path. That route takes us to the index action. On error, we simply re-render new.html, passing the conn and the changeset with the failed validations. We'll use the Phoenix input fields to handle the problem.

Show the validation errors for each form input field in lib/rumbl_web/templates/user/new.html.eex, like this:

```
ecto/listings/rumbl/lib/rumbl_web/templates/user/new.change1.html.eex
<%= if @changeset.action do %>
  <div class="alert alert-danger">
    <p>Oops, something went wrong! Please check the errors below.</p>
  </div>
<% end %>

<div>
  <%= text_input f, :name, placeholder: "Name" %>
  <%= error_tag f, :name %>
</div>
<div>
  <%= text_input f, :username, placeholder: "Username" %>
  <%= error_tag f, :username %>
</div>
```

The :action field of a changeset indicates an action we tried to perform on it, such as :insert. When we build a new changeset, the field is nil. If Phoenix renders our form with any action, we know the form action had validation errors. In our code, we first check for the existence of @changeset.action. If it's present, we show a validation notice at the top of the form. Next, we use the error_tag function defined in lib/rumbl_web/views/error_helpers.ex to display an error tag next to each form input with the validation error for each field.

Now try again to submit your form with invalid fields:

Presto!

If you've not yet appreciated the Ecto strategy for changesets, this code should help. The changeset had all validation errors because the Ecto changeset carries the validations and stores this information for later use. In addition to validation errors, the changesets also *track changes*!

Remember, we don't have to compromise our context by letting Ecto persistence details bleed through. We're actually surfacing *Phoenix form details* because changesets implement the Phoenix.HTML.FormData protocol.

Let's see how that works. Crack open IEx. If you have an old window already open, you can just recompile the current project:

```
iex> recompile()
iex> alias Rumbl.Accounts.User
iex> changeset = User.changeset(%User{username: "eric", name: "Eric"}, %{})
%Ecto.Changeset{changes: %{}, ...}

iex> import Ecto.Changeset
Ecto.Changeset

iex> changeset = put_change(changeset, :username, "ericmj")
%Ecto.Changeset{changes: %{username: "ericmj"}, ...}

iex> changeset.changes
%{username: "ericmj"}

iex> get_change(changeset, :username)
"ericmj"
```

Now you have a more complete picture. Ecto is using changesets as a bucket to hold everything related to a database change, before and after persistence. You can use this information to do more than see what changed. Ecto lets you write code to do the minimal required database operation to update a record. If a particular change must be checked against a database constraint, such as a unique index, changesets do that. If Ecto can enforce validations without hitting the database, you can do that too. You'll explore the broader changeset API, validations, and strategies as we build out the rest of our application.

Wrapping Up

It's a good time to pause and take stock of what we've done. It's been a busy chapter.

- We began the chapter by introducing Ecto and announcing our intention to replace the naive implementation in our context with a database-backed Ecto repository.

- We configured our new database and connected it to OTP, so that Elixir could do the right thing in the event our repository crashes.

- We created a schema, complete with information about each necessary field.

- We created a migration, to help us specify our database tables and automate doing and undoing any database changes.

- We created a changeset so Ecto could efficiently track and manage each change requested by our application.

- We integrated this change into our application.

We've already come a long way, and we're only a few chapters in. We're ready to handle some more sophisticated application features. Let's get rolling. In the next chapter, you'll use some of these new features to authenticate a user.

## CHAPTER 5

Authenticating Users

We have something that is starting to look like an application. Our database-backed Accounts context is wired to our controller using changesets and forms. Let's ramp up the sophistication with real login forms and sessions. Rather than use something off the shelf, we can build it ourselves. Along the way you'll learn more about managing change with *Ecto changesets* and chaining together functions using *plugs*. Finally, we'll introduce session handling so our application can track logged-in users.

As you've seen, Phoenix makes it easy to add functionality to your application from bottom to top. Authentication forms the foundation for your whole application's security system, though, so we're going to be sure each decision is right.

Preparing for Authentication

Authentication is one of those features that can make or break your whole application experience. Programmers need to be able to easily layer on the right services and to direct requests where they need to go. Administrators need to trust the underlying policies, and also to configure the password constraints. Initially, we'll plan our approach and install the necessary dependencies.

Our approach to authentication will be a conventional one. Users will provide credentials when registering. We'll store those in the database in a secure way. In our application, a *session* will contain the data about each individual user. We'll let Phoenix manage the details. A user starting a session will need to provide the credentials, and we'll check those against our database. We'll mark each user as authenticated in the session, so that users are granted access until their sessions expire or they log out. We will build these functions and expose those ideas into the Accounts context.

Above all else, we want this system to be secure. We won't write the dicey parts ourselves, and we'll make sure that we use approaches that are well understood to be secure. We'll use as much as we can from Phoenix, and we'll rely on Comeonin to handle the critical hashing piece.

Comeonin[1] is a specification for password hashing libraries. It provides up-to-date and secure hashing schemes. We will use the Pbkdf2 password hashing technique, as it does not require any native dependencies, but there are other options listed on Comeonin's documentation. Add :pbkdf2_elixir to your mix.exs dependencies to handle password hashing, like this:

```
defp deps do
  [
    ...,
    {:pbkdf2_elixir, "~> 1.0"}
  ]
end
```

:pbkdf2_elixir, like our other dependencies in mix.exs, is an application. An application is what you think it is: a collection of modules that work together and can be managed as a whole. So far, our application depends on :phoenix and :phoenix_ecto, as you'd expect, but also the :postgrex database driver, :gettext for internationalization, and now :pbkdf2_elixir for managing our password hashing.

Our application also relies on applications that ship as part of Elixir and Erlang. Those are not listed under deps, but within the application function in your mix.exs:

```
authentication/rumbl/mix.exs
def application do
  [
    mod: {Rumbl.Application, []},
    extra_applications: [:logger, :runtime_tools]
  ]
end
```

The application function tells Mix how to start our :rumbl application, and we configure Elixir to start :logger and :runtime_tools, which are part of the standard library.

Now run mix deps.get to fetch your new dependencies, like this:

```
$ mix deps.get
```

This command downloads the :pbkdf2_elixir dependency into deps directory. Elixir will make sure to start it before your own :rumbl application. Now that our preparations are out of the way, we're ready to begin the implementation.

---

1. https://github.com/riverrun/comeonin

Managing Registration Changesets

You've already seen a changeset for creating a new user, the one that handles the name and username. Let's review that now:

```
authentication/rumbl/lib/rumbl/accounts/user.ex
def changeset(user, attrs) do
  user
  |> cast(attrs, [:name, :username])
  |> validate_required([:name, :username])
  |> validate_length(:username, min: 1, max: 20)
end
```

The Ecto.Changeset.cast function converts a raw map of user input to a changeset, accepting only the :name and :username keys. Then, we fire a validation limiting the length of valid usernames to twenty characters. A failing validation places errors in the changeset so we can display them to the user.

As you might expect, you'll use *one changeset per use case*. Our existing changeset handles all the attributes except passwords. We can safely use it for updating nonsensitive information such as a form on a profile page. We'll build a separate changeset to manage more sensitive data such as credential changes.

For the password changeset, we'll add two new fields, :password and :password_hash. The :password field will contain the password in plain text, but for security reasons we won't store that field in the database. Instead, we will hash the password in the :password_hash field we added to the users table way back in Chapter 4, Ecto and Changesets, on page 59. Now, we'll define those two fields in the schema:

```
authentication/listings/rumbl/lib/rumbl/accounts/user.change1.ex
field :password, :string, virtual: true
field :password_hash, :string
```

We marked the :password field as virtual: true. Virtual schema fields in Ecto exist only in the struct, not the database.

Now let's create our separate changeset to handle user registrations:

```
authentication/listings/rumbl/lib/rumbl/accounts/user.change1.ex
def registration_changeset(user, params) do
  user
  |> changeset(params)
  |> cast(params, [:password])
  |> validate_required([:password])
  |> validate_length(:password, min: 6, max: 100)
  |> put_pass_hash()
end
```

There's not much to see here. We defined a registration_changeset function which creates a new changeset, casts the :password field and validates it. Then, our function delegates to the put_pass_hash function to compute and store the user hash in the database, like this:

```
authentication/listings/rumbl/lib/rumbl/accounts/user.change1.ex
defp put_pass_hash(changeset) do
  case changeset do
    %Ecto.Changeset{valid?: true, changes: %{password: pass}} ->
      put_change(changeset, :password_hash, Pbkdf2.hash_pwd_salt(pass))

    _ ->
      changeset
  end
end
```

We check to see if the changeset is valid so we won't waste time hashing an invalid or missing password. Then, we use comeonin to hash our password, following the instructions in its readme file. Finally, we put the result into the changeset as password_hash. If the changeset is invalid, we simply return it to the caller.

These password rules are light

 We're creating an intentionally lax password so readers can focus on learning concepts instead of memorizing passwords. You will want to use more strict password requirements in a production system.

Here you can see how easy it is to compose with changesets. We used our base User.changeset function to cast and validate the name and username parameters. Then we validated our virtual password field inside our registration changeset. Notice that it's trivial to validate our virtual password field, though we're not actually storing that value in the database! Persistence is not strongly coupled to our change policies.

Keep in mind that this is an example application, and you should configure your own password rules to fit your scenario. If you would like, OWASP[2] has an excellent set of guidelines you can follow depending on your specific requirements.

Let's take it for a spin.

---

2.   https://github.com/OWASP/CheatSheetSeries

Open up a console and follow along. If you've been following along and aren't working on a new console, you can safely skip alias RumblWeb.Router.Helpers, as: Routes.

Let's try out our changeset:

```
iex> alias Rumbl.Accounts.User
iex> alias RumblWeb.Router.Helpers, as: Routes
iex> changeset = User.registration_changeset(%User{}, %{
...>   username: "max", name: "Max", password: "123"
...> })
#Ecto.Changeset<...>
iex> changeset.valid?
false

iex> changeset.changes
%{
  name: "Max",
  username: "max",
  password: "123"
}
```

As we expected, creating a user with our registration changeset and a bad password results in an invalid changeset. When we inspect the changeset.changes, we can see that password_hash is missing because we didn't bother hashing a password we knew to be invalid.

Let's continue and see what happens when we create a valid registration changeset:

```
iex> changeset = User.registration_changeset(%User{}, %{
...>   username: "max", name: "Max", password: "asecret"
...> })
#Ecto.Changeset<
  action: nil,
  changes: %{
    name: "Max",
    username: "max",
    password: "asecret",
    password_hash:
      "$pbkdf2-sha512$r7zRM4aQgSUGlOy4483cFe1UouMC/9emcOI75MhgDQ6A9WNWBpfr."
  },
  errors: [],
  data: #Rumbl.Accounts.User<>,
  valid?: true
>
```

Check to see if it's valid, and see the changes:

```
iex> changeset.valid?
true

iex> changeset.changes
%{
  name: "Max",
  username: "max",
  password: "asecret",
  password_hash:
    "$pbkdf2-sha512$r7zRM4aQgSUGlOy4483cFe1UouMC/9emcOI75MhgDQ6A9WNWBpfr."
}
```

When given a valid username and password, our changeset applies the put_pass_hash function and puts a change for our password_hash field, but we now have an issue. The users we inserted up to this point lack account passwords, which won't be valid with the system's new behavior where we expect all accounts to have one. Let's fix that now by updating our existing users with properly hashed temporary passwords. Key this into your IEx session. If you're using an existing window, you may need to recompile with recompile:

```
iex> recompile()
iex> alias Rumbl.Repo
iex> for u <- Repo.all(User) do
...>   Repo.update!(User.registration_changeset(u, %{password: "temppass"}))
...> end
```

Now our new and existing users alike will have valid, secure passwords.

Creating Users

Now that things are working smoothly and safely, let's integrate that new code with our web layer through the public API we expose through the Accounts context. We'll need to replace Accounts.create_user with a function that performs proper account registration with passwords.

Since our UserController currently calls the Accounts.create_user function, we hope to get by with minimal changes. Our approach works fine but internally we are only using the base User.changeset which doesn't yet include our password hashing.

At this point, we could change the Accounts.create_user function to use the registration_changeset. Instead, we will explicitly build a new function to manage registration details. We'll maintain create_user to expose the details *any other API* will need to build users. So often, applications must create accounts to satisfy a number of different use cases, such as seeding example data, imports, or sending user invitations. For these cases, we want a workflow in our Accounts context that allows us to create a user without the full ceremony that end users use.

We will write a new Accounts.register_user function which wraps up all the details of end-user registration, while maintaining our API for simply creating a new user in the system. While we are at it, let's add a function to expose the registration changeset in the User schema. Open up your Accounts context and add these functions:

authentication/listings/rumbl/lib/rumbl/accounts.change1.ex
```
def change_registration(%User{} = user, params) do
  User.registration_changeset(user, params)
end

def register_user(attrs \\ %{}) do
  %User{}
  |> User.registration_changeset(attrs)
  |> Repo.insert()
end
```

Any view that requires the user passwords will need to use a specific changeset for registration. This new function isn't very exciting, but as we grow our application, our purpose-built functions will pay dividends by simplifying interactions with our controller. For example, as soon as we're ready to send welcome emails when a new user registers, we have a perfect place for this new code to live.

Next, we need to make a tiny change in the UserController. The create action must now call our new register_user function and the new action must pull in our registration changeset, like this:

authentication/listings/rumbl/lib/rumbl_web/controllers/user_controller.change1.ex
```
def new(conn, _params) do
  changeset = Accounts.change_registration(%User{}, %{})
  render(conn, "new.html", changeset: changeset)
end

def create(conn, %{"user" => user_params}) do
  case Accounts.register_user(user_params) do
    {:ok, user} ->
      conn
      |> put_flash(:info, "#{user.name} created!")
      |> redirect(to: Routes.user_path(conn, :index))

    {:error, %Ecto.Changeset{} = changeset} ->
      render(conn, "new.html", changeset: changeset)
  end
end
```

In create we use pattern matching to pick off the user_params and pass them to our new Accounts.register_user function. If our registration was successful, we redirect as before. If not, we simply render the new template again, with the changeset, which now has the errors from our failed validations.

Finally, we need to make one small change to our new user registration form to accept the user password. Open up lib/rumbl_web/templates/user/new.html.eex and add the following code above the submit button:

authentication/listings/rumbl/lib/rumbl_web/templates/user/new.change1.html.eex
```
<div>
  <%= password_input f, :password, placeholder: "Password" %>
  <%= error_tag f, :password %>
</div>
```

Now, we're ready to load the registration form at http://localhost:4000/users/new:

New User

Name

Username

Password

CREATE USER

You should be smiling now. Like plug pipelines, validations are a pipeline of functions that transform the changeset. Each validation is a step that transforms the changeset, explicitly tracking the changes and their validity. The actual change happens only when we call the repository in the context.

Now we should be able to visit http://localhost:4000/users/new and create new users with our registration changeset. We have a problem, though. Newly registered users are not automatically logged in, and users still can't log in or log out at will.

We need to create an authentication service and make it available throughout our system. You've used plugs created by others, but for this job it's time you learn to create your own. We'll implement authentication as a plug. That way we can add it to a pipeline in our router so other controllers can use it as needed.

The Anatomy of a Plug

Before we build our plug, let's take a deep dive into the Plug library and learn how plugs work from the inside. There are two kinds of plugs: *module plugs* and *function plugs*. A function plug is a single function. A module plug is a module that provides two functions with some configuration details. Either way, they work the same.

We have seen both kinds of plugs in use. From the endpoint module in lib/rumbl_web/endpoint.ex, you can see an example of a module plug:

```
plug Plug.RequestId
```

You specify a module plug by providing the module name. In the router, you can see an example of a function plug:

```
plug :protect_from_forgery
```

You specify a function plug with the name of the function as an atom. Because a module is just a collection of functions, it strengthens the idea that plugs are just functions.

For our first plug, we'll write a module plug that encapsulates all the authentication logic in one place.

Module Plugs

Sometimes you might want to share a plug across more than one module. In that case, you can use a module plug. To satisfy the Plug specification, a module plug must have two functions, named init and call.

The simplest possible module plug returns the given options on init and the given connection on call. This plug does nothing:

```
defmodule NothingPlug do
  def init(opts) do
    opts
  end

  def call(conn, _opts) do
    conn
  end
end
```

Remember, a typical plug transforms a connection. The main work of a module plug happens in call. In our NothingPlug, we simply pass the connection through without changes. The call will happen *at runtime*.

Sometimes, you might want to let the programmer change the behavior of a plug. We can do that work in the second argument to call, options. In our NothingPlug, we don't need any more information to do our job, so we ignore the options.

Sometimes, you might need Phoenix to do some heavy lifting to transform options. That's the job of the init function. Plug uses the result of init as the second argument to call. In development mode, Phoenix calls init at runtime, but in production mode, init is called only once, at *compile time*. This strategy makes init the perfect place to validate and transform options without slowing down every request so call can be as fast as possible. Since call is the workhorse of Plug, we want it to do as little work as possible.

For both module and function plugs, the request interface is the same. conn, the first argument, is the data we pass through every plug. It has the details for any request, and we morph it in tiny steps until we eventually send a response. All plugs take a conn and return a conn.

You'll see piped functions using a common data structure over and over in Elixir. The trick that makes this tactic work is having the right common data structure. Since Plug works with web APIs, our data structure will specify the typical details of the web server's domain.

In Phoenix, you'll see connections, usually abbreviated conn, literally everywhere. At the end of the day, the conn is only a Plug.Conn struct, and it forms the foundation for Plug.

Plug.Conn Fields

You can find great online documentation for Plug.Conn.[3] This structure has the various fields that web applications need to understand about web requests and responses. Let's look at some of the supported fields.

Request fields contain information about the inbound request. They're parsed by the adapter for the web server you're using. Cowboy is the default web server that Phoenix uses, but you can also choose to plug in your own. These fields contain strings, except where otherwise specified:

---

3.   http://hexdocs.pm/plug/Plug.Conn.html

host

The requested host. For example, www.pragprog.com.

method

The request method. For example, GET or POST.

path_info

The path, split into a List of segments. For example, ["admin", "users"].

req_headers

A list of request headers. For example, [{"content-type", "text/plain"}].

scheme

The request protocol as an atom. For example, :https.

You can get other information as well, such as the query string, the remote IP address, the port, and the like. For Phoenix, if a web request's information is available from the web server's adapter, it's in Plug.Conn.

Next comes a set of *fetchable fields*. A fetchable field is empty until you explicitly request it. These fields require a little time to process, so they're left out of the connection by default until you want to explicitly fetch them:

cookies

These are the request cookies with the response cookies.

params

These are the request parameters. Some plugs help to parse these parameters from the query string, or from the request body.

Next are a series of fields that are used to process web requests and keep information about the plug pipeline. Here are some of the fields you'll encounter:

assigns

This user-defined map contains anything you want to put in it. For instance, this is where we will keep the authenticated user for the current request.

halted

Sometimes a connection must be halted, such as a failed authorization. In this case, the halting plug sets this flag.

You can also find a secret_key_base for everything related to encryption.

Since the Plug framework handles the whole life cycle of a request, including both the request and the response, Plug.Conn provides fields for the response:

resp_body
> Initially an empty string, the response body will contain the HTTP response string when it's available.

resp_cookies
> The resp_cookies has the outbound cookies for the response.

resp_headers
> These headers follow the HTTP specification and contain information such as the response type and caching rules.

status
> The response code generally contains 200–299 for success, 300–399 for redirects, 400–499 for bad client requests such as not-found, and 500+ for server errors.

Finally, Plug supports some private fields reserved for the adapter and frameworks:

adapter
> Information about the underlying web server is stored here.

private
> This field has a map for the private use of frameworks.

Initially, a conn comes in almost blank and is filled out progressively by different plugs in the pipeline. For example, the endpoint may parse parameters, and the application developer will set fields primarily in assigns. Functions that render set the response fields such as status, change the state, and so on.

Plug.Conn also defines many functions that directly manipulate those fields, which makes abstracting the work of doing more complex operations such as managing cookies or sending files straightforward.

Now that you have a little more knowledge, we're ready to transform the connection by writing our first plug.

Writing an Authentication Plug

The authentication process works in two stages. First, we'll store the user ID in the session every time a new user registers or a user logs in. Second, we'll check if there's a new user in the session and store it in conn.assigns for every incoming request, so it can be accessed in our controllers and views. Let's start with the second part because it's a little easier to follow.

Create a file called lib/rumbl_web/controllers/auth.ex that looks like this:

```
authentication/listings/rumbl/lib/rumbl_web/controllers/auth.ex
defmodule RumblWeb.Auth do
  import Plug.Conn

  def init(opts), do: opts

  def call(conn, _opts) do
    user_id = get_session(conn, :user_id)
    user = user_id && Rumbl.Accounts.get_user(user_id)
    assign(conn, :current_user, user)
  end
end
```

Don't let the init function throw you off. It's just a simple function to allow compile time options. Plugs allow data to flow through an application at *run time* through the context. Without init, our plug can't accept any *compile time* options.

call checks if a :user_id is stored in the session. If one exists, we look it up and assign the result in the connection. assign is a function imported from Plug.Conn that slightly transforms the connection—in this case, storing the user (or nil) in conn.assigns. That way, the :current_user will be available in all downstream functions including controllers and views.

Let's add our plug to the router, at the end of the browser pipeline:

```
authentication/listings/rumbl/lib/rumbl_web/router.change1.ex
pipeline :browser do
  plug :accepts, ["html"]
  plug :fetch_session
  plug :fetch_flash
  plug :protect_from_forgery
  plug :put_secure_browser_headers
  plug RumblWeb.Auth
end
```

With our plug in place, we can begin to use this information downstream.

Restricting Access

The RumblWeb.Auth plug processes the request information and transforms the conn, adding :current_user to conn.assigns. Now, downstream plugs can use it to find out if a user is logged in.

We'll use this information to restrict access to pages where we list or show user information. Specifically, we don't want to allow users to access the :index and :show actions of RumblWeb.UserController unless they're logged in.

Open up RumblWeb.UserController and add the following function:

authentication/listings/rumbl/lib/rumbl_web/controllers/user_controller.change2.ex
```elixir
defp authenticate(conn) do
  if conn.assigns.current_user do
    conn
  else
    conn
    |> put_flash(:error, "You must be logged in to access that page")
    |> redirect(to: Routes.page_path(conn, :index))
    |> halt()
  end
end
```

If there's a current user, we return the connection unchanged. Otherwise we store a flash message and redirect back to our application root. We use halt(conn) to stop any downstream transformations.

Let's invoke the authenticate function from index to try it out:

authentication/listings/rumbl/lib/rumbl_web/controllers/user_controller.change2.ex
```elixir
def index(conn, _params) do
  case authenticate(conn) do
    %Plug.Conn{halted: true} = conn ->
      conn

    conn ->
      users = Accounts.list_users()
      render(conn, "index.html", users: users)
  end
end
```

Now visit http://localhost:4000/users, where we're redirected back to the root with a message telling us to log in, as shown in the figure on page 91.

We could make the same changes to the show action, invoking our plug and honoring halt. And we could do the same thing every time we require authentication. We'd also have code that's repetitive, ugly, and error prone. We need to *plug* the authenticate function for the actions to be protected. Let's do that.

Like endpoints and routers, controllers also have their own plug pipeline. Each plug in the controller pipeline is executed in order, before the action is invoked. The controller pipeline lets us explicitly choose which actions fire any given plug.

To plug the authenticate function, we must first make it a function plug. A function plug is any function that receives two arguments—the connection

You must be logged in to access that page

Welcome to Rumbl.io!

Rumbl out loud.

and a set of options—and returns the connection. With a minor tweak, we can satisfy that contract. You need only add an options variable, which you'll ignore:

authentication/listings/rumbl/lib/rumbl_web/controllers/user_controller.change3.ex
```
defp authenticate(conn, _opts) do
  if conn.assigns.current_user do
    conn
  else
    conn
    |> put_flash(:error, "You must be logged in to access that page")
    |> redirect(to: Routes.page_path(conn, :index))
    |> halt()
  end
end
```

Now let's plug it in our controller, right after alias Rumbl.Accounts.User:

authentication/listings/rumbl/lib/rumbl_web/controllers/user_controller.change3.ex
```
plug :authenticate when action in [:index, :show]
```

Then, change the index action back to its previous state, like this:

authentication/listings/rumbl/lib/rumbl_web/controllers/user_controller.change3.ex
```
def index(conn, _params) do
  users = Accounts.list_users()
  render(conn, "index.html", users: users)
end
```

Visit http://localhost:4000/users to see our plug in action. We redirect, exactly as we should.

Let's take a minute to appreciate the code we've written so far. A small change to our authentication lets us plug it before every action. We can also share it with any other controllers or even move it to a router pipeline, restricting whole sections of our application with minor changes. None of these features relies on magical inheritance mechanisms, only our explicit lists of functions in our plug pipelines.

At this point, you may also be wondering what happened with halt. When we changed the index action, we had to explicitly check if the connection halted or not, before acting on it. Plug pipelines explicitly check for halted: true between every plug invocation, so the halting concern is neatly solved by Plug.

In fact, you're seeing Elixir macro expansion in action. Let's take an arbitrary example. Suppose you write code like this:

```
plug :one
plug Two
plug :three, some: :option
```

It would compile to:

```
case one(conn, []) do
  %Plug.Conn{halted: true} = conn -> conn
  conn ->
    case Two.call(conn, Two.init([])) do
      %Plug.Conn{halted: true} = conn -> conn
      conn ->
        case three(conn, some: :option) do
          %Plug.Conn{halted: true} = conn -> conn
          conn -> conn
        end
    end
end
```

Elixir macros and macro expansion are beyond the scope of this book. What you need to know is that at some point in the compile process, Elixir would translate the first example to the second. Conceptually, not much is happening here, and that's exactly the beauty behind Plug. For each plug, we invoke it with the given options, check if the returned connection halted, and move forward if it didn't. It's a simple abstraction that allows us to express and compose both simple and complex functionality.

With all that said, we already have a mechanism for loading data from the session and using it to restrict user access. But we still don't have a mechanism to log the users in.

Logging In

Let's add a tiny function to RumblWeb.Auth that receives the connection and the user, and stores the user ID in the session:

```
authentication/listings/rumbl/lib/rumbl_web/controllers/auth.change1.ex
def login(conn, user) do
  conn
  |> assign(:current_user, user)
  |> put_session(:user_id, user.id)
  |> configure_session(renew: true)
end
```

As you recall, the Plug.Conn struct has a field called assigns. We call setting a value in that structure an *assign*. Our function stores the given user as the :current_user assign, puts the user ID in the session, and finally configures the session, setting the :renew option to true. The last step is extremely important and it protects us from session fixation attacks. It tells Plug to send the session cookie back to the client with a different identifier, in case an attacker knew, by any chance, the previous one.

Let's go back to the RumblWeb.UserController.create action and change it to call the login function after we insert the user in the database:

```
authentication/listings/rumbl/lib/rumbl_web/controllers/user_controller.change2.ex
def create(conn, %{"user" => user_params}) do
  case Accounts.register_user(user_params) do
    {:ok, user} ->
      conn
      |> RumblWeb.Auth.login(user)
      |> put_flash(:info, "#{user.name} created!")
      |> redirect(to: Routes.user_path(conn, :index))

    {:error, %Ecto.Changeset{} = changeset} ->
      render(conn, "new.html", changeset: changeset)
  end
end
```

Now visit http://localhost:4000/users/new, register a new user, and try to access the pages we restricted previously. As you can see, the user can finally access them.

Implementing Login and Logout

We made great progress in the last section. We created a module plug that loads information from the session, used this information to restrict user access, and finally stored users in the session.

We're almost done with our authentication feature. We need to implement both login and logout functionality, as well as change the layout to include links to those pages.

First things first. Before changing our controllers and views, let's expose a function that authenticates a given username and password. We will look up a user by username in the database and securely ensure that the user's password matches the one in the database. The Accounts context is a perfect place to define this function. Open up rumbl/accounts.ex and add the new function authenticate_by_username_and_pass, like this:

authentication/listings/rumbl/lib/rumbl/accounts.change2.ex
```
def authenticate_by_username_and_pass(username, given_pass) do
  user = get_user_by(username: username)

  cond do
    user && Pbkdf2.verify_pass(given_pass, user.password_hash) ->
      {:ok, user}

    user ->
      {:error, :unauthorized}

    true ->
      Pbkdf2.no_user_verify()
      {:error, :not_found}
  end
end
```

We use the existing get_user_by function to look up a User by username. If the user isn't found, we use comeonin's no_user_verify() function to simulate a password check with variable timing. This hardens our authentication layer against timing attacks,[4] which is crucial to keeping our application secure. If we find our user and the password matches, we return the user wrapped in an :ok tuple, otherwise we return {:error, :unauthorized} for a bad password, or {:error, :not_found} if the user does not exist for the given username.

Now we are ready to work on our login and logout pages. Let's add some new routes to lib/rumbl_web/router.ex:

authentication/listings/rumbl/lib/rumbl_web/router.change2.ex
```
scope "/", RumblWeb do
  pipe_through :browser # Use the default browser stack

  get "/", PageController, :index
  resources "/users", UserController, only: [:index, :show, :new, :create]
  resources "/sessions", SessionController, only: [:new, :create, :delete]
end
```

---

4. https://en.wikipedia.org/wiki/Timing_attack

We add three of the prepackaged REST routes for /sessions. We use the REST routes for GET /sessions/new to show a new session login form, POST /sessions to log in, and DELETE /sessions/:id to log out.

Next, we need a SessionController to handle those actions. Create a lib/rumbl_web/controllers/session_controller.ex, like this:

```
authentication/listings/rumbl/lib/rumbl_web/controllers/session_controller.ex
defmodule RumblWeb.SessionController do
  use RumblWeb, :controller

  def new(conn, _) do
    render(conn, "new.html")
  end
end
```

The new action simply renders our login form. We need a second action, create, to handle the form submission, like this:

```
authentication/listings/rumbl/lib/rumbl_web/controllers/session_controller.change1.ex
def create(
  conn,
  %{"session" => %{"username" => username, "password" => pass}}
) do
  case Rumbl.Accounts.authenticate_by_username_and_pass(username, pass) do
    {:ok, user} ->
      conn
      |> RumblWeb.Auth.login(user)
      |> put_flash(:info, "Welcome back!")
      |> redirect(to: Routes.page_path(conn, :index))

    {:error, _reason} ->
      conn
      |> put_flash(:error, "Invalid username/password combination")
      |> render("new.html")
  end
end
```

That create action picks off the inbound arguments for username as username, and for password as pass. Then, we call authenticate_by_username_and_pass. On success, we report a success flash message to the user and redirect to Routes.page_path. Otherwise, we report a failure message to our user and render new again.

Here we can appreciate the benefits of contexts once again. Instead of the controller dealing with all of the complexity, our context handles three return types: {:ok, user}, {:error, :not_found}, and {:error, :unauthorized}. The controller does not care about the details of how authentication works. The controller's job is to translate whatever our business logic returns into something meaningful for the user, which is quite trivial to do with pattern matching.

In particular, we choose to match only on {:error, _} to ignore the :unauthorized and :not_found reason codes, returning only a vague "Invalid username/password combination" message. We could have returned something like "Invalid password for username" or "Username not found", but this approach might raise privacy issues as anyone would be able to find whether an email is registered on the website.

We still need to create our view and template. Create a new lib/rumbl_web/views/session_view.ex file that looks like this:

authentication/listings/rumbl/lib/rumbl_web/views/session_view.ex
```
defmodule RumblWeb.SessionView do
  use RumblWeb, :view
end
```

Next, we need a session directory for our new view, so create a lib/rumbl_web/templates/session/new.html.eex with our new login form, like this:

authentication/listings/rumbl/lib/rumbl_web/templates/session/new.html.eex
```
<h1>Login</h1>

<%= form_for @conn,
            Routes.session_path(@conn, :create),
            [as: :session],
            fn f -> %>
  <div>
    <%= text_input f, :username, placeholder: "Username" %>
  </div>
  <div>
    <%= password_input f, :password, placeholder: "Password" %>
  </div>
  <%= submit "Log in" %>
<% end %>
```

We use form_for as in our new-user forms, but instead of passing a changeset, we pass the %Plug.Conn{} struct. Plug.conn structs are useful when you're creating forms that aren't backed by a changeset, such as a login or search form. To try out the new page, we have to logout, but we haven't written that functionality yet. As a temporary workaround, instead of logging out you can clear your browser cookies or start a new session in incognito mode, then visit /sessions/new to try some login attempts.

With a bad login, we see an error flash notice and our template rerendered as shown in the figure on page 97.

Now let's try a good login:

It works!

Presenting User Account Links

We've come a long way. We can now authenticate a user in a secure way. We're using a single function that we can reliably share across each feature of the application that needs it. Now, we can turn our attention to showing customized headers in our layout based on a user's authentication status. Let's start with a welcome message and a logout link.

We want to change the layout of the application to handle the new user features so that other views can also take advantage of these features. Let's update the layout in lib/rumbl_web/templates/layout/app.html.eex. Replace your <nav> section to look like this:

authentication/listings/rumbl/lib/rumbl_web/templates/layout/app.change1.html.eex
```
<section class="container">
  <nav role="navigation">
    <ul>
      <%= if @current_user do %>
        <li><%= @current_user.username %></li>
        <li>
          <%= link "Log out",
                to: Routes.session_path(@conn, :delete, @current_user),
                method: "delete" %>
        </li>
      <% else %>
        <li><%= link "Register", to: Routes.user_path(@conn, :new) %></li>
        <li><%= link "Log in", to: Routes.session_path(@conn, :new) %></li>
      <% end %>
    </ul>
  </nav>
  <a href="http://phoenixframework.org/" class="phx-logo">
    <img src="<%= Routes.static_url(@conn, "/images/phoenix.png") %>"
      alt="Phoenix Framework Logo"/>
  </a>
</section>
```

You can see our strategy. We test whether the user is authenticated by checking if the @current_user is present. Because RumblWeb.Auth.login stored the user under conn.assigns.current_user, it's automatically available as @current_user in our views. To put it more broadly, everything in conn.assigns is available in our views.

If the user is available, we show the username, followed by a logout link. Otherwise, we allow users to register themselves or log in. If you're watching closely, you can see that this template uses the Routes.session_path twice when building the login and logout links. Each link function uses it a little differently, as you'll see when we break it down.

The code uses the Phoenix helpers to build a link:

```
link "Log out",
  to: Routes.session_path(@conn, :delete, @current_user),
  method: "delete"
```

The link:

- Has the text Log out

- Links to the Routes.session_path path with the @conn connection, the :delete action, and the @current_user argument

- Uses the HTTP delete method

By passing the :method option to link, Phoenix generates a form tag instead of an anchor tag. Links without a specified HTTP method will default to GET, and Phoenix will render a simple link.

Let's head back to our browser and try it out. When we visit http://localhost:4000, we see the Log in link in the header:

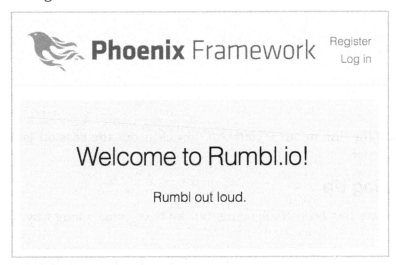

Now sign in with one of the accounts you created earlier:

And it works.

Now that we have a working dynamic header with a "Log out" link, we need to implement the delete action in our SessionController and handle clearing the user's session in our auth module. That's nearly trivial to do.

First let's do the work to delete the session in RumblWeb.Auth:

```
authentication/listings/rumbl/lib/rumbl_web/controllers/auth.change2.ex
def logout(conn) do
  configure_session(conn, drop: true)
end
```

This time we are invoking configure_session and setting :drop to true, which will drop the whole session at the end of the request. If you want to keep the session around, you could also delete only the user ID information by calling delete_session(conn, :user_id).

Now, we need only add the controller action. In lib/rumbl_web/controllers/session_controller.ex, add the delete action, like this:

```
authentication/listings/rumbl/lib/rumbl_web/controllers/session_controller.change2.ex
def delete(conn, _) do
  conn
  |> RumblWeb.Auth.logout()
  |> redirect(to: Routes.page_path(conn, :index))
end
```

Following the link in our layout will now clear out the session and redirect us to the root.

Wrapping Up

This chapter has been challenging, but we have come a long way. Let's take stock:

- We used our existing Accounts context to look up session users.

- We added the pbkdf2_elixir dependency to our project for password hashing.

- We built our own authentication layer.

- We built the associated changesets to handle validation of passwords.

- We implemented a module plug that loads the user from the session and made it part of our browser pipeline.

- We implemented a function plug and used it alongside some specific actions in our controller pipeline.

In the next chapter, you'll dive deeper into Ecto's waters by exploring relationships. We'll also begin to flesh out our application, using code generators to speed us along.

## CHAPTER 6

Generators and Relationships

So far, our Ecto tour has been pretty basic. We've read and written repository data, but we still haven't connected any schemas together. Relational databases like PostgreSQL are named that way for a reason. Dealing with related data is the defining characteristic of that whole family of databases, so management of relationships is the feature that makes or breaks any persistence layer. This chapter takes you on a deeper dive into Ecto by exploring how to tie our schemas together in the database.

Throughout this process, we'll make some design decisions. Our contexts will continue to be the overarching API that our controllers will access. Sometimes those contexts will tie together united concepts. Other times we'll use contexts to segregate the different concerns of our application.

Along the way, we'll use code generators to accelerate the process where it's possible, and you'll walk through what each of these generators does for us. When you're through, you'll know how to take greater advantage of some of the code generators in Phoenix, and you'll have a better understanding of how to layer together individual Ecto schemas with relationships, and group together related concepts in contexts.

Using Generators

To dig into Ecto, we're going to have to define relationships, and for that we need to extend the domain of our application. That's great, because our application is going to need those features. Let's define our problem in a little more detail.

Adding Videos and Annotations

The rumbl application will let users choose a video. Then, they can attach their comments, in real time. Users can play back these videos with comments over time. See what it looks like in the figure on page 102.

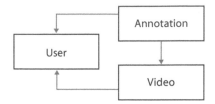

Users create videos. Then, users can create annotations on those videos. If you've ever seen *Mystery Science Theater 3000*, you know exactly what we're going for. In that show, some robots sat on the bottom of the screen, throwing in their opinions about bad science fiction.

Here's how it's going to work. Rather than building everything by hand as we did with the Accounts context and its User schema, we're going to use generators to build the skeleton—including the migration, context, controllers, and templates to bootstrap the process for us. It's going to happen fast, and we're going to move through the boilerplate quickly, so be sure to follow closely.

Generating Web Interfaces

Phoenix includes two Mix tasks to bootstrap web interfaces. phx.gen.html creates a simple HTTP scaffold with HTML pages, and phx.gen.json does the same for a REST-based API using JSON. They give you a simple scaffold for a traditional web-based application with CRUD (create, read, update, and delete) operations. You get migrations, a basic context, controllers, and templates for simple CRUD operations of a resource, as well as tests so you can hit the ground running. You won't write all your Phoenix code this way, but the generators are a great way to get up and running quickly. They can also help new users learn how the Phoenix layers fit together in the context of a working application.

Our application allows users to annotate videos in real time. We know up-front that we'll need a video resource, but we need to figure out where it will live within our application. When you're organizing code, think contexts first. Rumbl enables users to interact around videos in real time, and we can imagine a future expansion to real-time conversations around all types of multimedia---images, books, etc.—so a Multimedia context will give us a nice place to group this functionality.

Now that we know where videos will live, we'll start with a few fields, including:

- An associated User
- A creation time for the video
- A URL of the video location
- A title
- The type of the video

Later, our application will let users decorate these videos with annotations. But first, we need users to be able to create and show their videos. Let's use the phx.gen.html Mix task to generate our resource, like this:

```
$ mix phx.gen.html Multimedia Video videos user_id:references:users \
url:string title:string description:text

* creating lib/rumbl_web/controllers/video_controller.ex
* creating lib/rumbl_web/templates/video/edit.html.eex
* creating lib/rumbl_web/templates/video/form.html.eex
* creating lib/rumbl_web/templates/video/index.html.eex
* creating lib/rumbl_web/templates/video/new.html.eex
* creating lib/rumbl_web/templates/video/show.html.eex
* creating lib/rumbl_web/views/video_view.ex
* creating test/rumbl_web/controllers/video_controller_test.exs
* creating lib/rumbl/multimedia/video.ex
* creating priv/repo/migrations/20180408024739_create_videos.exs
* creating lib/rumbl/multimedia.ex
* injecting lib/rumbl/multimedia.ex
* creating test/rumbl/multimedia_test.exs
* injecting test/rumbl/multimedia_test.exs

Add the resource to your browser scope in lib/rumbl_web/router.ex:

    resources "/videos", VideoController
```

All of the preceding files should look familiar, because you wrote a similar stack of code for the user accounts layer by hand. Let's break that command down. Following the mix phx.gen.html command, we have:

- The name of the context: Multimedia
- The name of the module that defines the schema: Video
- The plural form of the schema name: videos
- Each field, with some type information

This mix command may be more verbose than you've seen elsewhere. In some frameworks, you might use simple one-time generator commands, which leave it up to the framework to inflect plural and singular forms as requests come and go. It ends up adding complexity to the framework, and indirectly, to your application. At the end of the day, you save only a few keystrokes every once in a while. *Such generators optimize the wrong thing.*

Sometimes it pays to be explicit. For all things internal, Phoenix frees you from memorizing unnecessary singular and plural conventions by consistently using singular forms in schemas, controllers, and views in most cases. In your application boundaries, such as URLs and table names, you provide a bit more information, because you can use pluralized names. Since creating plural forms is imperfect and rife with exceptions, the generator command is the perfect place to tell Phoenix *exactly what we need*.

It's time to follow up on the remaining instructions printed by the generator. First, we need to add the route to lib/rumbl_web/router.ex:

```
resources "/videos", VideoController
```

The question is: in which pipeline? Let's review what we know and come back to that question shortly.

Our Multimedia.Video is a REST resource, and these routes work just like the ones we created for Accounts.User. As with the index and show actions in UserController, we also want to restrict the video actions to logged-in users. We've already written the code for authentication in the user controller. Let's recap that now:

authentication/listings/rumbl/lib/rumbl_web/controllers/user_controller.change3.ex
```
defp authenticate(conn, _opts) do
  if conn.assigns.current_user do
    conn
  else
    conn
    |> put_flash(:error, "You must be logged in to access that page")
    |> redirect(to: Routes.page_path(conn, :index))
    |> halt()
  end
end
```

To share this function between routers and controllers, move it to RumblWeb.Auth, call it authenticate_user for clarity, make it public (use def instead of defp), import our controller functions for put_flash and redirect, and alias our router helpers:

relationships/listings/rumbl/lib/rumbl_web/controllers/auth.change1.ex
```
import Phoenix.Controller
alias RumblWeb.Router.Helpers, as: Routes

def authenticate_user(conn, _opts) do
  if conn.assigns.current_user do
    conn
  else
    conn
    |> put_flash(:error, "You must be logged in to access that page")
    |> redirect(to: Routes.page_path(conn, :index))
    |> halt()
  end
end
```

You might be tempted to import RumblWeb.Router.Helpers instead of defining an alias, but hold off on that impulse. The router depends on Rumbl.Auth so importing the router helpers in Rumbl.Auth would lead to a circular dependency and compilation would fail.

Save the auth.ex file. Since that module provides services our entire application will use, we'll want to make it easier to integrate. An import should do the trick. First, let's share authenticate_user function across all controllers and routers. We will write import RumblWeb.Auth, only: [authenticate_user: 2], where the number 2 is the number of arguments expected by authenticate_user. Crack open lib/rumbl_web.ex and make this change to your controller function:

relationships/listings/rumbl/lib/rumbl_web.change1.ex
```
def controller do
  quote do
    use Phoenix.Controller, namespace: RumblWeb

    import Plug.Conn
    import RumblWeb.Gettext
    import RumblWeb.Auth, only: [authenticate_user: 2] # New import
    alias RumblWeb.Router.Helpers, as: Routes
  end
end
```

In the same file, make a similar change to your router function:

relationships/listings/rumbl/lib/rumbl_web.change1.ex
```
def router do
  quote do
    use Phoenix.Router
    import Plug.Conn
    import Phoenix.Controller
    import RumblWeb.Auth, only: [authenticate_user: 2] # New import
  end
end
```

Next, in UserController, we want to use the newly imported function. Rename authenticate to authenticate_user, like this:

relationships/listings/rumbl/lib/rumbl_web/controllers/user_controller.change1.ex
```
plug :authenticate_user when action in [:index, :show]
```

Now, back to the router. Let's define a new scope called /manage containing the video resources. This scope pipes through the browser pipeline and our newly imported authenticate_user function, like this:

relationships/listings/rumbl/lib/rumbl_web/router.change1.ex
```
scope "/manage", RumblWeb do
  pipe_through [:browser, :authenticate_user]

  resources "/videos", VideoController
end
```

pipe_through can work with a single pipeline, and it also supports a list of them. Furthermore, because pipelines are also plugs, we can use authenticate_user directly in pipe_through.

We now have a whole group of actions that allow the users to manage content. In a business application, many of those groups of tasks would have a policy, or checklist. Our combination of plugs with pipe_through allows developers to mix and match those policies at will. You can use these techniques for any group of users that share your plug's policies, whether they are admins or anonymous users. Applications can use as many plugs and pipelines as they need to do a job, organizing them in scopes.

We're almost ready to give the generated code a try, but first we need to run the last of the generator's instructions. Go ahead and update the database by running migrations:

```
$ mix ecto.migrate
Compiling 24 files (.ex)
Generated rumbl app
[info] == Running Rumbl.Repo.Migrations.CreateVideos.change/0 forward
[info] create table videos
[info] create index videos_user_id_index
```

Next start your server:

```
$ mix phx.server
```

And we're all set. The migration created the new video table and an index to keep it fast. Head over to your browser and visit http://localhost:4000/manage/videos as a logged-in user. We see an empty list of videos:

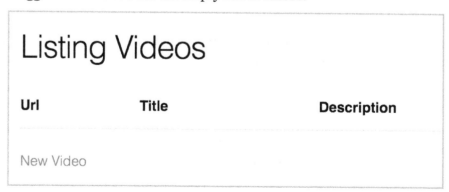

Now take it for a test drive. Click "New video" to create a video. We see the generated form for a new video in the figure on page 107.

New Video

Url

https://www.youtube.com/watch?v=zbbK0WOvWII

Title

ElixirConf Keynote

Description

ElixirConf Phoenix Keynote

SAVE

Fill out the form and click "Save". The application should create your video and redirect. We're not yet scoping our video lists to a given user, but we still have a great start. We know that code generators like this one aren't unique, that dozens of other tools and languages do the same. Still, it's a useful exercise that can rapidly ramp up your understanding of Phoenix and even Elixir. Let's take a quick glance at what was generated.

Examining the Generated Context, Controller, and View

The generated controller is complete. It contains the full spectrum of REST actions. The Multimedia context handles all of our heavy lifting.

The view looks like an empty module, but at this point we already know that it will pick all templates in lib/rumbl_web/templates/video and transform them into functions, such as render("index.html", assigns):

```
relationships/rumbl/lib/rumbl_web/views/video_view.ex
defmodule RumblWeb.VideoView do
  use RumblWeb, :view
end
```

Take some time and read through the template files in lib/rumbl_web/templates/video/ to see how Phoenix uses forms, links, and other HTML functions. There's no magic with Phoenix. Everything is explicit so you can see exactly what each function does. With the application boilerplate generated, we can shift our focus to Ecto relationships, starting with the generated migration.

First let's take a look at the generated Multimedia context in lib/rumbl/multimedia.ex:

```
relationships/listings/rumbl/lib/rumbl/multimedia.ex
defmodule Rumbl.Multimedia do
  import Ecto.Query, warn: false
  alias Rumbl.Repo
  alias Rumbl.Multimedia.Video

  def list_videos do
    Repo.all(Video)
  end

  def get_video!(id), do: Repo.get!(Video, id)

  def create_video(attrs \\ %{}) do
    %Video{}
    |> Video.changeset(attrs)
    |> Repo.insert()
  end

  def update_video(%Video{} = video, attrs) do
    video
    |> Video.changeset(attrs)
    |> Repo.update()
  end

  def delete_video(%Video{} = video) do
    Repo.delete(video)
  end

  def change_video(%Video{} = video) do
    Video.changeset(video, %{})
  end
end
```

The Accounts context we wrote by hand is similar, so this context should look familiar to you. It contains a logical grouping of functions you can use to work with our videos. After all, grouping like functions is what contexts is all about. Let's shift to the migrations code that will interact directly with the database to create our schema.

Generated Migrations

Let's open up the video migration in priv/repo/migrations:

relationships/listings/rumbl/priv/repo/migrations/20180408024739_create_videos.exs

```
def change do
  create table(:videos) do
    add :url, :string
    add :title, :string
    add :description, :text
    add :user_id, references(:users, on_delete: :nothing)

    timestamps()
  end

  create index(:videos, [:user_id])
end
```

Phoenix generates a migration for all the fields that we passed on the command line, like the migration we created by hand for our users table. You can see that our generator made effective use of the type hints we provided. In relational databases, *primary keys*, such as our automatically generated id field, identify rows. *Foreign keys*, such as our user_id field, point from one table to the primary key in another one. At the database level, this foreign key lets the database get in on the act of maintaining consistency across our two relationships. Ecto is helping us to do the right thing.

The change function handles two database changes: one for migrating up and one for migrating down. A migration up applies a migration, and a migration down reverts it. This way, if you make a mistake and need to move a single migration up or down, you can do so.

For example, let's say you meant to add a view_count field to your generated create_video migration before you migrated the database up. You could create a new migration that adds your new field. Since you haven't pushed your changes upstream yet, you can roll back, make your changes, and then migrate up again. First, you'd roll back your changes:

```
$ mix ecto.rollback
[info] == Running Rumbl.Repo.Migrations.CreateVideos.change/0 backward
[info] drop index videos_user_id_index
[info] drop table videos
[info] == Migrated in 0.0s
```

We verify that our database was fully migrated up. Then we run mix ecto.rollback to undo our CreateVideos migration. At this point, we could add our missing view_count field. We don't need a view_count at the moment, so let's migrate back up and carry on:

```
$ mix ecto.migrate
[info] == Running Rumbl.Repo.Migrations.CreateVideos.change/0 forward
[info] create table videos
[info] create index videos_user_id_index
```

The migration sets up the basic relationships between our tables and—now that we've migrated back up—we're ready to leverage those relationships in our schemas.

Building Relationships

After the migration, Ecto generated a schema. This file is responsible for identifying the fields in a way that ties in to both the database table and the Elixir struct. Now let's take a look at the schema in lib/rumbl/multimedia/video.ex:

```
relationships/listings/rumbl/lib/rumbl/multimedia/video.ex
schema "videos" do
  field :description, :string
  field :title, :string
  field :url, :string
  field :user_id, :id

  timestamps()
end
```

Our schema sets up a user_id field, of type :id, while our migration defines a :user_id foreign key. To relate our data at the schema level, we need to tell Ecto about our Video to User association. Replace your field :user_id, :id line in your video schema with the following association:

```
belongs_to :user, Rumbl.Accounts.User
```

Ecto will now use this information to build the right association between our schemas.

The video module also includes a changeset function, similar to the one that we defined for Accounts.User. The top of the pipeline kicks it all off. The cast function prepares tainted user input containing your specified fields for safe inclusion into the database. We require all fields to be present. cast uses a whitelist to tell Ecto which fields from user-input *may be allowed* in the input. validate_required is a validation that tells Ecto which fields *must be present* from that list of fields'.

```
relationships/listings/rumbl/lib/rumbl/multimedia/video.ex
@doc false
def changeset(video, attrs) do
  video
  |> cast(attrs, [:url, :title, :description])
  |> validate_required([:url, :title, :description])
end
```

The :user_id field is neither castable nor required in the previous example, because many times the field doesn't come from external data such as forms but, rather, directly from the application. That's exactly our case. We'll make sure to associate the current user from the session to each new video.

With our belongs_to in place, we now have a complete one-to-many association. Now a user effectively has many videos. By defining these relationships, we can now use Ecto's association features. Fire up a new iex -S mix session so we can put the new Video code through its paces.

Let's create a new video to see how our new association ties things together:

```
iex> {:ok, video} = Rumbl.Multimedia.create_video(%{
...>   title: "New Vidco", url: "http://example.com", description: "new video"
...> })
{:ok, %Rumbl.Multimedia.Video{...}}

iex> video.user
#Ecto.Association.NotLoaded<association :user is not loaded>
```

Ecto associations are explicit! When you want Ecto to fetch some records, you need to ask. When you don't ask, you can be sure that you won't get them. This decision may seem tedious at first, but it's useful. One of the most time-consuming things about dealing with persistence frameworks is that they can often fetch rows you don't need or fetch in inefficient ways. When these kinds of changes cascade, you can quickly run up a tab that you're unable to pay.

Digging deeper, you can see that referencing video.user returns Ecto.Assocation.Not-Loaded.

Let's load some videos, like this:

```
iex> video = Rumbl.Repo.preload(video, :user)

iex> video.user
nil
```

There's not much to see here yet, but we are making progress. Repo.preload accepts one name or a collection of association names. It loads the associated data for you—in this case, :user. After Ecto tries to fetch the association, we can reference the video.user, which returns nil since our video doesn't yet have an associated user. To make this even more meaningful, we need some associated data.

Let's attach a video to one of our users:

```
iex> alias Ecto.Changeset
iex> alias Rumbl.Repo

iex> user = Rumbl.Accounts.get_user_by(username: "josevalim")
%Rumbl.Accounts.User{...}

iex> changeset =
...>    video |> Changeset.change() |> Changeset.put_assoc(:user, user)
#Ecto.Changeset<...>

iex> video = Repo.update!(changeset)
%Rumbl.Multimedia.Video{...}

iex> video.user
%Rumbl.Accounts.User{username: "josevalim"}
```

Part of a framework's job is to make tedious things easier. In this case, Ecto.Changeset.put_assoc allows us to place an association as a change into the changeset with a little less ceremony. This is how you would make the same change without the useful put_assoc function:

```
iex> video = \
...>    video \
...>    |> Changeset.change() \
...>    |> Changeset.put_change(:user_id, user.id) \
...>    |> Repo.update!()

%Rumbl.Multimedia.Video{}
```

You didn't even have to remember the specific foreign key for the User association. Now that our video has a user, let's try preload again:

```
iex> video = Repo.get(Rumbl.Multimedia.Video, video.id)
%Rumbl.Multimedia.Video{
  ...,
  user: #Ecto.Association.NotLoaded<association :user is not loaded>,
}

iex> video = Repo.preload(video, :user)
%Rumbl.Multimedia.Video{
  ...,
  user: %Rumbl.Accounts.User{username: "josevalim"}
  user_id: 1
}
```

Preload is great for bundling data. Other times we may want to fetch the user associated with a video, without storing the user in the video struct, like this:

```
iex> query = Ecto.assoc(video, :user)
#Ecto.Query<...>

iex> Repo.one(query)
%Rumbl.Accounts.User{username: "josevalim"}
```

assoc is another convenient function from Ecto that returns an Ecto.Query with the user scoped to the given video. We convert this query into data by calling Repo.one. As you'll learn in the next chapter, we'll be able to further manipulate this query, allowing us to slice the data in any way we want.

If you're a careful reader, you might have noticed the one-way relationship between videos and users. We generally want to avoid having cyclic dependencies between our contexts. It is expected for the Video schema to depend on User, but if we also allow the User schema to reach out to schemas in other contexts, the responsibilities between the accounts and multimedia contexts will blur over time.

Now let's dig deeper into related data.

Managing Related Data

Our generated video controller gave us the CRUD basics, but as with any generated code, we're going to need to tailor it to our needs. We want to link videos with users for this social platform. To do so, we need to grab the current user from the connection and scope our operations against the user. Open up your lib/rumbl_web/controllers/video_controller.ex, and scroll to the create action:

```
def create(conn, %{"video" => video_params}) do
  case Multimedia.create_video(video_params) do
    {:ok, video} ->
      conn
      |> put_flash(:info, "Video created successfully.")
      |> redirect(to: Routes.video_path(conn, :show, video))

    {:error, %Ecto.Changeset{} = changeset} ->
      render(conn, "new.html", changeset: changeset)
  end
end
```

That's simple enough. We create a video with the create_video function and then redirect if it's successful, otherwise we render the errors. That's a good start, but it's not sufficient. We need to associate the video with the current user's session. That user is already in the connection at conn.assigns.current_user. We know that the put_assoc function in Ecto.Changeset does just that. Our multimedia context's create_video function has all of the basics and is ready for extension.

Let's rewrite our create_video to receive and associate a user to the video, like this:

relationships/listings/rumbl/lib/rumbl/multimedia.change1.ex
```
alias Rumbl.Accounts

def create_video(%Accounts.User{} = user, attrs \\ %{}) do
  %Video{}
  |> Video.changeset(attrs)
  |> Ecto.Changeset.put_assoc(:user, user)
  |> Repo.insert()
end
```

Our new implementation receives the user and puts it in the changeset with Ecto.Changeset.put_assoc, just like we did in iex. The last step is to provide the current user from the controller to the new create_video function we wrote in the Multimedia context. Similarly, we need to touch up the new and edit actions to use current_user in the change_video function, like this:

relationships/listings/rumbl/lib/rumbl_web/controllers/video_controller.change1.ex
```
Line 1  def create(conn, %{"video" => video_params}) do
     -    case Multimedia.create_video(conn.assigns.current_user, video_params) do
     -      {:ok, video} ->
     -        conn
     5        |> put_flash(:info, "Video created successfully.")
     -        |> redirect(to: Routes.video_path(conn, :show, video))

     -      {:error, %Ecto.Changeset{} = changeset} ->
     -        render(conn, "new.html", changeset: changeset)
    10    end
     -  end
```

On line 2 we passed our current user to our modified multimedia context function. This code gives us what we want, mostly. Notice the code conn.assigns.current_user. That code has a crucial task, and it's a task we're going to use in nearly all the actions of this controller. Though that code seems concise, it's code with a common job and we'll wind up repeating it often. We could define a current_user(conn) function, but we can do better. Let's add the current_user to the argument list for our actions. We'll do so with the custom action function in the controller, like this:

relationships/listings/rumbl/lib/rumbl_web/controllers/video_controller.change2.ex
```
def action(conn, _) do
  args = [conn, conn.params, conn.assigns.current_user]
  apply(__MODULE__, action_name(conn), args)
end
```

Each controller is also a plug. To call a controller, Phoenix invokes the default action function at the end of the controller pipeline. We're replacing it because we want to change the API for all of our controller actions. It's easy enough. We call apply to call our action the way we want. The apply function takes the module, the action name, and the arguments. Rather than explicitly using our module's name, we use the _MODULE_ directive, which expands to the current module, in atom form. Now, if our module name changes, we do not have to change our code along with it. The arguments are now the connection, the parameters, and the current user. Presto. Each action has a new signature.

Let's tweak new and create actions to receive all three parameters:

```
relationships/listings/rumbl/lib/rumbl_web/controllers/video_controller.change2.ex
def new(conn, _params, _current_user) do
  changeset = Multimedia.change_video(%Video{})
  render(conn, "new.html", changeset: changeset)
end

def create(conn, %{"video" => video_params}, current_user) do
  case Multimedia.create_video(current_user, video_params) do
    {:ok, video} ->
      conn
      |> put_flash(:info, "Video created successfully.")
      |> redirect(to: Routes.video_path(conn, :show, video))

    {:error, %Ecto.Changeset{} = changeset} ->
      render(conn, "new.html", changeset: changeset)
  end
end
```

The new action does not need to associate videos with users because new does not insert data into the database. However, if you want to associate them at this moment, there would be no harm either. Next, we make use of the new current_user parameter in the create action. This change is not just for utility. current_user can also help make our application more secure by reminding us to first scope any list of videos to the current user.

For all of the remaining actions, we will want to let each user manage only the videos that they created. We will need to expose a function in our Multimedia context to look up the videos for a given user. We will do so in two parts. user_videos_query will define an Ecto query to return a user's videos. Then, both the list_user_videos and get_user_video! functions will scope a request to the videos a user can see.

Let's do that now:

relationships/listings/rumbl/lib/rumbl/multimedia.change2.ex
```elixir
def list_user_videos(%Accounts.User{} = user) do
  Video
  |> user_videos_query(user)
  |> Repo.all()
end

def get_user_video!(%Accounts.User{} = user, id) do
  Video
  |> user_videos_query(user)
  |> Repo.get!(id)
end

defp user_videos_query(query, %Accounts.User{id: user_id}) do
  from(v in query, where: v.user_id == ^user_id)
end
```

The user_videos_query query fetches all of the videos with a matching user ID.
list_user_videos and get_user_video! make use of that shared query. We also see the
composeable nature of Ecto queries. For the most part, our new functions
are similar to the original list_videos and get_video! functions. The only difference
is that we pipe videos through the user query before invoking the repository.
Now, we need only use the new functions in the index, show, edit, update, and
delete actions:

relationships/listings/rumbl/lib/rumbl_web/controllers/video_controller.change2.ex
```elixir
Line 1  def index(conn, _params, current_user) do
2         videos = Multimedia.list_user_videos(current_user)
3         render(conn, "index.html", videos: videos)
4       end
5
6       def show(conn, %{"id" => id}, current_user) do
7         video = Multimedia.get_user_video!(current_user, id)
8         render(conn, "show.html", video: video)
9       end
```

On lines 2 and 7, we grabbed our current_user from the action and called our
new Multimedia.list_user_videos and Multimedia.get_user_video! functions to authorize
access. Now, users can only access the information from videos they own. If
the user provides an id from any other video, Ecto raises a not found error. Let's
do the same change to edit and update to ensure that they can only change
videos coming from the association. Now that we have the supporting functions, the change is easy:

relationships/listings/rumbl/lib/rumbl_web/controllers/video_controller.change2.ex
```elixir
Line 1  def edit(conn, %{"id" => id}, current_user) do
-         video = Multimedia.get_user_video!(current_user, id)
-         changeset = Multimedia.change_video(video)
-         render(conn, "edit.html", video: video, changeset: changeset)
5       end
```

```
  def update(conn, %{"id" => id, "video" => video_params}, current_user) do
    video = Multimedia.get_user_video!(current_user, id)

10  case Multimedia.update_video(video, video_params) do
      {:ok, video} ->
        conn
        |> put_flash(:info, "Video updated successfully.")
        |> redirect(to: Routes.video_path(conn, :show, video))

15
      {:error, %Ecto.Changeset{} = changeset} ->
        render(conn, "edit.html", video: video, changeset: changeset)
    end
  end
end
```

On lines 2 and 8 we called our new functions to authorize access. As before, we'll reject any other requests to change another's content, whether those change requests are malicious or simply our own bugs.

Finally, we need to do the same for delete:

relationships/listings/rumbl/lib/rumbl_web/controllers/video_controller.change2.ex

```
Line 1  def delete(conn, %{"id" => id}, current_user) do
  2     video = Multimedia.get_user_video!(current_user, id)
  3     {:ok, _video} = Multimedia.delete_video(video)
  4
  5     conn
  6     |> put_flash(:info, "Video deleted successfully.")
  7     |> redirect(to: Routes.video_path(conn, :index))
  8  end
```

Once again, we use Multimedia.get_user_video! to properly lock down access. After those changes, our users have a panel for managing their videos in a safe way. Using simple Ecto queries with well-named context functions, we built a solid authorization rule restricting deletes and updates to the video's formal owner. Our application is easier to read and more secure thanks to these changes.

In-context Relationships

So far, we've created a new context each time we create a new resource. However, one of the important ideas behind contexts is to group similar resources, meaning sometimes new resources should go into existing contexts. We already talked about how the Multimedia context could manage related entities such as videos, books and the like in the future.

Sometimes we'll define relationships within the same context. For example, let's add categories to our videos. Categories are simple resources. They have a single category name field that will be something like action, comedy or sci-fi.

We expect our categories to be mostly fixed. After we define a few of them, we don't expect them to change often. For this reason, we don't need to create a controller with a view and templates to manage them from user input. We can create them programatically instead.

Since all multimedia resources have categories and categories are only available to multimedia resources, it makes sense to define these categories within the Multimedia context. We will define the category schema as Multimedia.Category.

Should I Create Another Context?

Sometimes it may be tricky to determine if two resources belong to the same context or not. The fact two resources are related in the database does not imply they belong in the same context. Otherwise, almost all schemas would be within the Accounts context, as the majority of entities in a system belong to a user.

For example, users and videos are related, but they clearly belong in different contexts. On the other hand, categories and videos are also related, but we put them together, as categories are only available to multimedia resources and they do not bring much complexity on their own. In cases you are unsure how to group your resources, prefer distinct contexts per resource and refactor later if necessary. Otherwise you can easily end up with large contexts of loosely related entities. Similarly, if a context grows too large over time, you can always break it apart. To sum it up: When in doubt, put your new resource in its own context.

Let's once again use generators to define our categories, but this time we'll use a different generator. Let's study our options.

Schema and Context Generators

Up to this point, we've used the mix ecto.gen.migration generator and mix phx.gen.html. Those generators operate at two different ends of the spectrum when it comes to building our app. The migration generator has a very specific concern and generates only migration files while the html and json generators generate migrations, schemas, contexts, as well as controllers, views, and templates.

It just so happens there are two generators that fit between the HTML generator and the migration: context and schema generators. Let's briefly discuss those generators and when to use them. Remember, you can get more information about any generator by typing mix help GENERATOR_NAME in your terminal.

In the following examples, we'll use the upcoming Multimedia.Category as an example. Once we explore all options, we can make an informed generator choice. The candidates are:

- mix phx.gen.html Multimedia Category categories name:string. This command generates a controller, view, and template on the frontend. On the backend, it generates a Multimedia context, a Multimedia.Category schema, and a migration. This generator, and the similar mix phx.gen.json generator, are typically used when we want to define all conveniences to expose a resource over the web interface.

- mix phx.gen.context Multimedia Category categories name:string. This command makes a Multimedia context, a Multimedia.Category schema and the associated migration. This generator is useful for generating a resource with all of its context functions *without exposing that resource via the web interface.* Note that if the context already exists, which is the case for Multimedia, the generator will inject the new category functions into the existing context.

- mix phx.gen.schema Multimedia.Category categories name:string. This command creates a schema with a migration. It's useful for creating a resource when you want to define the context functions yourself.

- mix ecto.gen.migration create_categories. This generator builds a new empty migration. Useful when the schema and context are already laid out, and all you need is to update the database

In our case, we know our categories won't be managed via a web interface. That rules out mix phx.gen.html. We also know that we want a schema, so we can associate it with videos. That rules out mix ecto.gen.migration, as it does too little.

Therefore, we need to choose between mix phx.gen.context and mix phx.gen.schema. Both choices work fine. If you want Phoenix to generate more code than you need and then trim from there, you'll generate the context. If you'd rather generate the minimum amount of code and build what you need from scratch, you'll use the schema generator. Since categories don't need a web interface, our hunch is that we won't need most of the generated context functions so we'll pick the schema generator.

Enough exposition. Let's get down to business.

Generating Category Migrations

Generate the Multimedia.Category schema like this:

```
$ mix phx.gen.schema Multimedia.Category categories name:string

* creating lib/rumbl/multimedia/category.ex
* creating priv/repo/migrations/20180513025558_create_categories.exs

...

    $ mix ecto.migrate
---- END OF OUTPUT ----
```

As expected, the command generated a category schema and a migration. The schema is backed by the "categories" database table with a name column of type string.

Next, let's edit our migration to mark the name field as NOT NULL and create a unique index for it:

```
relationships/listings/rumbl/priv/repo/migrations/20180513025558_create_categories.change1.exs
defmodule Rumbl.Repo.Migrations.CreateCategories do
  use Ecto.Migration

  def change do
    create table(:categories) do
      add :name, :string, null: false

      timestamps()
    end

    create unique_index(:categories, [:name])
  end
end
```

Now we can add the referential constraints to our Video schema. A Video belongs to a Category, like so:

```
relationships/listings/rumbl/lib/rumbl/multimedia/video.change1.ex
Line 1  schema "videos" do
     2    field :description, :string
     3    field :title, :string
     4    field :url, :string
     5
     6    belongs_to :user, Rumbl.Accounts.User
     7    belongs_to :category, Rumbl.Multimedia.Category
     8
     9    timestamps()
    10  end
```

We created a simple belongs-to relationship, so we need to add the category_id to the permitted fields for our changeset:

relationships/listings/rumbl/lib/rumbl/multimedia/video.change1.ex

```
Line 1   @doc false
  2   def changeset(video, attrs) do
  3     video
  4     |> cast(attrs, [:url, :title, :description, :category_id])
  5     |> validate_required([:url, :title, :description])
  6   end
```

Now our API users can safely use category_id in the user input we provide to our changeset. Use mix ecto.gen.migration to generate a migration to add the category_id to our video table:

```
$ mix ecto.gen.migration add_category_id_to_video
* creating priv/repo/migrations
* creating priv/repo/migrations/20180513030504_add_category_id_to_video.exs
```

With the database table updated, this relationship will allow us to add a new category ID to our existing videos. Now open up your new priv/repo/migrations/xxx_add_category_id_to_video.exs and key this in:

relationships/listings/rumbl/priv/repo/migratio ... 80513030504_add_category_id_to_video.change1.exs

```
def change do
  alter table(:videos) do
    add :category_id, references(:categories)
  end
end
```

This code sets up a database constraint between videos and categories, one that will ensure that the category_id for a video exists. Finally, migrate your database with your two new migrations:

```
$ mix ecto.migrate
[info] == Running Rumbl.Repo.Migrations.CreateCategories.change/0 forward
[info] create table categories
[info] create index categories_name_index
[info] == Migrated in 0.0s
[info] == Running Rumbl.Repo.Migrations.AddCategoryIdToVideo.change/0 forward
[info] alter table videos
[info] == Migrated in 0.0s
```

We migrated our categories and added the proper foreign keys. The database will maintain the database integrity, regardless of what we do on the Phoenix side. With our relationships established, we can safely associate videos with categories in our user interface, by presenting a list of categories whenever a user creates or edits a video. To do that, we need to learn how to effectively query data. That's exactly what we have in store for you in the next chapter.

Wrapping Up

In this chapter, we generated a Video resource with a relationship to User and made changes to the generated code, learning a lot along the way:

- We used contexts throughout to craft an easy-to-maintain API layer for our application.

- We converted a private plug into a public function and shared it with our controllers and routers.

- You learned how to migrate and roll back changes to the database.

- We defined relationships between User and Video schemas and used functions from Ecto to build and retrieve associated data.

- We discussed the main generators Phoenix provides to scaffold our applications.

The next chapter will take everything up a notch by exploring Ecto queries and leveraging the database constraints. When we're done, you'll be able to ensure data uniqueness and use the database to maintain data integrity. Turn the page, and let's get started!

## CHAPTER 7

Ecto Queries and Constraints

In the previous chapter, we extended our application domain by associating videos to users and categories. Now we want our users to select which category a video belongs to upon video creation. To build this feature, you'll need to learn how to programmatically populate the database with a hardcoded list of categories and add those new features to our context. Along the way we'll explore some of the different ways you can use Ecto to retrieve data from the database.

We want to build our feature safely so that corrupt data can't creep into our database, so we'll spend some time working with database constraints. Database engines like PostgreSQL are called *relational* for a reason. A tremendous amount of time and effort has gone into tools and features that help developers define and enforce the relationships between tables. Instead of treating the database as pure dumb storage, Ecto uses the strengths of the database to help keep the data consistent. You'll learn about error-reporting strategies so you'll know when to report an error and when to let it crash, letting other application layers handle the problem.

Let's get started.

Seeding and Associating Categories

Let's associate videos and categories. The first step is to make sure categories actually exist in our database by using seed data. Then we will change our web interface to allow users to pick the category for a new video.

Setting Up Category Seed Data

We need to define a handful of initial categories for our application to use. We could start an IEx session and directly invoke the repository to do that, but this approach has some issues. If we do this work manually, each team-mate will have to do the same as soon as they want to take our application for a spin. Once our application grows in size, having to populate each table in our application with relevant data can get long and tedious.

Furthermore, categories won't have a web interface where we can manage them, so we need a mechanism to create them in production programatically. Elixir is a great language for writing scripts so let's create a small one to insert data in the database. We'll let that new script use a function in our Multimedia context to create the necessary records.

Phoenix already defines a convention for seeding data. Open up priv/repo/seeds.exs and read the comments Phoenix generated for us. Phoenix will make sure that our database is appropriately populated. We only need to drop in a script that uses our repository to directly add the data we want. Then, we'll be able to run Mix commands when it's time to create the data.

Since the seed script may be executed multiple times, namely every time more seed data is added, we need to make sure our seed script won't fail or won't generate duplicated categories every time it runs.

Let's see what happens when we create a category that already exists. Open up IEx and key this in:

```
iex> Rumbl.Repo.insert! %Rumbl.Multimedia.Category{name: "Test"}
%Rumbl.Multimedia.Category{
  __meta__: #Ecto.Schema.Metadata<:loaded, "categories">,
  id: 1,
  inserted_at: ~N[2019-05-19 13:06:12],
  name: "hello",
  updated_at: ~N[2019-05-19 13:06:12]
}
```

So far, so good. We used the insert! repository function, which will raise an error if anything goes wrong. Let's run the same command again:

```
iex> Rumbl.Repo.insert! %Rumbl.Multimedia.Category{name: "Test"}
** (Ecto.ConstraintError) constraint error when attempting to insert struct:

    * categories_name_index (unique_constraint)

...

The changeset has not defined any constraint.
```

Now Ecto has raised an a ConstraintError, letting us know that the unique_constraint defined in our database did not allow the operation to succeed. Ecto also tells us how to convert this constraint error into a changeset error, a technique we will employ later in this chapter.

However, in this particular case, instead of returning errors as part of a changeset, we would rather create the category only if it doesn't exist. Perhaps, we could write this operation as:

```
Repo.get_by(Category, name: name) || Repo.insert!(%Category{name: name})
```

While this behavior would likely be fine for our seed scripts, this idiom is inherently unsafe, and we should generally avoid it. For instance, if two users are trying to create a new category with the same name at the same time, the Repo.get_by(Category, name: name) would return nil to both, causing both of them to insert the same category. Thanks to our uniqueness constraint, only one of those operations will succeed and we will not get duplicate categories, but the other user would get an error page, leading to a poor user experience.

The answer to the problem is once more to let the database manage the data integrity. In particular, we want to let the database manage what happens when there is a conflict with the data we are inserting. This feature is commonly known as an "Upsert" because it is common to update the data whenever there is a conflict during an insert. In this case, we want to simply ignore the conflict.

Ecto allows us to do exactly that via the :on_conflict option:

```
iex> Rumbl.Repo.insert! %Rumbl.Multimedia.Category{name: "hello"},
...>    on_conflict: :nothing
%Rumbl.Multimedia.Category{
  __meta__: #Ecto.Schema.Metadata<:loaded, "categories">,
  id: nil,
  inserted_at: ~N[2019-05-19 13:06:22],
  name: "hello",
  updated_at: ~N[2019-05-19 13:06:22]
}
```

The default value for :on_conflict is :raise. Once we change it to :nothing, no exceptions are raised and you can see the returned category has a nil id, indicating that indeed the category was not inserted. Upserts allow us to do many different things in case of conflicts, from updating certain fields to even performing whole queries. The downside is that the upsert behaviour is often database specific, so make sure to explore the different options available to your database of choice. You can learn more about upserts in the documention for Repo.insert.[1]

---

1.   https://hexdocs.pm/ecto/Ecto.Repo.html#c:insert/2-upserts

Finally, let's expose this operation in our Multimedia context with a new function called create_category!, like this:

```
queries/listings/rumbl/lib/rumbl/multimedia.change1.ex
alias Rumbl.Multimedia.Category

def create_category!(name) do
  Repo.insert!(%Category{name: name}, on_conflict: :nothing)
end
```

Now, use the new function in the seeds script like this:

```
queries/listings/rumbl/priv/repo/seeds.change1.exs
alias Rumbl.Multimedia

for category <- ~w(Action Drama Romance Comedy Sci-fi) do
  Multimedia.create_category!(category)
end
```

We use the sigil ~w to define a list of words. Each word represents a category. We then traverse the list of category names, writing them to the database with the new Multimedia.create_category! function.

Let's run the seeds file with mix run:

```
$ mix run priv/repo/seeds.exs
```

Presto! We have categories.

Associating Videos and Categories

Now that we've populated our database with categories, we want to allow users to choose a category when creating or editing a video. To do so, we'll do all of the following:

- Fetch all category names and IDs from the database
- Sort them by the name
- Pass them into the view as part of a select input

To build this feature, we'll need to start with a query. Let's spend a little time with Ecto exploring queries a little more deeply. Fire up your project in IEx, and let's warm up with some queries:

```
iex> import Ecto.Query
iex> alias Rumbl.Repo
iex> alias Rumbl.Multimedia.Category
```

Importing Ecto.Query makes the Ecto query language available to us. That module plays some games with macros to provide a simple and beautiful query syntax with as little ceremony as possible. Since it's a framework in such a central part of database development, the tradeoff of more complexity for the library against more productivity for users makes sense. We also alias Repo and Category. If you find yourself always issuing the same set of commands in a project directory, you can include them in a file called .iex.exs. If you want more details, you can read about customizing iex.[2]

```
iex> query = from c in Category,
...>          select: c.name
iex> Repo.all query
```

First, we create a query. In this case:

- from is a macro that builds a query.
- c in Category means we're pulling rows (labeled c) from the Category schema.
- select: c.name means we're going to return only the name field.

Repo.all is simply a repository function that takes a query and returns all rows. You can see Ecto returns a few debugging lines that contain the exact SQL query we're sending to the database, and the resulting five category names:

```
[debug] QUERY OK source="categories" db=1.9ms
SELECT c0."name" FROM "categories" AS c0 []

["Action", "Drama", "Romance", "Comedy", "Sci-fi"]
```

Ecto's real purpose is to efficiently translate Elixir concepts into a language the database understands. For us, that language will be SQL. We can order category names alphabetically by passing the :order_by option to our query. We can also return a tuple from both the id and name fields.

Let's give it another try:

```
iex> Repo.all from c in Category,
...>          order_by: c.name,
...>          select: {c.name, c.id}
[
  {"Action", 1},
  {"Comedy", 4},
  {"Drama", 2},
  {"Romance", 3},
  {"Sci-fi", 5}
]
```

However, we rarely need to define the whole query at once. Ecto queries are *composable*, which means you can define the query bit by bit:

---

2. https://hexdocs.pm/iex/IEx.html

```
iex> query = Category
Category
iex> query = from c in query, order_by: c.name
#Ecto.Query<>
iex> query = from c in query, select: {c.name, c.id}
#Ecto.Query<>
iex> Repo.all(query)
[
  {"Action", 1},
  {"Comedy", 4},
  {"Drama", 2},
  {"Romance", 3},
  {"Sci-fi", 5}
]
```

This time, instead of building the whole query at once, we write it in small steps, adding a little more information along the way. You'll see this strategy quite frequently in Elixir because it allows us to use pipes to build complex queries from simpler ones, bit by bit. This strategy works because Ecto defines something called the queryable protocol. from receives a queryable, and you can use any queryable as a base for a new query. A queryable is an Elixir protocol. Recall that protocols like Enumerable (for Enum) define APIs for specific language features. This one defines the API for something that can be queried.

That's also why we can call Repo.all either as Repo.all(Category) or Repo.all(query): because both Category and query implement the so-called Ecto.Queryable protocol. By abiding by the protocol, you can quickly layer together sophisticated queries with Ecto.Query, maintaining clear boundaries between your layers and adding sophistication without complexity.

Let's talk briefly about which pieces of our categories will go where. We'll put query functions in our schema layer. Complex interactions, such as those between our multimedia and users, will go in in contexts. This organization will leave controllers as thin and simple as possible.

Let's implement the layered, composable query strategy. To make our queries compose well, we need functions that take a query as the first argument and return a query. We'll add an alphabetical function to our Category module which will sort the results:

queries/listings/rumbl/lib/rumbl/multimedia/category.change1.ex
```
import Ecto.Query

def alphabetical(query) do
  from c in query, order_by: c.name
end
```

To be more precise, our alphabetical function must receive and return a queryable. With our function in place, let's expose this new feature from a well-named function in our Multimedia context:

queries/listings/rumbl/lib/rumbl/multimedia.change1.ex
```
def list_alphabetical_categories do
  Category
  |> Category.alphabetical()
  |> Repo.all()
end
```

In our user interface, we plan to build a picker that will need names for our users and ids for our backend relationships. We added a Multimedia.list_alphabetical_categories to fetch the data in the order we want. Let's complete the circle by using our new functions to load all the categories in our VideoController and shape the data into a select drop-down within our VideoView:

queries/listings/rumbl/lib/rumbl_web/controllers/video_controller.change1.ex
```
plug :load_categories when action in [:new, :create, :edit, :update]

defp load_categories(conn, _) do
  assign(conn, :categories, Multimedia.list_alphabetical_categories())
end
```

We define a plug that calls our new Multimedia.list_alphabetical_categories function. We also specify the actions that need the categories in the when clause. Now, all sorted categories are available inside @categories in our templates for the actions we specified. You can see how adding our context layer simplifies our controller code.

Let's change the video form template at lib/rumbl_web/templates/video/form.html.eex to include a new select field:

queries/listings/rumbl/lib/rumbl_web/templates/video/form.change1.html.eex
```
<%= label f, :category_id, "Category"%>
<%= select f, :category_id, category_select_options(@categories),
    prompt: "Choose a category" %>
```

We added a new select field which builds a list of section options using category_select_options. Since that function is new, let's implement it inside our video view in lib/rumbl_web/views/video_view.ex, like this:

queries/listings/rumbl/lib/rumbl_web/views/video_view.change1.ex
```
defmodule RumblWeb.VideoView do
  use RumblWeb, :view

  def category_select_options(categories) do
    for category <- categories, do: {category.name, category.id}
  end
end
```

Remember, views are just modules with pure functions. We'll use the name as the label for each option in a select, and the id as the option value, and a simple for comprehension to walk through the available categories.

That's it. Now we can create videos with optional categories. We're doing so with query logic that lives in its own module so we'll be able to better test and extend those features. Try it out by visiting http://localhost:4000/manage/videos/new:

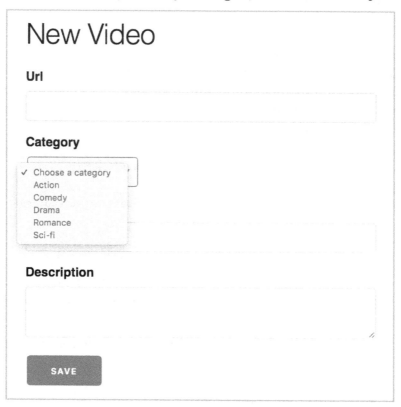

Before we finish this chapter, we'll add the proper mechanisms to ensure that the category sent by the user is valid. But first, let's take this opportunity to explore Ecto queries a little more deeply.

Diving Deeper into Ecto Queries

So far, you know Ecto queries like a YouTube dog knows how to ride a bike. We've written our first query and we know that queries compose, but we still haven't explored many concepts. It's time to take off the training wheels and see more-advanced examples.

Open up IEx once more, and let's retrieve a single user:

```
iex> import Ecto.Query
iex> alias Rumbl.Repo
iex> alias Rumbl.Accounts.User
iex> alias Rumbl.Multimedia.Video

iex> username = "josevalim"
"josevalim"

iex> Repo.one(from u in User, where: u.username == ^username)
...
%Rumbl.Accounts.User{username: "josevalim", ...}
```

We're using the same concepts you learned before:

- Repo.one means return one row.

- from u in User means we're reading from the Accounts.User schema.

- where: u.username == ^username means return the row where u.username == ^username. The ^ (caret) is used for injecting a value or expression for interpolation into an Ecto query

- When the select part is omitted, the whole struct is returned, as if we'd written select: u.

Repo.one doesn't mean "return the first result." It means "one result is expected, so if there's more, fail." This query language is a little different from what you may have seen before. This API is not just a composition of strings. By relying on Elixir macros, Ecto knows where user-defined variables are located, so it's easier to protect the user from security flaws like SQL-injection attacks.

Ecto queries also do a good part of the query normalization at compile time, so you'll see better performance while leveraging the information in our schemas for casting values at runtime. Let's see some of these concepts in action by using an incorrect type in a query:

```
iex> username = 123
123

iex> Repo.all(from u in User, where: u.username == ^username)
** (Ecto.Query.CastError) iex:7: value `123` in `where`
   cannot be cast to type :string in query:

from u in Rumbl.Accounts.User,
  where: u.username == ^123,
  select: u
```

The ^ operator interpolates values into our queries where Ecto can scrub them and safely put them to use, without the risk of SQL injection. Armed with our schema definition, Ecto is able to cast the values properly for us and match up Elixir types with the expected database types.

In other words, we define the repository and schemas and let Ecto changesets and queries tie them up together. This strategy gives developers the proper level of isolation because we mostly work with data, which is straightforward, and leave all complex operations to the repository.

The Query API

So far, we've used only the == operator in queries, but Ecto supports a wide range of them:

- Comparison operators: ==, !=, <=, >=, <, >
- Boolean operators: and, or, not
- Inclusion operator: in
- Search functions: like and ilike
- Null check functions: is_nil
- Aggregates: count, avg, sum, min, max
- Date/time intervals: datetime_add, date_add
- General: fragment, field, and type

In short, you can use many of the same comparison, inclusion, search, and aggregate operations for a typical query that you'd use in Elixir. You can see documentation and examples for many of them in the Ecto.Query.API documentation.[3] Those are the basic features you're going to use as you build queries. You'll use them from two APIs: keywords syntax and pipe syntax. Let's see what each API looks like.

Writing Queries with Keywords Syntax

The first syntax expresses different parts of the query by using a keyword list. For example, take a look at this code for counting all users with usernames starting with j or c. You can see keys for both :select and :where:

```
iex> Repo.one from u in User,
...>          select: count(u.id),
...>          where: ilike(u.username, "j%") or
...>                 ilike(u.username, "c%")
```

2

---

3.   http://hexdocs.pm/ecto/Ecto.Query.API.html

The u variable is bound as part of Ecto's from macro. Throughout the query, it represents entries from the User schema. If you attempt to access u.unknown or match against an invalid type, Ecto raises an error. Bindings are useful when our queries need to join across multiple schemas. Each join in a query gets a specific binding.

Let's also build a query to count all users:

```
iex> users_count = from u in User, select: count(u.id)
#Ecto.Query<from u in Rumbl.Accounts.User, select: count(u.id)>
```

Simple enough. We use from to build a query, selecting count(u.id). Now, let's say that we want to take advantage of this fantastic count feature to build some more-complex queries. Since the best usernames have a j, let's count the users that match a case-insensitive search for j, like this:

```
iex> j_users = from u in users_count, where: ilike(u.username, ^"%j%")
#Ecto.Query<from u in Rumbl.Accounts.User,
 where: ilike(u.username, ^"%j%"), select: count(u.id)>
```

Beautiful. You've built a new query, based on the old one. Although we've used the same binding as before, u, we didn't have to. You're free to name your query variables however you like, because Ecto doesn't use their names. The following query is equivalent to the previous one:

```
iex> j_users = from q in users_count, where: ilike(q.username, ^"%j%")
#Ecto.Query<from u in Rumbl.Accounts.User,
 where: ilike(u.username, ^"%j%"), select: count(u.id)>
```

You can use that composition wherever you have a query, be it written with the keyword syntax or the pipe syntax that you'll learn next.

Using Queries with the Pipe Syntax

Let's look at some other expressions. For example, let's build some queries with the Elixir pipe.

You've seen different query expressions constructed with key-value pairs. You can also build queries by piping through query macros.

Most often, you'll want to import from to build up a query against a queryable, but you can also use other query macros such as where and select where it makes sense. Each takes a queryable and returns a queryable, so you can pipe them together like this:

```
iex> User \
...> |> select([u], count(u.id)) \
...> |> where([u], ilike(u.username, ^"j%") or ilike(u.username, ^"c%")) \
...> |> Repo.one()
[debug] QUERY OK source="users" db=1.9ms
SELECT count(u0."id") FROM "users" AS u0 WHERE
((u0."username" ILIKE $1) OR (u0."username" ILIKE $2)) ["j%", "c%"]
2
```

Because each query is independent of others, we need to specify the binding manually for each one as part of a list. This binding is conceptually the same as the one we used in from u in User. We have a single binding, so we use a list with a single element, but we could use a longer list with more bindings if our query had joins.

The query syntax you choose depends on your taste and the problems you're trying to solve. The former syntax is probably more convenient for pulling together ad-hoc queries and solving one-off problems. The latter is probably better for building an application's unique complex layered query API. Each approach has its advantages.

Fragments

A poorly designed API will break down if it does not provide every feature that you need from the underlying storage you are trying to access. If Ecto gives you everything you need from the database layer beneath, that's great. If not, you do not have to panic and fork Ecto to build your own mapping layer. Since we cannot represent all possible queries in Elixir's syntax, we need a backup plan.

A programming truism is that the best abstractions offer an escape hatch, one that exposes the user to one deeper level of abstraction on demand. Ecto has such a feature, called the *query fragment.* A query fragment sends part of a query directly to the database but allows you to construct the query string in a safe way.

Imagine that you want to look up the user by username in a case-insensitive way. Though Ecto doesn't give us everything we need, you can access that feature by using an Ecto SQL fragment, like this:

```
from u in User,
    where: fragment("lower(username) = ?", ^String.downcase(name))
```

Using a fragment allows us to construct a fragment of SQL for the query but safely interpolate the String.downcase(name) code using a prepared statement.

Whether the interpolated values are Ecto query expressions or SQL fragments, Ecto safely escapes all interpolated values.

When everything else fails and even fragments aren't enough, you can always run direct SQL with Ecto.Adapters.SQL.query:

```
iex> Ecto.Adapters.SQL.query(Repo, "SELECT power($1, $2)", [2, 10])
[debug] QUERY OK db=2.0ms
SELECT power($1, $2) [2, 10]
{:ok,
 %Postgrex.Result{
   columns: ["power"],
   command: :select,
   connection_id: 33727,
   num_rows: 1,
   rows: [[1024.0]]
 }}
```

From the query result, you can fetch all kinds of information, such as the returned columns, the number of rows, and the result set itself. It's best to stick to Ecto query expressions wherever possible, but you have a safe escape hatch when you need it.

Querying Relationships

Ecto queries also offer support for associations. When working with relationships, you learned that Ecto associations are explicit, and we used Repo.preload to fetch associated data. Let's recap:

```
iex> video = Repo.one(from v in Video, limit: 1)
%Rumbl.Multimedia.Video{...}

iex> video.user
#Ecto.Association.NotLoaded<association :user is not loaded>

iex> video = Repo.preload(video, :user)
%Rumbl.Multimedia.Video{...}

iex> video.user
%Rumbl.Accounts.User{...}
```

However, we don't always need to preload associations as a separate step. Ecto allows us to preload associations directly as part of a query, like this:

```
iex> video = Repo.one(from v in Video, limit: 1,
...>             preload: [:user])
%Rumbl.Multimedia.Video{...}

iex> video.user
%Rumbl.Accounts.User{...}
```

Ecto also allows us to join on associations inside queries, filtering them in any way that makes sense:

```
iex> Repo.all from v in Video,
...>          join: u in assoc(v, :user),
...>          join: c in assoc(v, :category),
...>          where: c.name == "Comedy",
...>          select: {u, v}
[{%Rumbl.Accounts.User{...}, %Rumbl.Multimedia.Video{...}}]
```

This time, Ecto returns users and videos side by side as long as the video belongs to the Comedy category. We use a tuple in select, but we could also return each entry in a list, or even a map.

We expect that you'll find plenty of joy when you work with Ecto queries. They're flexible but also extremely readable. They're composable enough to flex but also rigid enough to offer type support and security when it comes to interacting with tainted external data. However, not all problems can be solved with queries. Sometimes, you'll need to use the underlying database to help manage database integrity. For those cases, Ecto provides *constraints*.

Constraints

Constraints allow us to use underlying relational database features to help us maintain database integrity. We used constraints to prevent duplicate categories in our application. There are many other ways we can leverage constraints.

For instance, when we create a video, we need to make sure that our category exists. We might be tempted to solve this problem by simply performing a query, but such an approach would be unsafe due to race conditions. In most cases, we would expect it to work like this:

1. The user sends a category ID through the form.
2. We perform a query to check if the category ID exists in the database.
3. If the category ID does exist in the database, we add the video with the category ID to the database.

However, someone could delete the category between steps 2 and 3, allowing us to ultimately insert a video without an existing category in the database. In any sufficiently busy application, that approach *will lead to inconsistent data* over time. Ecto has relentlessly pushed us to define references and indexes in our database because sometimes, doing a query won't be enough and we'll need to rely on database constraints.

In Phoenix, we use constraints to manage change in a way that combines the harsh protections of the database with Ecto's gentle guiding hand to report errors without crashing.

Let's firm up some terminology before we get too far:

constraint
An explicit database constraint. This might be a uniqueness constraint on an index, or an integrity constraint between primary and foreign keys.

constraint error
The Ecto.ConstraintError. This happens when Ecto identifies a constraint problem, such as trying to insert a record without specifying a required key.

changeset constraint
A constraint annotation added to the changeset that allows Ecto to convert constraint errors into changeset error messages.

changeset error messages
Beautiful error messages for the consumption of humans.

Relational databases deal with relationships between tables. A database constraint is a mechanism for restricting data in a table based on the needs of an application. For example, a given user_id must exist as the id field in a users table, or an email field must be unique. Ensuring data is consistent across records is a critical job that all database-backed applications need to handle.

Ecto allows developers to enjoy many of the guarantees databases offer in terms of data integrity. In fact, Ecto rewards developers for doing exactly this, both in the short term, by transforming constraint errors into user feedback, and in the long term by guaranteeing you won't be awake at 3:00 a.m. fixing bugs caused by inconsistent data. In the remainder of this chapter, we're going to walk you through how Ecto manages constraints.

Validating Unique Data

When we created the users table, we edited the migration to index the username field as unique:

```
create unique_index(:users, [:username])
```

Let's see what happens if we try to create a user with an existing username (as shown in the figure on page 138).

Ecto.ConstraintError at POST

constraint error when attempting to insert struct:

  * unique: users_username_index

If you would like to convert this constraint into an error, please
call unique_constraint/3 in your changeset and define the proper
constraint name. The changeset has not defined any constraint.

Oops. Our application blows up with a constraint error, similar to the one we saw when creating duplicated categories. If we inspect the error message in the terminal, or in the browser, we see:

```
[error] #PID<0.403.0> running RumblWeb.Endpoint terminated
Server: localhost:4000 (http)
Request: POST /users
** (exit) an exception was raised:
  ** (Ecto.ConstraintError) constraint error when attempting to insert struct:

  * unique: users_username_index

If you would like to convert this constraint into an error, please
call unique_constraint/3 in your changeset and define the proper
constraint name. The changeset has not defined any constraint.
```

We have seen ConstraintErrors before when inserting duplicate categories. For categories, we prevented the error by changing the referential constraints, but for duplicate usernames, we need to inform users filling in the form.

The previous error message tells us how to proceed next. It suggests converting the constraint error into a changeset error message by calling unique_constraint in the changeset.

Let's do that. Open up lib/rumbl/accounts/user.ex and change the changeset function:

```
queries/listings/rumbl/lib/rumbl/accounts/user.change1.ex
def changeset(user, attrs) do
  user
  |> cast(attrs, [:name, :username])
  |> validate_required([:name, :username])
  |> validate_length(:username, min: 1, max: 20)
  |> unique_constraint(:username)
end
```

We pipe the changeset into unique_constraint. By default, Ecto infers the constraint name for us, but it can also be given with the :name option. Calling unique_constraint won't perform any validation on the spot. Instead, it stores all the relevant information in the changeset. When it's time, the repository can convert those constraints into a human-readable error.

Let's try creating a user with an existing username once again:

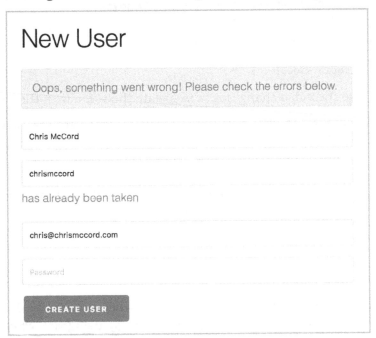

Excellent, this is exactly what we expected: a nice, beautiful, human-readable error. unique_constraint is only one of the different constraint mappings that changesets offer. The next kind of constraint is a foreign-key check.

Validating Foreign Keys

After taking some time to appreciate our unique_constraint, let's continue with our category relationship. When the user picks a category for the video, we could provide some meaningful feedback if the operation fails. Let's update our Video changeset, like this:

```
queries/listings/rumbl/lib/rumbl/multimedia/video.change1.ex
def changeset(video, attrs) do
  video
  |> cast(attrs, [:url, :title, :description, :category_id])
  |> validate_required([:url, :title, :description])
  |> assoc_constraint(:category)
end
```

That assoc_constraint converts foreign-key constraint errors into human-readable error messages and guarantees that a video is created only if the category exists in the database. Taking it for a spin, let's load some data inside iex -S mix:

```
iex> import Ecto.Query
iex> alias Rumbl.Repo
iex> alias Rumbl.Multimedia.{Video, Category}

iex> category = Repo.get_by(Category, name: "Drama")
%Rumbl.Multimedia.Category{...}

iex> video = Repo.one(from v in Video, limit: 1)
...
%Rumbl.Multimedia.Video{...}
```

Now let's use the video changeset to associate the video with the category:

```
iex> changeset = Video.changeset(video, %{category_id: category.id})
iex> Repo.update(changeset)
...
{:ok, %Rumbl.Multimedia.Video{...}}
```

We updated our video with a category that exists. The update works, but suppose we tried to update a video with a bad category:

```
iex> changeset = Video.changeset(video, %{category_id: 12345})
iex> Repo.update(changeset)
...
{:error, %Ecto.Changeset{}}
```

Oops. We couldn't update the video. Let's inspect the returned changeset further. IEx allows us to fetch a previous value by using v(n), where n is the number of the expression. You can also pass a negative value to grab the last n[th] expression:

```
iex> {:error, changeset} = v(-1)
iex> changeset.errors
[category: {"does not exist", []}]
```

As with unique_constraint, when we set up assoc_constraint, we no longer get Ecto.ConstraintError. Instead, they're converted into changeset error messages.

You can try to reproduce this constraint error via our web application in a couple of ways. For example, you could load the page, then remove the category from the database and submit the form after choosing the removed category. If you feel a bit more sneaky, you can fiddle the select options in the browser console, changing their value and then submitting the form.

As we move forward, you'll see how changesets are an essential part of Ecto. *Each changeset encapsulates the whole change policy*, including allowed fields, detecting change, validations, and messaging the user.

On Delete

Our constraints have helped us insert and update database data safely. They should also apply when we remove data.

Let's open up IEx once more:

```
iex> alias Rumbl.Repo
iex> alias Rumbl.Multimedia.Category

iex> category = Repo.get_by(Category, name: "Drama")
%Rumbl.Multimedia.Category{...}

iex> Repo.delete(category)
** (Ecto.ConstraintError) constraint error when attempting to delete
struct
```

We pick the Drama category because we added a video to it in the previous section. A video is tied to the category, so we can't delete the category because it would leave orphaned records.

We could solve this problem in several ways, described briefly here, that you can explore further on your own. The first one is to use changeset constraints. Like insert and update, Repo.delete also accepts a changeset, and you can use foreign_key_constraint to ensure that no associated videos exist when a category is deleted; otherwise you get a nice error message. The foreign_key_constraint function is like the assoc_constraint we used earlier, except it doesn't inflect the foreign key from the relationship. This is particularly useful when you want to show the user why you can't delete the category:

```
iex> import Ecto.Changeset
iex> changeset = change(category)
iex> changeset = foreign_key_constraint(changeset, :videos,
  name: :videos_category_id_fkey, message: "still exist")

iex> Repo.delete(changeset)
{:error,
 #Ecto.Changeset<
   ...,
   errors: [videos: {"still exist", []}],
   valid?: false
 >}
```

This time, we had to be a bit more explicit in the foreign_key_constraint call, because the foreign key has been set in the videos table. If needed, we could also add no_assoc_constraint to do the dirty work of lifting up the foreign-key name and setting a good error message. Check the Ecto docs for more information on no_assoc_constraint and other changeset constraint mappings.

Second, you could configure the database references to either cascade the deletions or simply make the videos.category_id columns NULL on delete. Let's open up the add_category_id_to_video migration:

```
add :category_id, references(:categories)
```

The references function accepts the :on_delete option, such as references(:categories, on_delete: :nothing), with one of the following:

:nothing
> The default.

:delete_all
> When the category is deleted, all videos in that category are deleted.

:nilify_all
> When a category is deleted, the category_id of all associated videos is set to NULL.

There's no best option here. For the category, which supports a has_many :videos relationship, :nilify_all seems like a good choice, because the category isn't an essential part of the video. However, when deleting a user, you likely want to delete all the videos created by that user, purging all of the user's data.

The final choice is to set up :on_delete when configuring has_many or belongs_to relationships in your schema, moving the logic effectively to the application domain. This choice, however, is only recommended when you can't perform one of the preceding operations. After all, *the work best suited to the database must be done in the database.*

Let It Crash

You might be expecting us to proceed to add *_constraint functions to all of our changesets, ensuring that all failed constraint checks are converted into human-readable error messages.

We're not going to do so, and we shouldn't. When we added a foreign_key_constraint to the video belongs_to :category relationship, we knew we wanted to allow the user to choose the video category later on. If a category is removed at some point between the user loading the page and submitting the request to publish the video, setting the changeset constraint allows us to show a nice error message telling the user to pick something else.

This isn't so uncommon. Maybe you've started to publish a new video on Friday at 5:00 p.m. but decide to finish the process next Monday. Someone has the whole weekend to remove a category, making your form data outdated.

On the other hand, let's take the :video belongs_to :user relationship. Our application is the one responsible for setting up the relationship between videos and users. If a constraint is violated, it can only be a bug in our application or a data-integrity issue.

In such cases, *the user can do nothing to fix the error,* so crashing is the best option. Something unexpected really happened. But that's OK. We know Elixir was designed to handle failures, and Phoenix allows us to convert them into nice status pages. Furthermore, we also recommend setting up a notification system that aggregates and emails errors coming from your application, so you can discover and act on potential bugs when your software is running in production.

Putting it another way: the *_constraint changeset functions are useful when the constraint being mapped is triggered by external data, often as part of the user request. *Using changeset constraints only makes sense if the error message can be something the user can take action on.*

Wrapping Up

In this chapter, we pushed Ecto a little harder. We started with queries and went deep into the query API. We explored constraints and how Ecto integrates with the database, ensuring that our data is kept clean and consistent. We also built a category layer. Along the way, you learned many things about the Phoenix philosophy:

- We learned how to seed data and how to use the :on_conflict option to manage data conflicts.

- We used Ecto's query API, which is independent of the repository API, to do some basic queries.

- We used two forms of queries, a keyword list–based syntax and a pipe-based syntax.

- We used fragments to pass SQL commands through the query API unchanged.

- We explored the different ways Ecto queries work with relationships, beyond data preloading.

- We wrote constraint-style validations for unique indexes and foreign-key violations.

- We learned how to choose between letting constraint errors go and when to report them to the user.

Next, you'll learn how to test everything we've seen so far.

## CHAPTER 8

Testing MVC

After reading through so many chapters, you might be wondering, "Where are all of the tests?" We strongly believe in writing tests as you go, but such an approach could be repetitive, awkward, and distracting in a book. Rather than present tests as we go, we decided to focus on presenting one concept at a time and save the tests for the end of each part. In this chapter, you'll see us use techniques to test everything we built in the first part of the book. We might not test every single line of code we've written so far, but we'll cover all of the concepts you'll need to test everything.

Regardless of what you're building or the language that you're using, many testing principles remain the same. Let's look at some of the principles we'd like to emphasize:

- Fast: We're going to make sure our tests run quickly and can run concurrently wherever possible.

- Isolated: We want to have the right level of isolation in our tests. Tests that are too isolated won't have enough context to be useful. Tests that aren't isolated enough will be difficult to understand and maintain.

- DRY (Don't Repeat Yourself): We want to eliminate unnecessary repetition in our tests.

- Repeatable: We want the same test on the same code to always yield the same result.

Both the Phoenix platform and Elixir have many features that simplify testing. Clean contracts between layers of the application make it easy to get to the right level of isolation. The focus on immutability, concurrency, and speed will help our tests run quickly. Functional programming will help keep our tests DRY and repeatable.

Before we go too much further, let's settle on some common terminology, since different testing terms mean different things depending on which framework or language you're using.

A *unit test* exercises a function for one layer of your application. For example, if you're testing a web calculator, unit tests would exercise the Calculator module supporting your arithmetic. You might dedicate one or more tests to the add function on your calculator module.

An *integration test* focuses on the way different layers of an application fit together. Our integration tests in this chapter will generally do a request to a controller to use the things we've created so far. A single test will begin at our endpoint, run through our pipelines, read from the database, and render templates through views just as Phoenix requests would.

You may also encounter types of tests that we don't cover here. For a larger project, you'd also possibly want to test how multiple actions work together. For example, a single *acceptance test case* might sign the user on, perform several calculations that might build on each other, and then sign off. You might also consider *performance testing* to see how your application performs under load. In this book, we focus strictly on unit and integration tests.

Enough background! We're going to work through the various layers of our application. We'll start with some of the tools we can use to run tests and shape the tests we write. Next, we'll work through some integration tests and then focus on unit-testing the individual components.

Let's get started.

Understanding ExUnit

When you're testing with Phoenix, the framework builds default tests for you that help you keep the basic structure of your tests straight. Those templates even go a long way toward showing you how to build tests to cover your MVC code. Still, it's best to start at the beginning: a walkthrough of using ExUnit, Elixir's testing framework. Let's take a look at a basic Elixir test, one without Phoenix involved at all.

ExUnit has three main macros. The setup macro specifies some setup code that runs once before each test. The test macro defines a single isolated test. The assert macro specifies something we believe to be true about our code. If the assertion is true, the test passes. If it's false, the test fails. Either way, ExUnit reports the results, accumulating a list of failures and exceptions. Let's use these three macros in a simple test:

```
defmodule MyTest do
  use ExUnit.Case, async: true

  setup do
    # run some tedious setup code
    :ok
  end

  test "pass" do
    assert true
  end

  test "fail" do
    assert false
  end
end
```

This code runs two tests. The first runs the setup function and then the pass test. The second again runs the setup function and then the fail test. The output will include a passing test and a failing test.

The async: true flag allows the tests in this module to run concurrently with tests defined in other modules. However, tests in the same module are always executed sequentially, in random order to avoid implicit dependencies between tests.

If you need to know more about Elixir tests, excellent online resources exist, such as the ExUnit documentation.[1] For now, let's move on to specifically testing Phoenix functions.

Using Mix to Run Tests

Most developers, including the authors of this book, write tests as they build their application, piece by piece. Such a flow works well for a developer's day, but might seem repetitive when writing a book. In our case, we're going to write tests at the end of the two main parts of our book. This one captures testing contexts and controllers.

Whether you knew it or not, Phoenix has already been generating default tests for you, such as test/rumbl_web/controllers/video_controller_test.exs, test/rumbl/accounts/, and test/rumbl/multimedia/. You can use those tests to better understand the overall testing philosophy and structure behind Phoenix. We can go ahead and remove those files and directories since they were built for generic functionality, not the features we've specifically built into our controller and contexts. We've added user authentication, validations, and the like to our videos, so we'll start fresh with our VideoController tests. Delete the test/rumbl_web/controllers/video_controller_test.exs

---

1. http://elixir-lang.org/docs/stable/ex_unit/ExUnit.Case.html

file now, followed by the test/rumbl/accounts and test/rumbl/multimedia directories, and then let's see where our test suite stands:

```
$ mix test
    1) test GET / (RumblWeb.PageControllerTest)
       test/rumbl_web/controllers/page_controller_test.exs:4
       Assertion with =~ failed
       code:  assert html_response(conn, 200) =~ "Welcome to Phoenix!"
       left:  "<!DOCTYPE html>\n<html lang=\"en\">\n  <head>\n
       <meta charset=\"utf-8\"/>\n
       <meta http-equiv=\"X-UA-Compatible\" content=\"IE=edge\"/>\n..."
       right: "Welcome to Phoenix!"
       stacktrace:
         test/rumbl_web/controllers/page_controller_test.exs:6: (test)


Finished in 0.09 seconds
3 tests, 1 failure
```

We have one basic test that was generated along with the standard Phoenix installation. Since our controller has some changes, the tests fail. Let's fix that so we can start our test additions clean and green, from a passing state. It looks like we were expecting our "Welcome to Phoenix!" message to exist, but we've changed that message along the way. Let's update the test:

```
testing_mvc/listings/rumbl/test/rumbl_web/controllers/page_controller_test.change1.exs
test "GET /", %{conn: conn} do
  conn = get conn, "/"
  assert html_response(conn, 200) =~ "Welcome to Rumbl.io!"
end
```

Now you can run your test with a better result. This time, let's run a single test, like this:

```
$ mix test test/rumbl_web/controllers/page_controller_test.exs:4
Including tags: [line: "4"]
Excluding tags: [:test]

.

Finished in 0.07 seconds
1 test, 0 failures
```

It passes! The page test we just fixed is an integration test because it tests the integration of our basic contexts with the Phoenix features that make it available with the web, page by page. We'll write plenty of those in a bit. Let's start with the context and application tests. Then, we'll test their integration with our web stack.

Creating Test Data

In this chapter we're going to write tests for user registration and our video controller. To do so, we need to be able to rapidly create video and user records to support our tests. Let's create some fixture functions for creating users and videos. Create a test/support/test_helpers.ex file and key this in:

```
testing_mvc/listings/rumbl/test/support/test_helpers.ex
defmodule Rumbl.TestHelpers do
  alias Rumbl.{
    Accounts,
    Multimedia
  }

  def user_fixture(attrs \\ %{}) do
    {:ok, user} =
      attrs
      |> Enum.into(%{
        name: "Some User",
        username: "user#{System.unique_integer([:positive])}",
        password: attrs[:password] || "supersecret"
      })
      |> Accounts.register_user()

    user
  end

  def video_fixture(%Accounts.User{} = user, attrs \\ %{}) do
    attrs =
      Enum.into(attrs, %{
        title: "A Title",
        url: "http://example.com",
        description: "a description"
      })

    {:ok, video} = Multimedia.create_video(user, attrs)

    video
  end
end
```

We add a user_fixture function that accepts a map of attributes and creates a persistent user with them. Then, we do the same with a function called video_fixture. That function must also take the Accounts.User that created the video. We'll use this file as a convenient base for common helpers like user_fixture.

Notice that the functions in those two files are extremely thin. They simply integrate with the context features we've already written. Such thin functions don't necessarily mean that your design is right, but it is a data point. By testing, we force our context APIs to satisfy the needs of two clients, both controllers and tests, and that often gives a good sanity check for our designs.

You might be tempted to automatically reach for complex factory libraries, as you would in other languages, or approaches that let you specify fixtures. For simple data with a few well-defined relationships and mostly static attributes, you might find that simple functions work much better. For applications like ours, such an approach has much less ceremony and will serve perfectly well.

Keep in mind, though, that absolutes of any kind can get you into trouble. A contract exists between your tests and your test data, whether you choose to make it explicit or not. The best approach is to start slowly with functions. Later, as your needs—such as faked unique or structured data—grow, you can decide to adopt a library based on the specific needs of your application. The context is the right place to anchor such data generation clients. Libraries are like macros. Don't use one when a simple function will do the job.

Testing Contexts

It's time to test the M of the MVC, models. Phoenix generates a module in test/support/data_case.ex to serve as a foundation for your tests that interact with the database. In our case, Accounts and Multimedia contexts both work with the database. The data_case handles setup and teardown of the database and integrates with Ecto.Sandbox to allow concurrent transactional tests. Crack it open and import the fixtures we just defined:

```
testing_mvc/listings/rumbl/test/support/data_case.change1.ex
Line 1  defmodule Rumbl.DataCase do
  -       use ExUnit.CaseTemplate
  -
  -       using do
  5         quote do
  -           alias Rumbl.Repo
  -
  -           import Ecto
  -           import Ecto.Changeset
  10          import Ecto.Query
  -           import Rumbl.DataCase
  -           import Rumbl.TestHelpers
  -         end
  -       end
  15
  -       setup tags do
  -         :ok = Ecto.Adapters.SQL.Sandbox.checkout(Rumbl.Repo)
  -
  -         unless tags[:async] do
  20          Ecto.Adapters.SQL.Sandbox.mode(Rumbl.Repo, {:shared, self()})
  -         end
```

```
   :ok
 end

 def errors_on(changeset) do
   Ecto.Changeset.traverse_errors(changeset, fn {message, opts} ->
     Regex.replace(~r"%{(\w+)}", message, fn _, key ->
       opts |> Keyword.get(String.to_existing_atom(key), key) |> to_string()
     end)
   end)
 end
end
```

Let's take a look in more detail.

On line 12 we import our test helpers inside the using block. The using block serves as a place for defining macros, common imports and aliases. We also see a setup block for handling transactional tests. A transactional test runs a test and rolls back any changes made during the test. This transactional technique allows tests to reset the database to a known state quickly between tests.

Phoenix also generates an errors_on function for quickly accessing a list of error messages for attributes on a given schema. You'll see that function come into play as we write tests for our contexts.

Testing User Accounts

Let's start with user account registration. In truth, most context-related functionality will be tested with our integration tests as they insert and update records, but not all. Error and exception flows are some of the trickiest parts of our application to get right. We will explicitly try to catch some error conditions as close to the breaking point as possible. For us, since our context layer is the one that interacts directly with our database code, we'll build such cases there. Create a new file test/rumbl/accounts_test.exs that looks like this:

testing_mvc/listings/rumbl/test/rumbl/accounts_test.exs
```
defmodule Rumbl.AccountsTest do
  use Rumbl.DataCase, async: true

  alias Rumbl.Accounts
  alias Rumbl.Accounts.User

  describe "register_user/1" do
    @valid_attrs %{
      name: "User",
      username: "eva",
      password: "secret"
    }
    @invalid_attrs %{}
```

```
15    test "with valid data inserts user" do
        assert {:ok, %User{id: id}=user} = Accounts.register_user(@valid_attrs)
        assert user.name == "User"
        assert user.username == "eva"
        assert [%User{id: ^id}] = Accounts.list_users()
20    end

      test "with invalid data does not insert user" do
        assert {:error, _changeset} = Accounts.register_user(@invalid_attrs)
        assert Accounts.list_users() == []
25    end

      test "enforces unique usernames" do
        assert {:ok, %User{id: id}} = Accounts.register_user(@valid_attrs)
        assert {:error, changeset} = Accounts.register_user(@valid_attrs)
30
        assert %{username: ["has already been taken"]} =
                 errors_on(changeset)

        assert [%User{id: ^id}] = Accounts.list_users()
35    end

      test "does not accept long usernames" do
        attrs = Map.put(@valid_attrs, :username, String.duplicate("a", 30))
        {:error, changeset} = Accounts.register_user(attrs)
40
        assert %{username: ["should be at most 20 character(s)"]} =
                 errors_on(changeset)
        assert Accounts.list_users() == []
      end
45
      test "requires password to be at least 6 chars long" do
        attrs = Map.put(@valid_attrs, :password, "12345")
        {:error, changeset} = Accounts.register_user(attrs)

50      assert %{password: ["should be at least 6 character(s)"]} =
               errors_on(changeset)
        assert Accounts.list_users() == []
      end
    end
55 end
```

On line 2, we use Rumbl.DataCase to set up our DB dependent tests. We pass the async: true option so the test runs concurrently. Then, on lines 15 and 22, we build valid and invalid users and assert the expected results of trying to register a new user account with Accounts.register_user. In the remaining tests, on lines 37, 46, and 27, our error checking is a bit more intentional. We set a username that's too long and assert that we got a specific error back. Likewise, we set a password that is too short and then test for a specific error.

We close by setting a password that is too short and then test for a specific error. For these tests, we use the errors_on function defined on Rumbl.DataCase. errors_on is convenient for quickly retrieving errors from the changeset. Keep in mind errors_on is just a function. You can create a custom version if you need to test custom behavior.

Now let's run our tests:

```
$ mix test test/rumbl/accounts_test.exs
.......

Finished in 0.1 seconds
5 tests, 0 failures
```

All green.

Next, let's introduce a testing feature in ExUnit called the describe block. Sometimes, you need to apply the same setup code to many different tests. Describe blocks allow us to apply different test setups to a whole block of tests. For example, we need a user record to test Accounts.authenticate_by_username_and_pass, so we create a describe block with its own setup and three tests, like this:

```
testing_mvc/listings/rumbl/test/rumbl/accounts_test.change1.exs
Line 1  describe "authenticate_by_username_and_pass/2" do
   -      @pass "123456"
   -
   -      setup do
   5        {:ok, user: user_fixture(password: @pass)}
   -      end
   -
   -      test "returns user with correct password", %{user: user} do
   -        assert {:ok, auth_user} =
   10             Accounts.authenticate_by_username_and_pass(user.username, @pass)
   -
   -        assert auth_user.id == user.id
   -      end
   -
   15     test "returns unauthorized error with invalid password", %{user: user} do
   -        assert {:error, :unauthorized} =
   -             Accounts.authenticate_by_username_and_pass(user.username, "badpass")
   -      end
   -
   20     test "returns not found error with no matching user for email" do
   -        assert {:error, :not_found} =
   -             Accounts.authenticate_by_username_and_pass("unknownuser", @pass)
   -      end
   -    end
```

Let's break it down. We start by defining a new describe block on line 4 which creates a user fixture having a hardcoded valid email and password.

Next, on line 8, we test that authenticate_by_username_and_pass returns our user when we provide a correct email and password. Following our valid authentication tests, we then test for the two possibile user authentication failures, a bad password or missing email on lines 15 and 20.

Now let's run our tests again:

```
$ mix test test/rumbl/accounts_test.exs
.......

Finished in 0.1 seconds
8 tests, 0 failures
```

We're still happily green.

Testing the Multimedia Context

Let's test the data access features in our Multimedia context. Create a new file at test/rumbl/multimedia_test.exs that looks like this:

testing_mvc/listings/rumbl/test/rumbl/multimedia_test.exs
```
defmodule Rumbl.MultimediaTest do
  use Rumbl.DataCase, async: true

  alias Rumbl.Multimedia
  alias Rumbl.Multimedia.Category

  describe "categories" do
    test "list_alphabetical_categories/0" do
      for name <- ~w(Drama Action Comedy) do
        Multimedia.create_category!(name)
      end

      alpha_names =
        for %Category{name: name} <-
          Multimedia.list_alphabetical_categories() do

          name
        end

      assert alpha_names == ~w(Action Comedy Drama)
    end
  end
end
```

We programmatically create categories and later fetch them. Our tests verify that they are in alphabetical order. Now let's run our tests:

```
$ mix test test/rumbl/multimedia_test.exs
.

Finished in 0.07 seconds
1 test, 0 failures
```

Success!

Everything looks good, so let's now test the video functions of our Multimedia context, which is a little more involved than the previous tests:

testing_mvc/listings/rumbl/test/rumbl/multimedia_test.change1.exs

```
Line 1  describe "videos" do
   -      alias Rumbl.Multimedia.Video
   -
   -      @valid_attrs %{description: "desc", title: "title", url: "http://local"}
   5      @invalid_attrs %{description: nil, title: nil, url: nil}
   -
   -      test "list_videos/0 returns all videos" do
   -        owner = user_fixture()
   -        %Video{id: id1} = video_fixture(owner)
  10        assert [%Video{id: ^id1}] = Multimedia.list_videos()
   -        %Video{id: id2} = video_fixture(owner)
   -        assert [%Video{id: ^id1}, %Video{id: ^id2}] = Multimedia.list_videos()
   -      end
   -
  15      test "get_video!/1 returns the video with given id" do
   -        owner = user_fixture()
   -        %Video{id: id} = video_fixture(owner)
   -        assert %Video{id: ^id} = Multimedia.get_video!(id)
   -      end
  20
   -      test "create_video/2 with valid data creates a video" do
   -        owner = user_fixture()
   -
   -        assert {:ok, %Video{} = video} =
  25          Multimedia.create_video(owner, @valid_attrs)
   -
   -        assert video.description == "desc"
   -        assert video.title == "title"
   -        assert video.url == "http://local"
  30      end
   -
   -      test "create_video/2 with invalid data returns error changeset" do
   -        owner = user_fixture()
   -        assert {:error, %Ecto.Changeset{}} =
  35          Multimedia.create_video(owner, @invalid_attrs)
   -      end
   -
   -      test "update_video/2 with valid data updates the video" do
   -        owner = user_fixture()
  40        video = video_fixture(owner)
   -        assert {:ok, video} =
   -          Multimedia.update_video(video, %{title: "updated title"})
   -        assert %Video{} = video
   -        assert video.title == "updated title"
  45      end
   -
```

```
        test "update_video/2 with invalid data returns error changeset" do
          owner = user_fixture()
          %Video{id: id} = video = video_fixture(owner)
50
          assert {:error, %Ecto.Changeset{}} =
            Multimedia.update_video(video, @invalid_attrs)

          assert %Video{id: ^id} = Multimedia.get_video!(id)
55      end

        test "delete_video/1 deletes the video" do
          owner = user_fixture()
          video = video_fixture(owner)
60        assert {:ok, %Video{}} = Multimedia.delete_video(video)
          assert Multimedia.list_videos() == []
        end

        test "change_video/1 returns a video changeset" do
65        owner = user_fixture()
          video = video_fixture(owner)
          assert %Ecto.Changeset{} = Multimedia.change_video(video)
        end
      end
```

We started by grouping our tests together with a new describe block for testing video functionality. On line 7, we create a video, picking off the id field with a pattern match. When we fetch a video, we verify correctness by matching against the id key of the Video record. Then, we do the same with a second video record. This test handles fetching a list of videos. Next, on line 15, we test the get_video function. We use the same technique to fetch a single video using get_video.

Next, on line 21 and 32 we test creation of videos with both valid and invalid user input. We verify a few attributes for the valid test and match against an error tuple for the invalid one. We're specifically testing our change set functionality. We used a similar approach to test video updates on lines 38 and 47.

Next, we tested delete_video. We ran assertions to verify both the :ok tuple and that the video no longer exists on a subsequent fetch.

Finally, we checked out the ability to return a changeset for tracking video changes on line 64. These tests cover a lot of ground, but they're quite simple.

Now let's run our tests:

```
$ mix test test/rumbl/multimedia_test.exs
.........

Finished in 0.2 seconds
9 tests, 0 failures
```

As expected, they are all green. Before we write more tests, let's take a short break and talk about the Ecto Sandbox.

Using Ecto Sandbox for Test Isolation and Concurrency

We mentioned that DataCase uses some aliases, imports, and macros to give us the functionality our tests need. One of the features that file provides is the *Ecto Sandbox*. The role of the sandbox is to undo all changes we have done to the database during our tests. These database transaction rollbacks give us test isolation.

The way the sandbox operates is quite efficient too: instead of deleting all of the data once the suite finishes, which would be expensive, it just wraps each test in a transaction. Once the test is done, the transaction is rolled back and everything behaves as if the data was never there.

While a database sandbox is commonplace in many web frameworks or database libraries, what sets the Ecto Sandbox apart is that it enables *concurrent testing within the same database*. In other words, you can run multiple tests that interact with the database at the same time, and they won't affect each other. *This is a big deal* since most developers must make compromises between slow tests that sequentially hit the DB and "fast" tests that stub out all DB calls altogether. With the Ecto Sandbox, we can make full use of the database and still use all of our machine resources, making sure the test suite runs as fast as it possibly can. We can do all of this without having to manage multiple database instances.

Note, however, that tests do not run concurrently by default. In order to enable concurrency, we need to pass the async: true true option when using Rumbl.Data-Case, which is exactly what we have done in both AccountsTest and MultimediaTest:

```
defmodule Rumbl.AccountsTest do
  use Rumbl.DataCase, async: true
```

Then back in Rumbl.DataCase, Phoenix defines a setup block that configures the sandbox for us:

```
testing_mvc/rumbl/test/support/data_case.ex
Line 1  setup tags do
     2    :ok = Ecto.Adapters.SQL.Sandbox.checkout(Rumbl.Repo)
     3
     4    unless tags[:async] do
     5      Ecto.Adapters.SQL.Sandbox.mode(Rumbl.Repo, {:shared, self()})
     6    end
     7
     8    :ok
     9  end
```

On line 2, we check out a connection from the sandbox. The sandbox wraps the connection in a transaction which is automatically rolled back at the end of the test. Then we check if the test is running asynchronously. If the test is not asynchronous, we make sure the connection is shared across all processes on line 5. We are going to see a use case for sharing the connection in Chapter 13, Testing Channels and OTP, on page 279.

You can find out more about how the sandbox works by checking out the Hex documentation.[2] Now let's move on to views and controllers.

Integration Tests

We've begun by testing our contexts. Since our contexts deal with database-backed applications, those tests checked the way we created, deleted, fetched, and updated data from the database. We also paid special attention to how we processed changes and errors. Our context API exposed those features through changesets.

Now it's time to shift to integration tests. One of our basic principles for testing is isolation, but that doesn't mean that the most extreme isolation is always the right answer. The interactions among parts of your software are the very things that make it interesting. When you test your Phoenix applications, getting the right level of isolation is critical. Sometimes, a function is the perfect level of isolation. Sometimes, though, you'll want to run a test that encompasses multiple layers of your application. This is the realm of the integration test.

Fortunately, we have a natural architectural barrier that enforces the perfect balance. We're going to fully test the route through the endpoint, as a real web request will do. That way, we'll execute each plug and pick up all of the little transformations that occur along the way. We won't have to do any complex test setup, and we won't have any mismatch between the ways the tests and production server use our application. We'll make sure our controller actions return success, redirect, or error codes as they should. We will test the behaviors we expect for authorization. To top it off, testing through the endpoint is superfast, so we pay virtually no penalty.

Warming Up with the Page Controller

Let's get started. Start by opening test/rumbl_web/controllers/page_controller_test.exs to take another look:

---

2. https://hexdocs.pm/ecto_sql/Ecto.Adapters.SQL.Sandbox.html

```
testing_mvc/rumbl/test/rumbl_web/controllers/page_controller_test.exs
defmodule RumblWeb.PageControllerTest do
  use RumblWeb.ConnCase

  test "GET /", %{conn: conn} do
    conn = get conn, "/"
    assert html_response(conn, 200) =~ "Welcome to Rumbl.io!"
  end
end
```

This test is pretty sparse, but let's see what we can glean. Notice RumblWeb.ConnCase. Phoenix adds a test/support/conn_case.ex file to each new project. That file extends Phoenix.ConnTest to provide the services your test suite will need to run locally. It will help your tests set up connections, call your endpoints with specific routes and the like. Open RumblWeb.ConnCase to see what's provided by default:

```
testing_mvc/rumbl/test/support/conn_case.ex
defmodule RumblWeb.ConnCase do
  use ExUnit.CaseTemplate

  using do
    quote do
      # Import conveniences for testing with connections
      use Phoenix.ConnTest
      alias RumblWeb.Router.Helpers, as: Routes

      # The default endpoint for testing
      @endpoint RumblWeb.Endpoint
    end
  end

  setup tags do
    :ok = Ecto.Adapters.SQL.Sandbox.checkout(Rumbl.Repo)

    unless tags[:async] do
      Ecto.Adapters.SQL.Sandbox.mode(Rumbl.Repo, {:shared, self()})
    end

    {:ok, conn: Phoenix.ConnTest.build_conn()}
  end
end
```

As you'd expect, we use Phoenix.ConnTest to set up that API. Next, it imports convenient aliases we'll use throughout our tests. Finally, it sets the @endpoint module attribute, which is required for Phoenix.ConnTest. This attribute lets Phoenix know which endpoint to call when you directly call a route in your tests.

Also notice our setup block. It sets up the Ecto Sandbox, as in DataCase, but the last line here is different. It returns {:ok, conn: ...}, which places a base conn into our test metadata, which flows into our page_controller_test as an optional second argument to the test macro.

These small bits of code let Phoenix tests use real endpoints, pipelines, and Plug.Conn connections that pass through your application code, just as the Phoenix framework would. After all, these are integration tests that should use the same paths production code uses whenever possible.

For example, in your page_controller_test, we called our controller with get conn, "/" rather than calling the index action on our controller directly. This practice ensures that we're testing the router and pipelines because we're using the controller the same way Phoenix does.

Phoenix also gives us some helpers to test responses and keep our tests clean, such as the assertion from page_controller_test:

```
assert html_response(conn, 200) =~ "Welcome to Rumbl.io!"
```

These functions pack a lot of punch in a single function call. The simple statement html_response(conn, 200) does the following:

- Asserts that the conn's response was 200
- Asserts that the response content-type was text/html
- Returns the response body, allowing us to match on the contents

If our request had been a JSON response, we could have used another response assertion called json_response to match on any field of a response body. For example, you might write a json_response assertion like this:

```
assert %{user_id: ^user_id} = json_response(conn, 200)
```

Keep in mind RumblWeb.ConnCase is just a foundation. You can personalize it to your own application as needed. Let's learn more about integration tests by writing our own VideoController tests from scratch, starting with the actions available while logged out.

Testing Logged-Out Users

We will need to create data so we will add factory helpers to our application so we can use user_fixture and video_fixture. Add import Rumbl.TestHelpers to your ConnCase using block to bring in our helpers in all our connection-related tests, like this:

```
testing_mvc/listings/rumbl/test/support/conn_case.change1.ex
Line 1  using do
   -      quote do
   -        # Import conveniences for testing with connections
   -        use Phoenix.ConnTest
   5        import Rumbl.TestHelpers
   -        alias RumblWeb.Router.Helpers, as: Routes
```

```
     # The default endpoint for testing
     @endpoint RumblWeb.Endpoint
10   end
 end
```

With our fixture functions accessible, we can start testing our VideoController. Create a file called test/rumbl_web/controllers/video_controller_test.exs and make it look like this:

testing_mvc/listings/rumbl/test/rumbl_web/controllers/video_controller_test.exs
```
defmodule RumblWeb.VideoControllerTest do
  use RumblWeb.ConnCase, async: true

  test "requires user authentication on all actions", %{conn: conn} do
    Enum.each([
      get(conn, Routes.video_path(conn, :new)),
      get(conn, Routes.video_path(conn, :index)),
      get(conn, Routes.video_path(conn, :show, "123")),
      get(conn, Routes.video_path(conn, :edit, "123")),
      put(conn, Routes.video_path(conn, :update, "123", %{})),
      post(conn, Routes.video_path(conn, :create, %{})),
      delete(conn, Routes.video_path(conn, :delete, "123")),
    ], fn conn ->
      assert html_response(conn, 302)
      assert conn.halted
    end)
  end
end
```

Since our video controller is locked behind user authentication, we want to make sure that our authentication pipeline halts every action. Since all of those tests are the same except for the routes, we use Enum.each to iterate over all of the routes we want, and we make the same assertion for each response. Since we're verifying a halted connection that kicks logged-out visitors back to the home page, we assert a html_response of 302.

Let's try our tests out:

```
$ mix test test/rumbl_web
....

Finished in 0.1 seconds
4 tests, 0 failures
```

And they pass. Now that we've tested all routes as logged-out users, we need to check the behavior as logged-in users.

Preparing for Logged-In Users

You might be tempted to place the user_id in the session for the Auth plug to pick up, like this:

```
conn()
|> fetch_session()
|> put_session(:user_id, user.id)
|> get("/videos")
```

This approach is a little messy because it assumes an implementation. We don't want to store anything directly in the session, because we don't want to leak implementation details. Alternatively, we could do a direct request to the session controller every time we want to log in. However, this would quickly become expensive, because most tests will require a logged-in user. There's a better way.

Instead, we choose to test our login mechanism in isolation and build a bypass mechanism for the rest of our test cases. We simply pass any user through in our conn.assigns as a pass-through for our Auth plug. Update your web/controllers/auth.ex, like this:

```
testing_mvc/listings/rumbl/lib/rumbl_web/controllers/auth.change1.ex
def call(conn, _opts) do
  user_id = get_session(conn, :user_id)

  cond do
    conn.assigns[:current_user] ->
      conn

    user = user_id && Rumbl.Accounts.get_user(user_id) ->
      assign(conn, :current_user, user)

    true ->
      assign(conn, :current_user, nil)
  end
end
```

We've rewritten our call function using cond to check for multiple conditions, with our new condition at the top. Its sole job is to match on the current_user already in place in the assigns. If we see that we already have a current_user, we return the connection as is.

Let's be clear. What we're doing here is controversial. We're adding this code to make our implementation more testable. We think the trade-off is worth it. We are *improving the contract*. If a user is in the conn.assigns, we honor it, no matter how it got there. We have an improved testing story that doesn't require us to write mocks or any other elaborate scaffolding.

Now, all of our tests for logged-in users will be much cleaner.

Testing Logged-In Users

Now, we're free to add tests. We add a new test for /videos to test/rumbl_web/controllers/video_controller_test.exs, like this:

```
testing_mvc/listings/rumbl/test/rumbl_web/controllers/video_controller_test.change1.exs
setup %{conn: conn, login_as: username} do
  user = user_fixture(username: username)
  conn = assign(conn, :current_user, user)

  {:ok, conn: conn, user: user}
end

test "lists all user's videos on index", %{conn: conn, user: user} do
  user_video  = video_fixture(user, title: "funny cats")
  other_video = video_fixture(
    user_fixture(username: "other"),
    title: "another video")

  conn = get conn, Routes.video_path(conn, :index)
  assert html_response(conn, 200) =~ ~r/Listing Videos/
  assert String.contains?(conn.resp_body, user_video.title)
  refute String.contains?(conn.resp_body, other_video.title)
end
```

In our setup block, we seed a user to the database by using our user_fixture helper function. ConnCase takes care of running our tests in isolation. Any seeded fixtures in the database will be wiped between test blocks.

However, our new setup block causes the previous tests to break, because they expect a connection without a logged-in user. To fix our failing tests, let's use describe blocks and tags.

Using Tags

Some of our tests require logging in and some don't. Let's wrap our new test case in a describe block to allow setup for only logged-in users. We'll also use a :login_as tag to specify which user we'd like to log in. Tagging allows you to mark specific tests with attributes you can use later. You can access these attributes from the test context blocks. Tests outside of the describe block will then skip the login requirement:

```
testing_mvc/listings/rumbl/test/rumbl_web/controllers/video_controller_test.change2.exs
Line 1  describe "with a logged-in user" do

  -       setup %{conn: conn, login_as: username} do
  -         user = user_fixture(username: username)
  5         conn = assign(conn, :current_user, user)

  -         {:ok, conn: conn, user: user}
  -       end

  -
  10      @tag login_as: "max"
  -       test "lists all user's videos on index", %{conn: conn, user: user} do
  -         user_video  = video_fixture(user, title: "funny cats")
  -         other_video = video_fixture(
  -           user_fixture(username: "other"),
  15          title: "another video")

  -         conn = get conn, Routes.video_path(conn, :index)
  -         response = html_response(conn, 200)
  -         assert response =~ ~r/Listing Videos/
  20        assert response =~ user_video.title
  -         refute response =~ other_video.title
  -       end
  -     end
```

We wrapped our setup block and video listing tests in a new describe block. Then, on line 10, we add a :login_as tag with our username. We consume that :login_as tag on line 3. Since Ex::Unit passes tags along with the test context, we can simply match on the tag, grabbing the value opposite the :login_as tag as username.

The tag module attribute accepts a keyword list or an atom. Passing an atom is a shorthand way to set flag style options. For example @tag :logged_in is equivalent to @tag logged_in: true. We rewrite our setup block to grab the config map, which holds our metadata with the conn and tags which we use to populate our user fixture.

Our tests now pass, because they only seed the database when necessary. We can also use the tags to run tests only matching a particular tag, like this:

```
$ mix test test/rumbl_web --only login_as
Including tags: [:login_as]
Excluding tags: [:test]

.

Finished in 0.1 seconds
5 tests, 0 failures, 4 skipped
```

Perfect. In short, we'll use tags anywhere we want to mark attributes for a block of tests and describes to scope setups to a block of tests. Our tests now exercise the video listing, but we still haven't used the controller to create a video. Let's build a test to create a video, making sure to define the new code *inside* our logged-in describe block like this:

```
testing_mvc/listings/rumbl/test/rumbl_web/controllers/video_controller_test.change3.exs
alias Rumbl.Multimedia

@create_attrs %{
  url: "http://youtu.be",
  title: "vid",
  description: "a vid"}
@invalid_attrs %{title: "invalid"}

defp video_count, do: Enum.count(Multimedia.list_videos())

@tag login_as: "max"
test "creates user video and redirects", %{conn: conn, user: user} do
  create_conn =
    post conn, Routes.video_path(conn, :create), video: @create_attrs

  assert %{id: id} = redirected_params(create_conn)
  assert redirected_to(create_conn) ==
    Routes.video_path(create_conn, :show, id)

  conn = get conn, Routes.video_path(conn, :show, id)
  assert html_response(conn, 200) =~ "Show Video"

  assert Multimedia.get_video!(id).user_id == user.id
end

@tag login_as: "max"
test "does not create vid, renders errors when invalid", %{conn: conn} do
  count_before = video_count()
  conn =
    post conn, Routes.video_path(conn, :create), video: @invalid_attrs
  assert html_response(conn, 200) =~ "check the errors"
  assert video_count() == count_before
end
```

In this example, we want to test the successful and unsuccessful paths for creating a video. To keep things clear and easy to understand, we create some module attributes for both valid and invalid changesets. This touch keeps our intentions clear. With one tweak, we can keep our tests DRY so changes in validations require only trivial adjustments to our controller tests. We'll have another set of tests we can use to fully handle our changesets, but for now this strategy will work fine.

Next, we create the test case for the successful case. We use the create route with our valid attributes and then assert that we're returning the right values and redirecting to the right place. Then, we confirm that our test impacts the database in the ways we expect. We don't need to test all of the attributes, but we should pay attention to the elements of this operation that are likely to break. We assert that our new record exists and has the correct owner. This test makes sure that our happy path is indeed happy.

Writing negative integration tests is a delicate balance. We don't want to cover all possible failure conditions, as those must be fully covered when unit testing the context. Instead, we're handling concerns we choose to expose to the user, especially those that change the flow of our code. We test the case of trying to create an invalid video, the redirect, error messages, and so on.

Our other persistence tests will follow much the same approach. You can find the full CRUD test listing in the downloadable source code for the book.[3]

As you recall, we left a hole in our code coverage when we worked around authentication. Let's shift gears and handle the authorization cases of our controller. We must test that other users cannot view, edit, update, or destroy videos of another user. Crack open our test case and key this in. Remember, since we're not logged in, we want to add this test outside of our logged-in describe block:

```
testing_mvc/listings/rumbl/test/rumbl_web/controllers/video_controller_test.change4.exs
test "authorizes actions against access by other users", %{conn: conn} do
  owner = user_fixture(username: "owner")
  video = video_fixture(owner, @create_attrs)
  non_owner = user_fixture(username: "sneaky")
  conn = assign(conn, :current_user, non_owner)

  assert_error_sent :not_found, fn ->
    get(conn, Routes.video_path(conn, :show, video))
  end
  assert_error_sent :not_found, fn ->
    get(conn, Routes.video_path(conn, :edit, video))
  end
  assert_error_sent :not_found, fn ->
    put(conn, Routes.video_path(conn, :update, video, video: @create_attrs))
  end
  assert_error_sent :not_found, fn ->
    delete(conn, Routes.video_path(conn, :delete, video))
  end
end
```

---

3. http://pragprog.com/book/phoenix/source_code

That test does a lot, so let's break it down. First we create a new user to act as the owner for a video. Then, we set up our conn to log in a newly created user named sneaky, one that doesn't own our existing video. Using descriptive variable names in tests can provide that extra bit of documentation to make your test's intentions clear.

We use the same approach we used when we tested the basic path without logging in. In this case, the context is raising the Ecto.NoResultsError, since there is no video with the given ID associated to the given user. Instead of letting this error blow up in the user's face, there is a protocol between Plug and Ecto where Plug is told to treat all Ecto.NoResultsError as a 404 response status, which we can also refer to as :not_found. We use a new function called assert_error_sent to test precisely that an error happened but it became a 404 when handled by Phoenix.

Though we don't cover every controller action, these test cases provide a pretty good cross section for the overall approach. For practice, you can use these techniques to round out our integration tests.

As we work from the top down, we have one plug that we extracted into its own module, since it plays a critical role across multiple sections of our application. We'll test that plug next, in isolation. We're going to adhere to our principle for getting the right level of isolation.

Unit-Testing Plugs

If your code is worth writing, it's worth testing. Earlier, we bypassed our authentication plug, so we should test it now. The good news is that since our plug is essentially a function, it's relatively easy to build a set of tests that will confirm that it does what we need.

Create a test/rumbl_web/controllers/auth_test.exs and key in the following contents. We're going to break the test file into parts to keep things simple.

First, test the authenticate_user function that does the lion's share of the work:

testing_mvc/listings/rumbl/test/rumbl_web/controllers/auth_test.exs
```elixir
defmodule RumblWeb.AuthTest do
  use RumblWeb.ConnCase, async: true
  alias RumblWeb.Auth

  test "authenticate_user halts when no current_user exists",
      %{conn: conn} do

    conn = Auth.authenticate_user(conn, [])
    assert conn.halted
  end
```

```
  test "authenticate_user for existing current_user",
      %{conn: conn} do
    conn =
      conn
      |> assign(:current_user, %Rumbl.Accounts.User{})
      |> Auth.authenticate_user([])

    refute conn.halted
  end
end
```

That's as simple as it gets. If we try to authenticate without a user, we shouldn't authenticate. Otherwise, we should.

Let's run that much to make sure things continue to work:

```
$ mix test test/rumbl_web/controllers/auth_test.exs
.

1)
test authenticate_user halts when no current_user exists (RumblWeb.AuthTest)
test/rumbl_web/controllers/auth_test.exs:5
** (KeyError) key :current_user not found in: %{}
code: conn = Auth.authenticate_user(conn, [])
stacktrace:
  (rumbl) lib/rumbl_web/controllers/auth.ex:47: Auth.authenticate_user/2
  test/rumbl_web/controllers/auth_test.exs:8: (test)

Finished in 0.05 seconds
2 tests, 1 failure
```

That was surprising. What happened?

Since our Auth plug assumes that a :current_user assign exists in the connection, the test errors.

Let's try to quickly fix this by injecting a nil :current_user in our first test case, like this:

```
conn =
  conn
  |> assign(:current_user, nil)
  |> Auth.authenticate_user([])
```

Now let's rerun the tests:

```
$ mix test test/rumbl_web/controllers/auth_test.exs
1)
test authenticate_user halts when no current_user exists (RumblWeb.AuthTest)
test/rumbl_web/controllers/auth_test.exs:5
** (ArgumentError) flash not fetched, call fetch_flash/2
code: |> Auth.authenticate_user([])
```

```
stacktrace:
  (phoenix) lib/phoenix/controller.ex:1265: Phoenix.Controller.get_flash/1
  (phoenix) lib/phoenix/controller.ex:1247: Phoenix.Controller.put_flash/3
  (rumbl) lib/rumbl_web/controllers/auth.ex:51: Auth.authenticate_user/2
  test/rumbl_web/controllers/auth_test.exs:11: (test)

Finished in 0.06 seconds
2 tests, 1 failure
```

Another error.

It looks like our authenticate_user raised an error because it puts a message in the flash, which isn't available. If you look at the :browser pipeline in the router, you see that it plugs fetch_flash to set up the flash.

So let's do the same:

```
conn =
  conn()
  |> fetch_flash()
  |> Auth.authenticate_user([])
```

We receive a ** (ArgumentError) session not fetched, call fetch_session/2 error. We could attempt to solve this one too, but we would get yet another error about the Plug.Session not being configured.

The issue here is that we want to unit test authenticate_user but it depends on other functionality from the Plug pipeline. These are the kinds of issues that integration testing through the endpoint avoids.

We could reimplement our whole endpoint and router pipeline in order to test authenticate_user but Phoenix gives us another option. For unit tests, Phoenix includes a bypass_through test helper that allows us to do a request that goes through the whole pipeline but bypasses the router dispatch. This approach gives you a connection wired up with all the transformations your specific tests require, such as fetching the session and adding flash messages:

testing_mvc/listings/rumbl/test/rumbl_web/controllers/auth_test.change1.exs
```
setup %{conn: conn} do
  conn =
    conn
    |> bypass_through(RumblWeb.Router, :browser)
    |> get("/")

  {:ok, %{conn: conn}}
end

test "authenticate_user halts when no current_user exists", %{conn: conn} do
  conn = Auth.authenticate_user(conn, [])
  assert conn.halted
end
```

```
test "authenticate_user for existing current_user", %{conn: conn} do
  conn =
    conn
    |> assign(:current_user, %Rumbl.Accounts.User{})
    |> Auth.authenticate_user([])
  refute conn.halted
end
```

We add a setup block, which calls bypass_through, passing our router and the :browser pipeline to invoke. Then we perform a request with get, which accesses the endpoint and stops at the browser pipeline, as requested. The path given to get isn't used by the router when bypassing; it's simply stored in the connection. This gives us all the requirements for a plug with a valid session and flash message support. Next, we pull the conn from the context passed to the test macro and use our bypassed conn as the base for our test blocks.

Now let's rerun our tests:

```
$ mix test test/rumbl_web/controllers/auth_test.exs
..

Finished in 0.08 seconds
2 tests, 0 failures
```

And boom. Now test the rest of our Auth plug, like the login and logout features:

testing_mvc/listings/rumbl/test/rumbl_web/controllers/auth_test.change2.exs
```
test "login puts the user in the session", %{conn: conn} do
  login_conn =
    conn
    |> Auth.login(%Rumbl.Accounts.User{id: 123})
    |> send_resp(:ok, "")

  next_conn = get(login_conn, "/")
  assert get_session(next_conn, :user_id) == 123
end
```

Here, we test our ability to log in. We create a new connection called login_conn. We take a basic conn, log the user in with Auth.login, and call send_resp, which sends the response to the client with a given status and response body. To make sure that our new user survives the next request, we make a new request with that connection and make sure the user is still in the session. That's easy enough. A test for logout is similar:

```
testing_mvc/listings/rumbl/test/rumbl_web/controllers/auth_test.change2.exs
test "logout drops the session", %{conn: conn} do
  logout_conn =
    conn
    |> put_session(:user_id, 123)
    |> Auth.logout()
    |> send_resp(:ok, "")

  next_conn = get(logout_conn, "/")
  refute get_session(next_conn, :user_id)
end
```

We create a connection, put a user_id into our session, and then call Auth.logout. To make sure the logout will persist through a request, we then make a request with get, and finally make sure that no user_id is in the session.

Now, let's test the main interface for our plug—the call function, which calls the plug directly to wire up the current_user from the session:

```
testing_mvc/listings/rumbl/test/rumbl_web/controllers/auth_test.change3.exs
Line 1  test "call places user from session into assigns", %{conn: conn} do
          user = user_fixture()
  -       conn =
  -         conn
  5         |> put_session(:user_id, user.id)
  -         |> Auth.call(Auth.init([]))
  -
  -       assert conn.assigns.current_user.id == user.id
  -     end
 10
  -     test "call with no session sets current_user assign to nil", %{conn: conn} do
  -       conn = Auth.call(conn, Auth.init([]))
          assert conn.assigns.current_user == nil
  -     end
```

The tests are simple and light. On line 2, we create a user for the test. Next, on line 5, we place that user's ID in the session. On line 6, we call Auth.call, and then assert that the current_user in conn.assigns matches our seeded user. We know that *logged-in users can get in*.

We have a workable positive test, but it's also important to test the negative condition. We want to make sure that *logged-out users stay out*. The test looks a lot like the positive test, but we never put any user in the session, and we match on nil instead.

Now let's run our new tests:

```
$ mix test test/rumbl_web/controllers/auth_test.exs
.........

Finished in 1.9 seconds
9 tests, 0 failures
```

All pass, but if you look closely, we have a problem. We are waiting two seconds for nine small tests. The test time is growing quickly. You have probably been noticing how the test times have crept up as we have seeded more and more users. If your tests are slow, you won't run them as much. We have to fix it.

The reason our tests are slow is that we seed users with our registration changeset, which hashes passwords. Hashing passwords is intentionally expensive. Doing this extra bit of work makes our passwords harder to crack, but we don't need all of that security in the test environment.

Let's ease up the number of hashing rounds to speed up our test suite by adding this configuration line to config/test.exs:

testing_mvc/listings/rumbl/config/test.change1.exs
```
config :pbkdf2_elixir, :rounds, 1
```

Now let's rerun our authentication tests:

```
$ mix test test/rumbl_web/controllers/auth_test.exs
.........

Finished in 0.1 seconds
9 tests, 0 failures
```

One-tenth of a second! Time to shift into views.

Testing Views and Templates

As we've said, any code worth writing is code worth testing, and your views are no exception. As you saw in Chapter 3, Controllers, on page 41, Phoenix templates are simply functions in a parent's view module. You can test these functions like any other. In this section, you'll see how to test views and templates in isolation.

Create a test/rumbl_web/views/video_view_test.exs and key this in:

testing_mvc/listings/rumbl/test/rumbl_web/views/video_view_test.exs
```
Line 1  defmodule RumblWeb.VideoViewTest do
     -    use RumblWeb.ConnCase, async: true
     -    import Phoenix.View
     -
```

```
 5   test "renders index.html", %{conn: conn} do
       videos = [
         %Rumbl.Multimedia.Video{id: "1", title: "dogs"},
         %Rumbl.Multimedia.Video{id: "2", title: "cats"}
       ]
10
       content = render_to_string(
         RumblWeb.VideoView,
         "index.html",
         conn: conn,
15       videos: videos)

       assert String.contains?(content, "Listing Videos")

       for video <- videos do
20         assert String.contains?(content, video.title)
       end
     end

     test "renders new.html", %{conn: conn} do
25       owner = %Rumbl.Accounts.User{}
       changeset = Rumbl.Multimedia.change_video(%Rumbl.Multimedia.Video{})
       categories = [%Rumbl.Multimedia.Category{id: 123, name: "cats"}]

       content =
30         render_to_string(RumblWeb.VideoView, "new.html",
           conn: conn,
           changeset: changeset,
           categories: categories
         )
35
       assert String.contains?(content, "New Video")
     end
   end
```

Our test needs some videos, so on line 5, we set up our required @videos assigns. With all of the prerequisites in place, we call Phoenix.View.render_to_string to render our HTML template as a simple string. Then, we make sure that all of the video titles are present on the page.

On line 24, we again set up our necessary @changeset and @categories assigns before rendering our template as a string and asserting that our render contents place us on the new video page.

Sometimes, views are simple enough that your integration tests will be enough. Many other times, you won't test the templates directly, but the functions that you create to help move the logic away from the templates and into code. Our goal with this section is to once again highlight the fact that because a template is just a function in the view, templates are easy to test because they aren't coupled with the controller layer. And this will apply to any function you create in your view, because all arguments are received explicitly. With Phoenix, you'll have all of the tools you need to do so easily. We've covered a lot of ground so it's a good time to wrap up.

Wrapping Up

With these final tests, we're finally done. We've accomplished a lot.

We started by writing some unit tests. The goal of these tests is to check a single layer of our application in isolation. We tested our basic contexts, the user and multimedia contexts. Since both of these contexts provided persistence services, we made sure to exercise the database. The Ecto.Sandbox preserved isolation and allowed concurrent testing and the describe keyword allowed us to apply setup code to multiple tests at once, saving duplication. We paid special attention to change sets which surface errors and change tracking through the API.

Next we worked with integration tests. The goal of integration tests is to test the layers of our application working together. Our integration tests used not only controller code but also the entire Phoenix pipeline and used actual endpoints to make sure to exercise the whole application stack. We used tagging to specify individual users to create data or log in. We also used Phoenix helpers to make multiple assertions in a compact way. To preserve the entire Plug pipeline, we wrote a bypass to skip only the authentication plugs.

Finally, we tested our plugs and views. Since these were simple functions, it was easy and fast to test them.

Raise a cheer, because we're through Part I! You should now be able to use Plug, Ecto, and Phoenix to build traditional request/response features for your application and test each of those concepts. Part II will be even more exciting, focusing on the features that prompted the creation of Phoenix. You'll see channels, OTP, and more. Get ready. We're going to push Phoenix harder.

Part II

Writing Interactive and Maintainable Applications

In Part II, we'll explore the features that will help you build a new generation of web applications. You'll learn to use channels to build highly concurrent interactive applications using a new set of abstractions. Then, you'll learn to build service layers with the OTP API, the famous Erlang library for building supervised, fault-tolerant services. You'll manage all of this with Mix, Elixir's build tool, allowing us to break a single monolithic application into smaller ones, separately maintainable but conveniently integrated. Finally, you'll learn to test channels and OTP features. You'll learn to build interactive applications that scale well and are easy to understand.

## CHAPTER 9

Watching Videos

We've accomplished quite a bit. We've built some basic web application features in a short time. We used Plug to build pipelines of functions that let us build organized, DRY code. We used Ecto to deal with our relational database in a functional way, favoring explicitness over hidden behaviors. We also organized our code into contexts to provide the domain API for other layers of our application to use. Phoenix wired it all together into a streamlined workflow, with live reloading, HTML support, and more.

Everything we've done so far highlights how well Phoenix encourages beautiful and maintainable applications. Those improvements bring a slightly different look to traditional web development, but nothing you've seen up to now is drastically different from what you already knew.

Now you're ready to see what makes Phoenix shine. This chapter starts with preparing some common ground by adding a page to watch videos. Then you'll look into Ecto custom types, which allow you to integrate your own requirements into queries, changesets, and structs. Along the way, we'll continue to expand our business logic within the Multimedia context, adding new application features one at a time. At the close of this chapter you'll customize URLs by tapping into the extensible power behind Elixir's protocols.

Tighten your seat belts. This ride will be unforgettable.

Watching Videos

Our rumbl application will allow us to add messages to videos in real time. We'll do some groundwork to make this process more convenient when the time comes. We'll tweak our views to make it easy to watch videos. Then, we'll create a new controller explicitly for watching a video, along with its view and template. Next, we'll tweak the router to pick up our new routes. Finally, we'll add some JavaScript to plug in to YouTube's API. You'll work through these features quickly, because they don't involve much new ground.

Let's let the user watch a video. First let's enhance our layout header with a link to My Videos for the current user in lib/rumbl_web/templates/layout/app.html.eex:

watching_videos/listings/rumbl/lib/rumbl_web/templates/layout/app.change1.html.eex
```
<nav role="navigation">
  <ul>
    <%= if @current_user do %>
      <li><%= @current_user.username %></li>
      <li><%= link "My Videos", to: Routes.video_path(@conn, :index) %></li>
      <li>
        <%= link "Log out",
              to: Routes.session_path(@conn, :delete, @current_user),
              method: "delete" %>
      </li>
    <% else %>
      <li><%= link "Register", to: Routes.user_path(@conn, :new) %></li>
      <li><%= link "Log in", to: Routes.session_path(@conn, :new) %></li>
    <% end %>
  </ul>
</nav>
```

Clicking My Videos routes a logged-in user directly to VideoController.index action.

This action is restricted to the current user, thanks to our scoping rules in the controller. In fact, there's no public URL we can share with our friends when it comes to watching videos. Let's address this by creating a WatchController for watching user videos, available to any user. Create a new lib/rumbl_web/controllers/watch_controller.ex file and key this in:

watching_videos/listings/rumbl/lib/rumbl_web/controllers/watch_controller.ex
```
defmodule RumblWeb.WatchController do
  use RumblWeb, :controller

  alias Rumbl.Multimedia

  def show(conn, %{"id" => id}) do
    video = Multimedia.get_video!(id)
    render(conn, "show.html", video: video)
  end
end
```

Now, let's create a new template directory for the controller in lib/rumbl_web/templates/watch and add a new show.html.eex template file with these contents:

watching_videos/listings/rumbl/lib/rumbl_web/templates/watch/show.html.eex

```
<div class="row">
  <div class="column column-60">
    <h1><%= @video.title %></h1>
    <%= content_tag :div, id: "video",
        data: [id: @video.id, player_id: player_id(@video)] do %>
    <% end %>
  </div>

  <div class="column annotations">
    <h3>Annotations</h3>

    <div id="msg-container">
    </div>

    <div>
      <textarea id="msg-input"
                rows="3"
                placeholder="Comment..."></textarea>

      <button id="msg-submit" class="button column"
              type="submit">
        Post
      </button>
    </div>
  </div>
</div>
```

The template is mostly markup, with the exception of the title and the video div, which includes the id, data-id, and data-player-id attributes. We extract the player ID from the video url field by a function aptly named player_id. Since templates are just functions in the view module, the view is the perfect place to define such a function.

Create a new lib/rumbl_web/views/watch_view.ex and make it look like this:

watching_videos/listings/rumbl/lib/rumbl_web/views/watch_view.ex

```
defmodule RumblWeb.WatchView do
  use RumblWeb, :view

  def player_id(video) do
    ~r{^.*(?:youtu\.be/|\w+/|v=)(?<id>[^#&?]*)}
    |> Regex.named_captures(video.url)
    |> get_in(["id"])
  end
end
```

Unfortunately, YouTube URLs come in a variety of formats. We need a regular expression to extract the video ID from the URL. Regular expressions are beyond the scope of this book, but here are the basics. A regular expression[1]

---

1. http://www.regular-expressions.info/

uses patterns to match specific patterns within strings. We're naming a pattern called id and then piping our expression into a function called named_captures, which extracts the id field given our URL name. Then, we build a map that returns the id key with its value.

Finally, let's add an entry to our router's :browser pipeline to the new WatchController:

watching_videos/listings/rumbl/lib/rumbl_web/router.change1.ex
```
scope "/", RumblWeb do
  pipe_through :browser # Use the default browser stack

  get "/", PageController, :index
  resources "/users", UserController, only: [:index, :show, :new, :create]
  resources "/sessions", SessionController, only: [:new, :create, :delete]
  get "/watch/:id", WatchController, :show
end
```

Now let's change the link for each entry in the My Videos page to point to watch instead of show. Open up lib/rumbl_web/templates/video/index.html.eex and replace show with this:

watching_videos/listings/rumbl/lib/rumbl_web/templates/video/index.change1.html.eex
```
<table>
  <thead>
    <tr>
      <th>Title</th>
      <th></th>
      <th></th>
      <th></th>
    </tr>
  </thead>
  <tbody>
<%= for video <- @videos do %>
    <tr>
      <td><%= video.title %></td>
      <td><%= link "Edit", to: Routes.video_path(@conn, :edit, video) %></td>
      <td>
        <%= link "Delete", to: Routes.video_path(@conn, :delete, video),
                     method: :delete,
                     data: [confirm: "Are you sure?"] %>
      </td>
      <td>
        <%= link "Watch", to: Routes.watch_path(@conn, :show, video),
                     class: "button" %>
      </td>
    </tr>
<% end %>
  </tbody>
</table>
```

First, we changed the table header to simplify the listing. We trimmed the headings to only the title with three empty headings for our edit, delete, and watch links. To match, we removed our url and description columns. We used the Routes.watch_path helper generated by the new route.

Not much exciting is happening here but this early preparation will lead to a great fireworks show later. Now, things will start to get a little more interesting. Let's add the JavaScript required to let us watch videos.

Adding JavaScript

webpack[2] is a build tool written in Node.js. We'll use webpack to build, transform, and minify[3] JavaScript and CSS code. Processing assets in this way makes your page load much more efficiently. webpack not only takes care of JavaScript but also CSS and all of our application assets, such as images.

The asset structure is laid out in the assets directory:

```
assets/
├── css/
├── js/
├── static/
├── vendor/
├── package.json
└── webpack.config.js
```

We put everything in assets/static that doesn't need to be transformed by webpack. The build tool will simply copy those static assets just as they are to priv/static, where they'll be served by Plug.Static in our endpoint.

We keep CSS and JavaScript files in their respective directories. The vendor directory is used to keep any third-party tools you need, such as jQuery. This structure helps us organize code, but we're also being practical. Let's see why.

Open up assets/js/app.js and take a look as its contents:

```
// We need to import the CSS so that webpack will load it
import css from "../css/app.css"

// webpack automatically bundles all modules in your
// entry points. Those entry points can be configured
// in "webpack.config.js".
//
// Import dependencies
//
```

---

2. https://webpack.js.org
3. https://blog.stackpath.com/glossary/minification/

```
import "phoenix_html"

// Import local files
// ...
// import socket from "./socket"
```

Phoenix configures webpack to use ECMAScript 6 (ES6)—the latest JavaScript specification we'll use in this book—to provide the necessary import statements. webpack wraps the contents for each JavaScript file you add to assets/js in a function and collects them into priv/static/js/app.js. That's the file loaded by browsers at the end of lib/rumbl_web/templates/layout/app.html.eex when we call Routes.static_url(@conn, "/js/app.js").

Since each file is wrapped in a function, it won't be automatically executed by browsers unless you explicitly import it in your app.js file. In this way, the app.js file is like a manifest. It's where you import and wire up your JavaScript dependencies. For example, we have imported phoenix_html as it provides some functionality to our HTML forms and buttons.

The assets/vendor directory is the exception to this rule. If you add an external JavaScript file to assets/vendor, it'll be automatically concatenated to your priv/static/app.js bundle and executed when your page loads. That way, external dependencies are never imported and available on the global JavaScript scope, such as window.

You can configure the webpack tool in the assets/webpack.config.js file. Take a look at it on your own time. The file is short and simple, so you can easily tell what's happening.

webpack ships with a command-line tool, and using it is straightforward. You need to know only a few commands:

```
$ webpack
$ webpack --watch
$ webpack --mode production
```

Since each of these commands builds your assets for a different context, let's talk about each in turn. webpack just compiles the assets into static files and copies the results to priv/static before exiting. During development as you're actively working on your JavaScript, you can add the -watch option. After you do so, webpack will monitor the files and automatically recompile them as they change. Use the --mode production flag to do everything you need to generally prepare your JavaScripts and style sheets for production, such as building and minifying them.

In all likelihood, you'll never type the first couple commands directly, because Phoenix does it for you. If you open up your config/dev.exs, you see this line:

```
watchers: [node: ["node_modules/webpack/bin/webpack.js",
  "--mode", "development", "--watch-stdin", "--colors",
  cd: Path.expand("../assets", __DIR__)]]
```

That code will automatically run webpack --watch-stdin when your Phoenix app starts in development. The --watch-stdin option makes the webpack program abort when Phoenix shuts down.

With the webpack introduction out of the way, it's time to write some JavaScript. First, we'll create a Player object to receive the data-player-id and embed the YouTube video. Later, we'll use the Player object to send and receive information about the video so we'll know exactly when an annotation is added.

Create a new file called assets/js/player.js with these contents:

```
watching_videos/listings/rumbl/assets/js/player.js
let Player = {
  player: null,

  init(domId, playerId, onReady){
    window.onYouTubeIframeAPIReady = () => {
      this.onIframeReady(domId, playerId, onReady)
    }
    let youtubeScriptTag = document.createElement("script")
    youtubeScriptTag.src = "//www.youtube.com/iframe_api"
    document.head.appendChild(youtubeScriptTag)
  },

  onIframeReady(domId, playerId, onReady){
    this.player = new YT.Player(domId, {
      height: "360",
      width: "420",
      videoId: playerId,
      events: {
        "onReady":  (event => onReady(event) ),
        "onStateChange": (event -> this.onPlayerStateChange(event) )
      }
    })
  },

  onPlayerStateChange(event){ },
  getCurrentTime(){ return Math.floor(this.player.getCurrentTime() * 1000) },
  seekTo(millsec){ return this.player.seekTo(millsec / 1000) }
}
export default Player
```

That's a fairly long example, so we should break it down piece by piece.

First, we will be creating a Player object that wires up YouTube's special window.onYouTubeIframeAPIReady callback. We inject a YouTube iframe tag, which will trigger our event when the player is ready.

Next, we implement a onIframeReady function to create the player with the YouTube iframe API. We finish by adding convenience functions like getCurrentTime and seekTo, since we want to bind messages to a point in time for the video playback.

This abstraction is more than a convenient wrapper. It builds an API for video players with the most important features for our application. Our Player API will insulate us from changes in YouTube and also let us add other video players over time. Our onYouTubeReady function needs the HTML container ID to hold the iframe. We'll pass this in from higher up in our JavaScript stack in a moment.

 Chris says:
Why webpack?

Instead of building yet another asset-build tool, the Phoenix team decided to leverage one of the many tools available in the Node.js ecosystem. webpack is the de facto choice in the Node.js community and the Phoenix team loves its adoption, solid documentation, and minimal out-of-the-box configuration.

We know this choice might not resonate with all developers, so Phoenix allows you to use the build tool of your choice. Not a single line of code in Phoenix knows about webpack. All the configuration is in your application. You can even skip webpack altogether when creating a new app by using the --no-webpack option. If you can tell your build tool to compile your static files to priv/static, you're good to go. You can even change your config/dev.exs file so Phoenix sets up a watcher for your favorite tool.

Our YouTube player is all set, but YouTube's JavaScript API expects a specific video ID, and all we have is the URL.

Remember, our player.js file won't be executed unless we import it. Let's do this in assets/js/app.js by importing the Player and starting it with the video and player ID if one exists:

```
watching_videos/listings/rumbl/assets/js/app.change1.js
import Player from "./player"
let video = document.getElementById("video")

if(video) {
  Player.init(video.id, video.getAttribute("data-player-id"), () => {
    console.log("player ready!")
  })
}
```

Next, let's tidy up our annotations box with a sprinkle of CSS. Create an assets/css/video.css file and key this in:

```
watching_videos/listings/rumbl/assets/css/video.css
.annotations {
  border-left: 1px solid #eaeaea;
}
#msg-container {
 min-height: 260px;
}
```

Now we can import our new video.css file in assets/css/app.css so our application can use it, like this:

```
watching_videos/listings/rumbl/assets/css/app.change1.css
/* This file is for your main application css. */

@import "./phoenix.css";
@import "./video.css";
```

We imported video.css after phoenix.css, a style sheet Phoenix includes for default styling.

Next, we'll create a new video with a YouTube URL, and you're now ready to watch it:

You can even start sharing the video URL with your friends with a URL that looks like /watch/13—but that's ugly. URLs for videos should use words, not numbers. Let's fix that.

Creating Slugs

We want our videos to have a unique URL-friendly identifier, called a *slug*. This approach lets us have a unique identifier that will build URLs that are friendlier to people and search engines. We need to create the slug from the title so we can represent a video titled Programming Elixir as a URL-friendly slug, such as 1-programming-elixir, where 1 is the video ID.

The first step is to add a slug column to the database:

```
$ mix ecto.gen.migration add_slug_to_videos
```

We generate a new migration. Remember, your name will differ based on the timestamp attached to the front of the file, but you can find the new file in the priv/repo/migrations directory. Let's fill it in like this:

watching_videos/listings/rumbl/priv/repo/migrations/20180721193825_add_slug_to_videos.exs
```
def change do
  alter table(:videos) do
    add :slug, :string
  end
end
```

Our new migration uses the alter macro, which changes the schema for both up and down migrations. With the migration in place, let's apply it to the database:

```
$ mix ecto.migrate
[info] == Running Rumbl.Repo.Migrations.AddSlugToVideos.change/0 forward
[info] alter table videos
[info] == Migrated in 0.0s
```

Next, we need to add the new field to the video schema in lib/rumbl/multimedia/video.ex, beneath the other fields:

```
field :slug, :string
```

The whole premise of a slug is that you can automatically generate a permanent field from other fields, some of which may be updatable. Let's do this by changing the changeset function, like this:

watching_videos/listings/rumbl/lib/rumbl/multimedia/video.change1.ex
```
def changeset(video, attrs) do
  video
  |> cast(attrs, [:url, :title, :description, :category_id])
  |> validate_required([:url, :title, :description])
  |> assoc_constraint(:category)
  |> slugify_title()
end
```

```elixir
defp slugify_title(changeset) do
  case fetch_change(changeset, :title) do
    {:ok, new_title} -> put_change(changeset, :slug, slugify(new_title))
    :error -> changeset
  end
end

defp slugify(str) do
  str
  |> String.downcase()
  |> String.replace(~r/[^\w-]+/u, "-")
end
```

We modify the generated changeset, just as we did the changeset for the password. We build the slug field within our changeset. The code couldn't be simpler. The pipe operator makes it easy for us to tell a story with code.

If a change is made to the title, we build a slug based on the new title with the slugify function. Otherwise, we simply return the changeset. slugify downcases the string and replaces nonword characters with a - character. cast, assoc_constraint, fetch_change and put_change are all functions defined in Ecto.Changeset, imported at the top of our video module.

Don't miss the importance of what we've done here. We're once again able to change how data gets into the system, without touching the controller and without using callbacks or any other indirection. All of the changes to be performed by the database are clearly outlined in the changeset. At this point, you've learned all the concepts behind changesets, and the benefits are becoming clearer:

- Because Ecto separates changesets from the definition of a given record, we can have a separate change policy for each type of change. We could easily add a JSON API that creates videos, including the slug field, for example.

- Changesets filter and cast the incoming data, making sure sensitive fields like a user role cannot be set externally, while conveniently casting them to the type defined in the schema.

- Changesets can validate data—for example, the length or the format of a field—on the fly, but validations that depend on data integrity are left to the database in the shape of constraints.

- Changesets make our code easy to understand and implement because they can compose easily, allowing us to specify each part of a change with a function.

In short, Ecto cleanly encapsulates the concepts of change, and we benefit tremendously as users. Now that we can generate slugs for the videos, let's make sure we use them in our links.

Extending Phoenix with Protocols

To use slugs when linking to the video page, let's open up the lib/rumbl_web/templates/video/index.html.eex template and see how links are generated:

```
<%= link "Watch", to: Routes.watch_path(@conn, :show, video),
                class: "button" %>
```

RumblWeb.Router generates the Routes.watch_path. It's available to our controller code because of the Routes alias in lib/rumbl_web.ex. When we pass a struct like video to watch_path, Phoenix automatically extracts its ID to use in the returned URL. To use slugs, we could simply change the route call to the following:

```
Routes.watch_path(@conn, :show, "#{video.id}-#{video.slug}")
```

This approach is easy to plug in, but it has a giant flaw. It's brittle because it's not DRY. Each place we need a link, we need to build the URL with the id and slug fields. If we forget to use the same structure in any of the future watch_path calls, we'll end up linking to the wrong URL. There's a better way.

We can customize how Phoenix generates URLs for the videos. Phoenix and Elixir have the perfect solution for this. Phoenix knows to use the id field in a Video struct because Phoenix defines a protocol, called Phoenix.Param. By default, this protocol extracts the id of the struct, if one exists.

However, since Phoenix.Param is an Elixir protocol, we can customize it for any data type in the language, including the ones we define ourselves. Let's do so for the Video struct. Create a new lib/rumbl_web/param.ex file with the following content:

```
watching_videos/listings/rumbl/lib/rumbl_web/param.ex
defimpl Phoenix.Param, for: Rumbl.Multimedia.Video do
  def to_param(%{slug: slug, id: id}) do
    "#{id}-#{slug}"
  end
end
```

We're implementing the Phoenix.Param protocol for the Rumbl.Multimedia.Video struct. The protocol requires us to implement the to_param function, which receives the video struct itself. We pattern-match on the video slug and ID and use it to build a string as our slug. Our param.ex file will serve as a home for other protocol implementations as we continue building our application.

The beauty behind Elixir protocols is that we can implement them for any data structure, anywhere, any time. We can place our implementation in the same file as the video definition, or anywhere else that makes sense. Because we can get Phoenix parameters without changing Phoenix or the Video module itself, we get a much cleaner polymorphism than we would otherwise.

Let's give this a try in IEx:

```
iex> video = %Rumbl.Multimedia.Video{id: 1, slug: "hello"}
%Rumbl.Multimedia.Video{id: 1, slug: "hello", ...}

iex> alias RumblWeb.Router.Helpers, as: Routes

iex> Routes.watch_path(%URI{}, :show, video)
"/watch/1-hello"
```

We build a video and then call Routes.watch_path, passing our video as an argument. The new path uses both the id and slug fields. Note that we give the URI struct to watch_path instead of the usual connection. The URI struct is part of Elixir's standard library, and all route functions accept it as their first argument. This convenience is particularly useful when building URLs outside of your web request. Think emails, messages, and so on. Let's play a bit with this idea:

```
iex> url = URI.parse("http://example.com/prefix")
%URI{...}

iex> Routes.watch_path(url, :show, video)
"/prefix/watch/1-hello"

iex> Routes.watch_url(url, :show, video)
"http://example.com/prefix/watch/1-hello"
```

You can also ask your endpoint to return the struct_url, based on the values you've defined in your configuration files:

```
iex> url = RumblWeb.Endpoint.struct_url()
%URI{...}
iex> Routes.watch_url(url, :show, video)
"http://localhost:4000/watch/1-hello"
```

With Phoenix.Param properly implemented for our videos, we can try it out. Start your server back up with mix phx.server, then access "My Videos" and click the "Watch" link for any existing video.

Well, that was less than ideal. You see a page with an error that looks something like this:

```
value `"13-hello-world"` in `where` cannot be cast to type :id in query:

from v in Rumbl.Multimedia.Video,
  where: v.id == ^"13-",
  select: v
```

Primary keys in Ecto have a default type of :id. For now, we can consider :id to be an :integer. When a new request goes to /watch/13-hello-world, the router matches 13-hello-world as the id parameter and sends it to the controller. In the controller, we try to make a query by using the id, and it complains. Let's look at the source of the problem:

```
def show(conn, %{"id" => id}) do
  video = Multimedia.get_video!(id)
  render(conn, "show.html", video: video)
end
```

WatchController.show is taking the id parameter and passing it to our Multimedia.get_video context function. Let's continue digging and open up lib/rumbl/multimedia.ex:

```
def get_video!(id), do: Repo.get!(Video, id)
```

That's the problem. We're doing a Repo.get! by using the id field, which is now a string instead of an integer. Let's fix that now.

Before doing a database query comparing against the id column, we need to cast 13-hello-world to an integer.

Extending Schemas with Ecto Types

Sometimes, the basic type information in our schemas isn't enough. In those cases, we'd like to improve our schemas with types that have a knowledge of Ecto. For example, we might want to associate some behavior to our id fields. A *custom type* allows us to do that. Let's implement one and place it in lib/rumbl/multimedia/permalink.ex. Our new *behaviour*, meaning an implementation of our interface, looks like this:

```
watching_videos/listings/rumbl/lib/rumbl/multimedia/permalink.ex
defmodule Rumbl.Multimedia.Permalink do
  @behaviour Ecto.Type

  def type, do: :id

  def cast(binary) when is_binary(binary) do
    case Integer.parse(binary) do
      {int, _} when int > 0 -> {:ok, int}
      _ -> :error
    end
  end

  def cast(integer) when is_integer(integer) do
    {:ok, integer}
  end

  def cast(_) do
    :error
  end
```

```elixir
  def dump(integer) when is_integer(integer) do
    {:ok, integer}
  end

  def load(integer) when is_integer(integer) do
    {:ok, integer}
  end
end
```

Behaviour or Behavior?

The Elixir and Erlang documentation use the European spelling of "behaviour" so we'll stick with that one when we refer to the actual Elixir concept. We'll use the "ior" spelling when we are talking about "behavior," the word.

Rumbl.Multimedia.Permalink is a custom type defined according to the Ecto.Type behaviour. It expects us to define four functions:

type   Returns the underlying Ecto type. In this case, we're building on top of :id.

cast   Called when external data is passed into Ecto. It's invoked when values in queries are interpolated or also by the cast function in changesets.

dump   Invoked when data is sent to the database.

load   Invoked when data is loaded from the database.

By design, the cast function often processes end-user input. We should be both lenient and careful when we parse it. For our slug—that means for binaries—we call Integer.parse to extract only the leading integer. On the other hand, dump and load handle the struct-to-database conversion. We can expect to work only with integers at this point because cast does the dirty work of sanitizing our input. Successful casts return integers. dump and load return :ok tuples with integers or :error.

Let's give our custom type a try with iex -S mix. Since we changed code in lib, you need to restart any running session.

```elixir
iex> alias Rumbl.Multimedia.Permalink, as: P
iex> P.cast("1")
{:ok, 1}
iex> P.cast(1)
{:ok, 1}
```

Integers and strings work as usual. That's great. Let's try something more complex:

```elixir
iex> P.cast("13-hello-world")
{:ok, 13}
```

Perfect. An integer followed by a string, such as the ones we build with our protocol, works just as it should. Let's try something that should break, like a string followed by an integer:

```
iex> P.cast("hello-world-13")
:error
```

And it breaks, just as it should. As long as the string starts with a positive integer, we're good to go. The last step is to tell Ecto to use our custom type for the id field in lib/rumbl/multimedia/video.ex:

```
watching_videos/listings/rumbl/lib/rumbl/multimedia/video.change2.ex
@primary_key {:id, Rumbl.Multimedia.Permalink, autogenerate: true}
schema "videos" do
```

Because Ecto automatically defines the id field for us, we can customize the primary key with the @primary_key module attribute. Just give it a tuple with the primary key name (:id). We tacked on the autogenerate: true option because our database autogenerates id values.

And that's that. Access the page once again, and it should load successfully. By implementing a protocol and defining a custom type, we made Phoenix work exactly how we wanted without tightly coupling it to our implementation. Ecto types go way beyond simple casting, though. We've already seen the community handle field encryption, data uploading, and more, all neatly wrapped and contained inside an Ecto type.

Wrapping Up

In this chapter, we accomplished a lot. We built a controller for watching videos and extended our context to provide the necessary domain logic. We then laid some foundation so we can play our videos in YouTube. Finally, we also created friendly URLs. Along the way:

- You learned to use webpack to support development-time reloading and minimization for production code.

- We used generators to create an Ecto migration.

- We used changesets to create slugs.

- We used protocols to seamlessly build URLs from those new slugs.

In the next chapter, you're going to reach the long-awaited channels topic. You'll learn to use Phoenix to build fully interactive features that show off Elixir's concurrency and consistency. Turn the page, because the energy only goes up from here!

## CHAPTER 10

Using Channels

If you dabbled in Phoenix before buying this book, at this point you're probably wondering why we've come so far and barely mentioned channels. The truth is that for the interactive applications we care about the most, channels are simpler to build so there's less to talk about.

Think about everything you've learned so far. Up until now, a browser made an isolated request and Phoenix delivered an isolated response. We had to spend plenty of time on pipelines and code organizational tools that let you do everything necessary to tie an individual user to each request and remember the exact state of the conversation. You know it well. A browser makes a request and the web server returns a response:

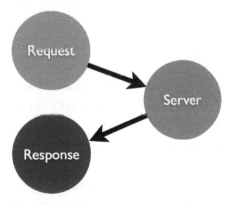

We build applications that way for a good reason. Each request is stateless, so it's easy to scale. When the programming language simply can't keep many connections around, it makes sense to do a little extra work so the web server can treat every request as a new one.

Sometimes, though, that programming model has too much overhead for the types of applications we want to build. Programs must be longer, programmers must work harder to reason about them, and the server has to work harder to process them.

This chapter will focus on the highly interactive problems that Phoenix solves so well. These problems don't lend themselves to a request/response flow. Think live chats, Google Maps, kayak.com, and twitter.com. In that world, a single client on a page connects directly with a process on the server called a channel, like this:

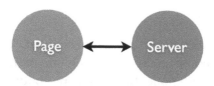

It *looks* simpler because for the programmer it *is* simpler. Since Elixir can scale to millions of simultaneous processes that manage millions of concurrent connections, you don't have to resort to request/response to make things easy to scale or even manage. A client connects to a channel and then sends and receives messages. That's it.

It's now cool again to have applications where the clients and servers just, you know, talk directly to each other. That's why this chapter is much shorter than the request/response paradigm covered in Part I, and it's also why Phoenix is such a big deal.

The Channel

A Phoenix channel is a conversation. The channel sends messages, receives messages, and keeps state. We call the messages *events*, and we put the state in a struct called socket.

A Phoenix conversation is about a *topic*, and it maps onto application concepts like a chat room, a local map, a game, or in our case, the annotations on a video. More than one user might be interested in the same topic at the same time. Channels give you tools to organize your code and the communication among users. The concept that makes channels so powerful in Elixir is that *each user's conversation on a topic has its own isolated, dedicated process.*

Here's the kicker. Whereas request/response interactions are *stateless*, conversations in a long-running process can be *stateful*. This means that for more-sophisticated user interactions like interactive pages or multiplayer games, you don't have to work so hard to keep track of the conversation by using cookies, databases, or the like. Each call to a channel simply picks up where the last one left off.

This approach only works if your foundation guarantees true isolation and concurrency. True isolation means that one crashing process won't impact other subscribed users. True concurrency means lightweight abstractions that won't bleed into one another. Your channels will *scale* in the dimensions that are most important to you, including code complexity, performance, and manageability.

You may be thinking that channels can't be this simple, but they are. Your channels application will have to worry about three things, each on both the client and the server:

- Making and breaking connections
- Sending messages
- Receiving messages

In this chapter, you'll learn each of those basic building blocks in greater detail. We're primarily going to be building the interactive portion of our application. We'll allow users to build annotations in real time, and rumbl will play back all video annotations for a user. We'll do this in two parts. First, on the client side, we need to build some client code to make a connection, send messages, and receive messages. We'll write our code in ES6, the latest generation of JavaScript. Then, on the server side, we'll do the same. We'll establish a connection and then write channels code to process each request in the conversation.

When we're done, we'll take advantage of some Phoenix infrastructure called Channel Presence. We'll write a little bit of code so users of Rumbl will be able to tell exactly who's logged in.

There's plenty to do, so let's get started.

Phoenix Clients with ES6

We're going to start on the client, using ECMAScript 6[1] JavaScript features. We'll build a bare-bones client to simply establish a connection. Over time, we'll build up our client to add annotations and play them back.

---

1. https://babeljs.io/docs/learn-es2015/

Remember, each Phoenix conversation is on a topic, so we'll need to be able to identify a topic. In our case, our topics will be videos. We'll create a Video object. That client-side construct will connect to Phoenix directly.

 Chris says:
Why ES6/ES2015 JavaScript?

Language features you've wished for years to land in JavaScript—string interpolation, a module system, destructuring assignment, and more—are now within reach. When you *transpile* a language, you're translating it to a more common form. Since it's possible to transpile ES6 to the widely available ES5 JavaScript, you can use ES6 today while supporting all mainstream browsers. This leaves you no reason to not go all-in on ES6. Plus, planned browser enhancements mean you have the bonus of waiting a couple years, and suddenly your ES6 code will be supported natively throughout the web.

Let's create a separate file for our Video object in assets/js/video.js. It's a long file, but it's not too complicated, especially when broken into parts:

channels/listings/rumbl/assets/js/video.js
```
Line 1  import Player from "./player"

        let Video = {

5         init(socket, element){ if(!element){ return }
            let playerId = element.getAttribute("data-player-id")
            let videoId  = element.getAttribute("data-id")
            socket.connect()
            Player.init(element.id, playerId, () => {
10            this.onReady(videoId, socket)
            })
          },

          onReady(videoId, socket){
15          let msgContainer = document.getElementById("msg-container")
            let msgInput     = document.getElementById("msg-input")
            let postButton   = document.getElementById("msg-submit")
            let vidChannel   = socket.channel("videos:" + videoId)
            // TODO join the vidChannel
20        }
        }
        export default Video
```

We first import our Player, the abstraction that lets us play videos and extract the exact time for any given frame so we can correctly place our annotations. Next, we define an init function to set up the player and pluck our video ID from the element attributes. We will then start the socket connection with socket.connect() and initialize our player while running a this.onReady() callback when the player has loaded. Within onReady, we define a handful of DOM variables for our Video player. We have the container for annotations, the input control, and the button for creating a new annotation. Pay special attention to vidChannel, which we'll use to connect our ES6 client to our Phoenix VideoChannel. For now we just instantiate it, but we'll join the conversation with the server in a moment.

Our topics need an identifier. By convention, ours takes the form "videos:" + videoId. In our application, this topic will let us easily send events to others interested in the same topic.

Let's tweak our video player to use this new Video object.

We were previously initializing and importing our video player in assets/js/app.js, like this:

```
import Player from "./player"
let video = document.getElementById("video")

if(video) {
  Player.init(video.id, video.getAttribute("data-player-id"), () => {
    console.log("player ready!")
  })
}
```

It would be better to tweak that code to compensate for the initialization we're doing in video.js. Let's tweak it to start only the Video object, like this:

```
channels/listings/rumbl/assets/js/app.change1.js
import socket from "./socket"
import Video from "./video"

Video.init(socket, document.getElementById("video"))
```

We import the Video object that we just created from its local module path. Next, we initialize the video with our connection called socket (more on this later) and the DOM element whose ID is video. Now load up your last video, and you should see it loaded into a YouTube player as before—but if you view your browser's JavaScript console, you see that the channel join is failing:

```
Unable to join > {reason: "unmatched topic"}
```

With our video up and running and vidChannel initialized, our client is trying to join a video channel that we haven't implemented yet. Let's flip back to the server side for a bit and fix this. It's time to create a channel and establish the conversation with our client.

Preparing Our Server for the Channel

In the request/response world, each request established a connection, which we represented in Plug.Conn. We then used ordinary functions to transform that connection until it had the response we wanted to send back to the client. Each plug didn't use the same conn per se, but each transformation was conceptually on the same request. Each time you had a new request, you'd start from scratch with a new conn struct. Said another way, for each request, a new conn would flow through all of the pipelines and then die.

In channels, the flow is different. A client establishes a new connection with a socket. After the connection is made, that socket will be transformed through the life of the connection.

At the high level, your socket is the ongoing conversation between client and server. It has all of the information necessary to do its job. When you make a connection, you're creating your initial socket, and that same socket will be transformed with each new received event, through the whole life of the whole conversation.

You need to do a couple of things to make a connection. First, you decide whether to allow the connection. Next, you create the initial socket, including any custom application setup your application might need.

Let's hack up a quick connection to see how things work. In our ES6 example, Phoenix created an assets/js/socket.js with an example socket connection and channel code. Replace the file contents with this minimal socket connection:

```
channels/listings/rumbl/assets/js/socket.change1.js
import {Socket} from "phoenix"

let socket = new Socket("/socket", {
  params: {token: window.userToken},
  logger: (kind, msg, data) => { console.log(`${kind}: ${msg}`, data) }
})

export default socket
```

That simple connection is as basic as it gets. Phoenix isn't doing anything fancy for us here. You can see that the ES6 client imports the Socket object. Then let socket = new Socket("/socket", ...) causes Phoenix to instantiate a new socket at our endpoint. We pass params and an optional logger callback, which includes helpful debugging logging in the JavaScript console. If you peek in lib/rumbl_web/endpoint.ex, you can see where the "/socket" is declared. This definition is the *socket mount point*:

```
socket "/socket", RumblWeb.UserSocket,
  websocket: true,
  longpoll: false
```

Each socket macro establishes a *socket mount* providing all configuration for a single user socket. The UserSocket module serves as the starting point for all socket connections. As you'll see later in this chapter, it's responsible for authenticating, and also for wiring up default socket information for all channels.

Our socket mount also defines the transport layers that will handle the connection between client and the server. You see the two default transport that Phoenix supports, longpoll and websocket. You can even build your own transport for more exotic use cases. Peek inside the lib/rumbl_web/channels/user_socket.ex to see the UserSocket in action:

```
defmodule RumblWeb.UserSocket do
  use Phoenix.Socket

  # channel "room:*", RumblWeb.RoomChannel

  def connect(_params, socket, _connect_info) do
    {:ok, socket}
  end

  def id(_socket), do: nil
end
```

UserSocket will use a single connection to the server to handle all of your channel processes. Phoenix will handle getting the right message to the right channel.

Regardless of the transport, the end result is the same. You operate on a shared socket abstraction, and Phoenix takes care of the rest. The beauty of this is that you no longer have to worry how the user is connected. Whether on older browsers over long-polling, native iOS WebSockets, or a custom transport like CoAP[2] for embedded devices, your backend channel code remains precisely the same. This is the new web. You'll be able to quickly adapt your applications as new transport protocols become important to you.

In our UserSocket, we have two simple functions: connect and id. The id function lets us identify the socket based on some state stored in the socket itself, like the user ID. The connect function decides whether to make a connection. It receives the connection parameters, the connection socket, and a map of advanced connection information. In our case, id returns nil, and connect simply lets everyone in. We're effectively allowing all connections as anonymous users by default.

---

2. http://coap.technology/

We'll be adding socket authentication with our RumblWeb.Auth system in a moment, but for now, let's leave these defaults. We added socket.connect() after we initialized our Player in video.js to establish the connection to the server. If we open up the JavaScript console in our browser and refresh one of our video pages, we see the following logger output:

```
transport: connected to
ws://localhost:4000/socket/websocket?token=undefined&vsn=2.0.0
```

We have a working connection! Let's create the channel on the Phoenix side.

Creating the Channel

It's time to write some code to process connections. To review what you know so far, a channel is a conversation on a topic. Our topic has an identifier of videos:video_id, where video_id is a dynamic ID matching a record in the database. In our application, we want a user to get all events for a topic, which to us means a user will get all annotations for a given video, regardless of who created them.

More generally, at their most basic level, topics are strings that serve as identifiers. They often take the form of topic:subtopic, where topic is often a resource name and subtopic is often an ID, but any string is a valid topic.

Since topics are organizing concepts, we'll include topics where you'd expect: as parameters to functions and in our URLs to identify conversations. Just as the client passes a URL with an :id parameter to represent a resource for a controller, we'll provide a topic ID to scope our channel connections.

Joining a Channel

Now that we've established a socket connection, our users can join a channel. In general, when clients join a channel, they must provide a topic. They'll be able to join any number of channels and any number of topics on a channel.

We need a VideoChannel for our application, so let's start by including a channel definition in our UserSocket:

```
channels/listings/rumbl/lib/rumbl_web/channels/user_socket.change1.ex
defmodule RumblWeb.UserSocket do
  use Phoenix.Socket

  ## Channels
  channel "videos:*", RumblWeb.VideoChannel
```

Transports route events into your UserSocket, where they're dispatched into your channels based on topic patterns that you declare with the channel macro.

Our videos:* convention categorizes topics with a resource name, followed by a resource ID.

Let's move on to the code that will process each incoming event.

Building the Channel Module

Now, it's time to create the module that will handle our specific VideoChannel. It'll allow connections through join and also let users disconnect and send events. For consistency with OTP naming conventions, this book sometimes refers to these features as *callbacks*. Let's start with join. Create a file called lib/rumbl_web/channels/video_channel.ex, like this:

channels/listings/rumbl/lib/rumbl_web/channels/video_channel.ex
```elixir
defmodule RumblWeb.VideoChannel do
  use RumblWeb, :channel

  def join("videos:" <> video_id, _params, socket) do
    {:ok, assign(socket, :video_id, String.to_integer(video_id))}
  end
end
```

Here we see the first of our channel callbacks: join. Clients can join topics on a channel. We return {:ok, socket} to authorize a join attempt or {:error, socket} to deny one.

For now, we let all clients join any video topic. We extract the video ID using pattern matching: "videos:" <> video_id will match all topics starting with "videos:" and assign the rest of the topic to the video_id variable. We then add the video ID to socket.assigns. Remember, sockets will hold all of the state for a given conversation. Each socket can hold its own state in the socket.assigns field, which typically holds a map.

For channels, *the socket is transformed in a loop rather than a single pipeline.* In fact, the socket state will remain for the duration of a connection. That means the socket state we add in join will be accessible later as events come into and out of the channel. This small distinction leads to an enormous difference in efficiency between the channels API and the controllers API.

With our channel in place, let's join it from the client. Open up assets/js/video.js and update your listing:

channels/listings/rumbl/assets/js/video.change1.js
```javascript
onReady(videoId, socket){
  let msgContainer = document.getElementById("msg-container")
  let msgInput     = document.getElementById("msg-input")
  let postButton   = document.getElementById("msg-submit")
  let vidChannel   = socket.channel("videos:" + videoId)
```

```
 6
 7    vidChannel.join()
 8      .receive("ok", resp => console.log("joined the video channel", resp) )
 9      .receive("error", reason => console.log("join failed", reason) )
10  }
```

On lines 5 through 9, we create a new channel object, vidChannel, from our socket and give it our topic. We build the topic by joining the "videos:" string with our video ID, which we plucked from the div element in our WatchView's show.html.eex template.

We see our joined message in the JavaScript web console output:

```
transport: connected to ws://localhost:4000/socket/websocket...
push: videos:1 phx_join (1, 1) – {}
receive: ok videos:1 phx_reply (1) – {response: {}, status: "ok"}
joined the video channel – {}
```

Likewise, our server output confirms that we've established our conversation:

```
[info] JOIN "videos:1" to RumblWeb.VideoChannel
  Transport:  :websocket
  Serializer: Phoenix.Socket.V2.JSONSerializer
  Parameters: %{}
[info] Replied videos:1 :ok
```

And we're joined!

Sending and Receiving Events

Everything we've done so far is setting us up to do one thing: process events. Just as controllers receive requests, channels receive events. With channels, we receive a message containing an event name, such as new_message, and a payload of arbitrary data.

Each channel module has three ways to receive events. You'll learn more about these callback functions in detail soon. For now, know that handle_in receives direct channel events, handle_out intercepts broadcast events, and handle_info receives OTP messages.

Taking Our Channels for a Trial Run

To test-drive everything we've put together so far, let's make our join function send our channel client a :ping message every five seconds, like this:

```
channels/listings/rumbl/lib/rumbl_web/channels/video_channel.change1.ex
def join("videos:" <> video_id, _params, socket) do
  :timer.send_interval(5_000, :ping)
  {:ok, socket}
end
```

```
def handle_info(:ping, socket) do
  count = socket.assigns[:count] || 1
  push(socket, "ping", %{count: count})

  {:noreply, assign(socket, :count, count + 1)}
end
```

The handle_info callback is invoked whenever an Elixir message reaches the channel. In this case, we match on the periodic :ping message and increase a counter every time it arrives.

Our new handle_info takes our socket, takes the existing count (or a default of 1), and increases that count by 1. We then return a tagged tuple. :noreply means we're not sending a reply, and the assign function transforms our socket by adding the new count. Conceptually, we're taking a socket and returning a transformed socket. This implementation bumps the count in :assigns by 1, each time it's called.

We've got the server-side implementation. We just need to call it now. Add the following line to video.js, immediately below your vidChannel declaration:

```
vidChannel.on("ping", ({count}) => console.log("PING", count) )
```

Now check out your web console, and you see a ping event being pushed from the server every five seconds, with an accumulated counter:

```
receive:  videos:1 ping
PING 1

receive:  videos:1 ping
PING 2

receive:  videos:1 ping
PING 3
```

Our channel process is alive and well!

handle_info is basically a loop. Each time, it returns the socket as the last tuple element for all callbacks. This way, we can maintain state. We simply push the ping event, and the JavaScript client picks up these events with the channel.on(event, callback) API. These events can arrive on the client at any time, but later you'll see how channels support synchronous messaging for handle_in responses.

This is the primary difference between channels and controllers. Controllers process a *request*. Channels hold a *conversation*.

Annotating Videos

Our channels are functioning but they're not doing any real work yet. Let's use them to build our real-time annotations. Since annotations need to happen in real time to stay in sync with videos, channels is the perfect way to build them. We'll need to add video annotation to our multimedia context and allow new users to access them as they join the channel. Before we get too far into extending our Multimedia context, let's start simple and build out the channel messaging first. Later, we can circle back and complete the annotation features when we're happy with our client-server channel communication.

Our WatchView's show.html.eex template is already mocked up with an annotations container and post button that we've plucked from the page to establish our msgContainer and postButton variables. Let's use these two elements to begin our real-time annotations support. Open up your video.js and update the listing below your vidChannel declaration with the following code:

```
channels/listings/rumbl/assets/js/video.change3.js
let vidChannel      = socket.channel("videos:" + videoId)

postButton.addEventListener("click", e => {
  let payload = {body: msgInput.value, at: Player.getCurrentTime()}
  vidChannel.push("new_annotation", payload)
            .receive("error", e => console.log(e) )
  msgInput.value = ""
})

vidChannel.on("new_annotation", (resp) => {
  this.renderAnnotation(msgContainer, resp)
})

vidChannel.join()
  .receive("ok", resp => console.log("joined the video channel", resp) )
  .receive("error", reason => console.log("join failed", reason) )
},

renderAnnotation(msgContainer, {user, body, at}){
  // TODO append annotation to msgContainer
}
```

Let's break it down. First, we handle the click event on the post button. The push function on our vidChannel takes the contents of our message input and sends it to the server, then clears the input control.

On lines 5 and 6, you can see the channel's synchronous messaging in action. When we push an event to the server, we can opt to receive a response. It's not a true synchronous operation, but it's a big win for code readability. It lets us compose client-side messaging in line with our Elixir process handling. It also provides request/response–style messaging over a socket connection.

Now, we have to handle new events sent by the server. When users post new annotations, the server will broadcast those new events to the client, triggering a new_annotation event. On line 10, we receive those new_annotation events, calling a stubbed renderAnnotation function. Let's now implement renderAnnotation to display our annotations on the page. You will need to update your listing with the following code:

channels/listings/rumbl/assets/js/video.change4.js

```
Line 1  esc(str){
          let div = document.createElement("div")
          div.appendChild(document.createTextNode(str))
          return div.innerHTML
5       },

        renderAnnotation(msgContainer, {user, body, at}){
          let template = document.createElement("div")

10        template.innerHTML = `
        <a href="#" data-seek="${this.esc(at)}">
          <b>${this.esc(user.username)}</b>: ${this.esc(body)}
        </a>
          `
15        msgContainer.appendChild(template)
          msgContainer.scrollTop = msgContainer.scrollHeight
        }
```

We implement the renderAnnotation function to append an annotation to our message container. First, we define an esc function on line 1 to safely escape user input before injecting values into the page. This strategy protects our users from XSS attacks. Next, on line 7, we use our esc function to safely build a DOM node with the user's name and annotation body and append it to the msgContainer list. Then, we finish by scrolling the container to the right point.

Adding Annotations on the Server

With our client-side event handling in place, let's wire up the server side of the conversation. Replace your VideoChannel with this:

channels/listings/rumbl/lib/rumbl_web/channels/video_channel.change2.ex

```
defmodule RumblWeb.VideoChannel do
  use RumblWeb, :channel

  def join("videos:" <> video_id, _params, socket) do
    {:ok, socket}
  end
```

```elixir
def handle_in("new_annotation", params, socket) do
  broadcast!(socket, "new_annotation", %{
    user: %{username: "anon"},
    body: params["body"],
    at: params["at"]
  })

  {:reply, :ok, socket}
end
end
```

We ditch our ping messaging and add the second major kind of callback, han-dle_in. This function will handle all incoming messages to a channel, pushed directly from the remote client.

Look at the function head. This particular callback handles the new_annotation events pushed from the client. Since we aren't persisting to the database yet, we simply broadcast new_annotation events to all the clients on this topic with broadcast!

The broadcast! function sends an event to all users on the current topic. It takes three arguments: the socket, the name of the event, and a payload, which is an arbitrary map. Within the body of our callback, we can send as many messages as we'd like.

Behind the scenes, broadcast! uses Phoenix's Publish and Subscribe (PubSub) system to send the message to all processes listening on the given topic. Phoenix PubSub is distributed out of the box; if there are multiple machines running Phoenix, they will all receive the message as long as they are connect-ed via distributed Erlang.

When we're done with the function, we send back a reply with a status and the socket. The status is the customary Elixir :ok or :error. We could also have used :noreply with the socket if we didn't want to reply to the client.

Let's try it out. This time, open up multiple browser windows side by side to see how broadcast! is relaying messages to all users who've joined our video topic:

It works! We now have a conversation going between client and server, and you can get a glimpse into how our real-time annotations will be orchestrated.

This Is a Bad Idea

Forwarding a raw message payload without inspection is a big security risk.

Note that we didn't forward along the raw payload, such as:

```
broadcast!(socket, "new_annotation", Map.put(params, "user", %{
  username: "anon"
}))
```

This would have worked, but it would have been extremely dangerous. Broadcasting events delivers the payload to *all* clients on this topic. If we don't properly structure the payload from the remote client before forwarding the message along as a broadcast, we're effectively allowing a client to broadcast arbitrary payloads across our channel. If you want your application to be secure, you want to control the payload as closely as you can.

We've delivered our annotations to the client, but we've yet to persist them. Before we can do that, we need to have the current user in the socket in our channels. We've put it off as long as we can. It's time to tackle authentication.

Socket Authentication

For request/response–type applications, session-based authentication makes sense. For channels, *token authentication* works better because the connection is a long-duration connection. With token authentication, we assign a unique token to each user. Tokens allow for a secure authentication mechanism that doesn't rely on any specific transport.

Programmers often ask why they can't access their session cookies in a channel. The answer is that this would be insecure over WebSockets because of cross-domain attacks. Also, cookies would couple channel code to the WebSocket transport, eliminating future transport layers. Fortunately, Phoenix has a better way: the Phoenix.Token.

Our current_user is already authenticated in the application by our RumblWeb.Auth plug. All we need to do is generate a token for our authenticated user and pass that to our socket on the frontend. The first step is to expose the token to the client side in our lib/rumbl_web/templates/layout/app.html.eex layout, like this:

channels/listings/rumbl/lib/rumbl_web/templates/layout/app.change1.html.eex
```
<script>window.userToken = "<%= assigns[:user_token] %>"</script>
<script type="text/javascript"
        src="<%= Routes.static_url(@conn, "/js/app.js") %>"></script>
</body>
```

Just before our app.js script, we render a script tag that attaches a userToken variable to the window from our layout assigns.

Next, we need to add the :user_token to conn.assigns whenever we have a current user. We already have code to assign the current user in RumblWeb.Auth, so let's handle this there:

channels/listings/rumbl/lib/rumbl_web/controllers/auth.change1.ex
```
Line 1  def call(conn, _opts) do
   -      user_id = get_session(conn, :user_id)
   -
   -      cond do
   5        user = conn.assigns[:current_user] ->
   -          put_current_user(conn, user)
   -
   -        user = user_id && Rumbl.Accounts.get_user(user_id) ->
   -          put_current_user(conn, user)
   10
   -        true ->
   -          assign(conn, :current_user, nil)
   -      end
   -    end
   15
   -    def login(conn, user) do
   -      conn
   -      |> put_current_user(user)
   -      |> put_session(:user_id, user.id)
   20     |> configure_session(renew: true)
   -    end
   -
   -    defp put_current_user(conn, user) do
   -      token = Phoenix.Token.sign(conn, "user socket", user.id)
   25
   -      conn
   -      |> assign(:current_user, user)
   -      |> assign(:user_token, token)
   -    end
```

We add a private put_current_user function to place a freshly generated user token and the current_user into conn.assigns, which we call on lines 6, 9, and 18. Now, any time a user session exists, both :current_user and :user_token will be set, and the :user_token will hold the signed-in user ID.

The last step is to pass the user token to the Socket constructor on the client, and then verify it in our UserSocket.connect callback. If you open up your assets/js/socket.js file, you can see that we prepared for this by passing up the window.userToken value as a token parameter, like this:

```
channels/listings/rumbl/assets/js/socket.change1.js
let socket = new Socket("/socket", {
  params: {token: window.userToken},
  logger: (kind, msg, data) => { console.log(`${kind}: ${msg}`, data) }
})
```

Any :params we pass to the socket constructor will be available as the first argument in UserSocket.connect. Let's verify the params on connect and store our current_user ID in the socket. Update your UserSocket with the following code:

```
channels/listings/rumbl/lib/rumbl_web/channels/user_socket.change2.ex
@max_age 2 * 7 * 24 * 60 * 60

def connect(%{"token" => token}, socket, _connect_info) do
  case Phoenix.Token.verify(
    socket,
    "user socket",
    token,
    max_age: @max_age
  ) do
    {:ok, user_id} ->
      {:ok, assign(socket, :user_id, user_id)}

    {:error, _reason} ->
      :error
  end
end

def connect(_params, _socket, _connect_info), do: :error

def id(socket), do: "users_socket:#{socket.assigns.user_id}"
```

We use Phoenix.Token.verify to verify the user token provided by the client. We pass a max_age, ensuring that tokens are only valid for a certain period of time; in this case, we set the value to about two weeks. If the token is valid, we receive the user_id and store it in our socket.assigns while returning {:ok, socket} to establish the connection. If the token is invalid, we return :error, denying the connection attempt by the client.

Remember, the socket keeps its state for the whole duration of the connection, not just for a single response. Any socket.assigns you place in the socket during connect will be available in your channel's socket.assigns map.

Now, refresh your page. The application should work as before, but now with user authentication. We have a logged-in user. so we can move on to persist our annotations.

Persisting Annotations

Now that we have in-memory annotations going across all connected clients through an authenticated user, let's extend our multimedia context to attach those annotations to videos and users in the database. You've seen how we manage schemas and relationships with Ecto so the process will be straightforward. In this case, we're creating annotations on videos. Each new annotation will belong to both a user and a video.

You can use the phx.gen.schema generator, like this:

```
$ mix phx.gen.schema Multimedia.Annotation annotations body:text \
at:integer user_id:references:users video_id:references:videos

* creating lib/rumbl/multimedia/annotation.ex
* creating priv/repo/migrations/20180726203443_create_annotations.exs

Remember to update your repository by running migrations:

    $ mix ecto.migrate
$
---- END OF OUTPUT ----
```

And now you can migrate your database:

```
$ mix ecto.migrate

[info] == Running Rumbl.Repo.Migrations.CreateAnnotations.change/0 forward
[info] create table annotations
[info] create index annotations_user_id_index
[info] create index annotations_video_id_index
[info] == Migrated in 0.1s

$
```

Our migrations are in, with our new table and two new indexes.

Next, we need to wire up our new relationships to our Accounts.User and Multimedia.Video schemas. Both users and videos will have annotations, but we need to decide where to surface these schema details within our contexts. Details like these will make or break an API. Allowing access to every possible type of data that may ever be associated with a user would probably lead to a tedious, bloated API and conflate the purpose of our Accounts context. We'll provide only enough functions to comfortably do the job at hand.

For now, we'll tentatively expose annotations strictly through the Multimedia context since the Accounts.User schema should not need to know about Multimedia.Annotations. If an application needs change in the future, we can revisit this decision. Add the has_many relationship to the Multimedia.Video schema blocks in lib/rumbl/multimedia/video.ex, like this:

```
has_many :annotations, Rumbl.Multimedia.Annotation
```

Next, let's update our generated Annotation schema in lib/rumbl/multimedia/annotation.ex. Right now, both user_id and video_id are simple schema fields. We'll want to manage annotation lists through Ecto so let's upgrade them to be first class belongs_to relationships, like this:

channels/listings/rumbl/lib/rumbl/multimedia/annotation.change1.ex

```
schema "annotations" do
  field :at, :integer
  field :body, :string

  belongs_to :user, Rumbl.Accounts.User
  belongs_to :video, Rumbl.Multimedia.Video

  timestamps()
end
```

We will want to read and write our video annotations from within our channels. Just as we did within our controllers, we'll want to access those features from our Multimedia context rather than the schema. Let's add those features to our context. Open up lib/rumbl/multimedia.ex and add functions to list and create annotations, like so:

channels/listings/rumbl/lib/rumbl/multimedia.change1.ex

```
Line 1  alias Rumbl.Multimedia.Annotation

     -  def annotate_video(%Accounts.User{id: user_id}, video_id, attrs) do
     -    %Annotation{video_id: video_id, user_id: user_id}
     5    |> Annotation.changeset(attrs)
     -    |> Repo.insert()
     -  end
     -
     -  def list_annotations(%Video{} = video) do
    10    Repo.all(
     -      from a in Ecto.assoc(video, :annotations),
     -        order_by: [asc: a.at, asc: a.id],
     -        limit: 500,
     -        preload: [:user]
    15    )
     -  end
```

On line 3, we added an annotate_video function, which accepts a user, video ID, and attributes for the annotation. In that function, we build an annotation struct with the video ID and user ID. We pipe that struct to changeset to create our changeset, and then pipe the completed record to Repo.insert. We could have used Ecto.Changeset.put_assoc to put both user and video associations, but setting the foreign keys directly gives the same end result.

To fetch a list of annotations for a given video, we defined the list_annotations on line 9. It's just a simple Ecto query. We put in a high limit to make sure we don't bring back too many records to handle, and we preloaded the user. Remember, if you want to use data in an association, you need to fetch it explicitly. You've seen queries like this before in Chapter 6, Generators and Relationships, on page 101.

Now, all that remains is to head back to our VideoChannel and integrate our callbacks to use the new context features. Open up the video channel and make these modifications:

```
channels/listings/rumbl/lib/rumbl_web/channels/video_channel.change3.ex
Line 1  alias Rumbl.{Accounts, Multimedia}

    -   def join("videos:" <> video_id, _params, socket) do
    -     {:ok, assign(socket, :video_id, String.to_integer(video_id))}
    5   end

    -   def handle_in(event, params, socket) do
    -     user = Accounts.get_user!(socket.assigns.user_id)
    -     handle_in(event, params, user, socket)
    10  end

    -   def handle_in("new_annotation", params, user, socket) do
    -     case Multimedia.annotate_video(user, socket.assigns.video_id, params) do
    -       {:ok, annotation} ->
    15          broadcast!(socket, "new_annotation", %{
    -             id: annotation.id,
    -             user: RumblWeb.UserView.render("user.json", %{user: user}),
    -             body: annotation.body,
    -             at: annotation.at
    20          })
    -           {:reply, :ok, socket}

    -         {:error, changeset} ->
    -           {:reply, {:error, %{errors: changeset}}, socket}
    25     end
    -   end
```

First, we ensure that all incoming events have the current user by defining a new handle_in/3 function on line 7. It catches all incoming events, looks up the user from the socket assigns, and then calls a handle_in/4 clause with the socket user as a third argument.

Next, we call our Multimedia.annotate_video function. On success, we broadcast to all subscribers as before. Otherwise, we return a response with the changeset errors. After we broadcast, we acknowledge the success by returning {:reply, :ok, socket}.

We could have decided not to send a reply with {:noreply, socket}, but it's common practice to acknowledge the result of the pushed message from the client. This approach allows the client to easily implement UI features such as loading statuses and error notifications, even if we're only replying with an :ok or :error status and no other information.

Since we also want to notify subscribers about the user who posted the annotation, we render a user.json template from our UserView on line 17. Let's implement that now:

```
channels/listings/rumbl/lib/rumbl_web/views/user_view.change1.ex
defmodule RumblWeb.UserView do
  use RumblWeb, :view
  alias Rumbl.Accounts

  def first_name(%Accounts.User{name: name}) do
    name
    |> String.split(" ")
    |> Enum.at(0)
  end

  def render("user.json", %{user: user}) do
    %{id: user.id, username: user.username}
  end
end
```

Now let's head back to the app and post a few annotations. Watch your server logs as the posts are submitted, and you can see your insert logs:

```
[debug] INCOMING "new_annotation" on "videos:1" to RumblWeb.VideoChannel
  Parameters: %{"at" => 0, "body" => "testing"}

begin []
[debug] QUERY OK db=20.3ms
INSERT INTO "annotations" ("at","body","user_id","video_id",...
[debug] QUERY OK db=0.6ms
commit []
```

And we have persisted data!

We have a problem, though. Refresh your page, and the messages disappear from the UI. They're still in the database, but we need to pass the messages to the client when a user joins the channel. We could do this by pushing an event to the client after each user joins, but Phoenix provides a 3-tuple join signature to both join the channel and send a join response at the same time.

Let's update our VideoChannel's join callback to pass down a list of annotations:

```
channels/listings/rumbl/lib/rumbl_web/channels/video_channel.change4.ex
alias RumblWeb.AnnotationView

def join("videos:" <> video_id, _params, socket) do
  video_id = String.to_integer(video_id)
  video = Multimedia.get_video!(video_id)

  annotations =
    video
    |> Multimedia.list_annotations()
    |> Phoenix.View.render_many(AnnotationView, "annotation.json")

  {:ok, %{annotations: annotations}, assign(socket, :video_id, video_id)}
end
```

Here, we rewrite join to get the video from our Multimedia context. Then, we list the video's annotations combined with something new. We compose a response by rendering an annotation.json view for every annotation in our list. Instead of building the list by hand, we use Phoenix.View.render_many. The render_many function collects the render results for all elements in the enumerable passed to it. We use the view to present our data, so we offload this work to the view layer so the channel layer can focus on messaging.

Create an AnnotationView in lib/rumbl_web/views/annotation_view.ex to serve as each individual annotation, like this:

```
channels/listings/rumbl/lib/rumbl_web/views/annotation_view.ex
defmodule RumblWeb.AnnotationView do
  use RumblWeb, :view

  def render("annotation.json", %{annotation: annotation}) do
    %{
      id: annotation.id,
      body: annotation.body,
      at: annotation.at,
      user: render_one(annotation.user, RumblWeb.UserView, "user.json")
    }
  end
end
```

Notice the render_one call for the annotation's user. Phoenix's view layer neatly embraces functional composition. The render_one function provides conveniences such as handling possible nil results.

Lastly, we return a 3-tuple from join of the form {:ok, response, socket} to pass the response down to the join event. Let's pick up this response on the client to build the list of messages.

Update your vidChannel.join() callbacks to render a list of annotations received on join:

`channels/listings/rumbl/assets/js/video.change5.js`

```js
vidChannel.join()
  .receive("ok", ({annotations}) => {
    annotations.forEach( ann => this.renderAnnotation(msgContainer, ann) )
  })
  .receive("error", reason => console.log("join failed", reason) )
```

Refresh your browser and see your history of messages appear immediately!

Now that we have our message history on join, we need to schedule the annotations to appear synced up with the video playback. Update video.js, like the following:

`channels/listings/rumbl/assets/js/video.change6.js`

```js
  vidChannel.join()
    .receive("ok", resp => {
      this.scheduleMessages(msgContainer, resp.annotations)
    })
    .receive("error", reason => console.log("join failed", reason) )
},

renderAnnotation(msgContainer, {user, body, at}){
  let template = document.createElement("div")
  template.innerHTML = `
  <a href="#" data-seek="${this.esc(at)}">
    [${this.formatTime(at)}]
    <b>${this.esc(user.username)}</b>: ${this.esc(body)}
  </a>
  `

  msgContainer.appendChild(template)
  msgContainer.scrollTop = msgContainer.scrollHeight
},

scheduleMessages(msgContainer, annotations){
  clearTimeout(this.scheduleTimer)
  this.schedulerTimer = setTimeout(() => {
    let ctime = Player.getCurrentTime()
    let remaining = this.renderAtTime(annotations, ctime, msgContainer)
    this.scheduleMessages(msgContainer, remaining)
  }, 1000)
},
```

```
renderAtTime(annotations, seconds, msgContainer){
  return annotations.filter( ann => {
    if(ann.at > seconds){
      return true
    } else {
      this.renderAnnotation(msgContainer, ann)
      return false
    }
  })
},

formatTime(at){
  let date = new Date(null)
  date.setSeconds(at / 1000)
  return date.toISOString().substr(14, 5)
},
```

There's a lot of code here, but it's relatively simple. Instead of rendering all annotations immediately on join, we schedule them to render based on the current player time. The scheduleMessages function starts an interval timer that fires every second. Now, each time our timer ticks, we call renderAtTime to find all annotations occurring at or before the current player time.

In renderAtTime, we filter all the messages by time while rendering those that should appear in the timeline. For those yet to appear, we return true to keep a tab on the remaining annotations to filter on the next call. Otherwise, we render the annotation and return false to exclude it from the remaining set.

You can see the end result. We have a second-by-second annotation feed based on the current video playback. Refresh your browser and let's give it a shot. Try posting a few new annotations at different points, and then refresh. Start playing the video, and then watch your annotations appear synced up with the playback time, as you can see in the screenshot on page 217.

We wired up a data-seek attribute on our renderAnnotation template, but we haven't done anything with it yet. Let's support having the annotations clickable so we can jump to the exact time the annotation was made by clicking it. Add this click handler above your vidChannel.join():

channels/listings/rumbl/assets/js/video.change6.js
```
msgContainer.addEventListener("click", e => {
  e.preventDefault()
  let seconds = e.target.getAttribute("data-seek") ||
                e.target.parentNode.getAttribute("data-seek")
  if(!seconds){ return }

  Player.seekTo(seconds)
})
```

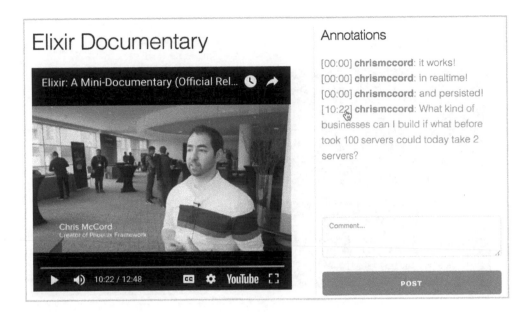

Now, clicking an annotation will move the player to the time the annotation was made. Cool!

Before we get too excited, we have one more problem to solve. We need to address a critical issue when dealing with disconnects between the client and server.

Handling Disconnects

Any stateful conversation between a client and server must handle data that gets out of sync. This problem can happen with unexpected disconnects, or a broadcast that isn't received while a client is away. We need to handle both cases. Let's find out how.

Our JavaScript client can disconnect and reconnect for a number of different reasons. Our server might be restarted, a rumbler might drive under a bridge, or our Internet connection may just be poor. We simply can't assume network reliability when designing our real-time systems. Fire up your server and visit one of your videos. Post a few annotations and then kill the server in your terminal. The client immediately begins trying to reestablish a connection using exponential back-off. Wait a few seconds. Then, you can restart the server with mix phx.server. Within a few seconds, you'll see something similiar to what is shown in the screenshot on page 218.

That's not good. When the client reconnected, our client rejoined our VideoChannel and the server returned all the annotations for this video, causing our client to append duplicate annotations to the ones it already had. You might be tempted to have the client detect duplicate annotations and ignore them, but we want to fetch as little data as required from the server, so there's a better way.

We can track a last_seen_id on the client and bump this value every time we see a new annotation. Then whenever we rejoin following a crash or disconnect, we can send our last_seen_id to the server. That way, we send only the data we missed. This technique keeps us from worrying about buffering messages on the server for clients that might never reconnect. We get back only the data that we need. Let's make it happen.

Open up your assets/js/video.js and make the following changes to your vidChannel instantiation:

```
channels/listings/rumbl/assets/js/video.change7.js
Line 1  onReady(videoId, socket){
     2    let msgContainer = document.getElementById("msg-container")
     3    let msgInput     = document.getElementById("msg-input")
     4    let postButton   = document.getElementById("msg-submit")
     5    let lastSeenId   = 0
     6    let vidChannel   = socket.channel("videos:" + videoId, () => {
     7      return {last_seen_id: lastSeenId}
     8    })
```

On line 7, we added a new variable declaration to track our client's lastSeenId. We also use *channel params* for the first time. The second argument to socket.channel adds a params callback as a second argument. The socket.channel function accepts an optional params object or callback. Phoenix will now send those custom params when a user joins the channel. Our function simply returns our last seen ID.

Our client is sending the last_seen_id parameter, but we still need to keep track of this value. Let's do that now:

```
channels/listings/rumbl/assets/js/video.change7.js
Line 1  vidChannel.on("new_annotation", (resp) => {
   -      lastSeenId = resp.id
   -      this.renderAnnotation(msgContainer, resp)
   -    })
   5
   -    vidChannel.join()
   -      .receive("ok", resp => {
   -        let ids = resp.annotations.map(ann => ann.id)
   -        if(ids.length > 0){ lastSeenId = Math.max(...ids) }
  10        this.scheduleMessages(msgContainer, resp.annotations)
   -      })
   -      .receive("error", reason => console.log("join failed", reason) )
```

On line 2, we update lastSeenId. Our client will pass it up to the channel on subsequent joins. We modify this value whenever we receive a new_annotation event from the server.

Next, we use a similar approach on line 8 within our ok callback on join. We receive the list of annotations in the response as before, but this time we grab the max annotation ID from the list and store it as the lastSeenId. Now, whenever we call vidChannel.join()—such as after reconnects—our parameter function will fire, providing the last_seen_id. Let's handle this new parameter on the server side within our VideoChannel. To list annotations since a given ID, we need to expose this feature from our Multimedia context. Open up lib/rumbl/multimedia.ex and make the following change to your list_annotations function:

```
channels/listings/rumbl/lib/rumbl/multimedia.change2.ex
Line 1  def list_annotations(%Video{} = video, since_id \\ 0) do
   2      Repo.all(
   3        from a in Ecto.assoc(video, :annotations),
   4          where: a.id > ^since_id,
   5          order_by: [asc: a.at, asc: a.id],
   6          limit: 500,
   7          preload: [:user]
   8      )
   9    end
```

We added an optional since_id argument which defaults to zero. Then we added a where clause in our query on line 4 to use this new value. With our context changes in place, we need to update our channel to look for last_seen_id. Open lib/rumbl_web/channels/video_channel.ex and update the join function:

```
channels/listings/rumbl/lib/rumbl_web/channels/video_channel.change5.ex
Line 1  def join("videos:" <> video_id, params, socket) do
   -      last_seen_id = params["last_seen_id"] || 0
   -      video_id = String.to_integer(video_id)
   -      video = Multimedia.get_video!(video_id)
   5
   -      annotations =
   -        video
   -        |> Multimedia.list_annotations(last_seen_id)
   -        |> Phoenix.View.render_many(AnnotationView, "annotation.json")
   10
   -      {:ok, %{annotations: annotations}, assign(socket, :video_id, video_id)}
   -    end
```

On line 2, we use the params as the second argument to join/3. We check for an existing last_seen_id value. To cover a fresh connection, we provide a default value of 0 since the user has yet to see an annotation.

Next, we modify our call to Multimedia.list_annotations by passing our last_seen_id on line 8.

That's it! If we try to re-create our duplicate entries, we'll see the client and server remain properly in sync across disconnects and reconnects using the last_seen_id approach in the channel params. Our approach is simple and direct.

Now our workers can do work on Rumbl and we know that work will leave our data in a reliable state. Next, we'll build a feature to make our application feel a little more social. Let's make a list of who's online.

Tracking Presence on a Channel

Let's track which users are watching a video. This problem may seem easy on the surface, but it's a notoriously difficult computer science problem when multiple servers are involved. The users may be stored in different places, and we'll need to access them. We'll also need to clean up the data when users disconnect. If the connections between servers fail, we'll need to make some decisions about how to calculate and present exactly who is present.

Luckily, we won't have to solve any of these problems because we can rely on Channel Presence to solve them for us. When we're done, we'll have no single point of failure and no single source of truth, an excellent attribute for a distributed solution. Since the entire solution is based on the standard Elixir library, you won't have to add dependencies. Since it's built on OTP, it is self-healing.

Generating Presence Files

We'll write a shockingly small amount of code to do all of this work. To get started, use the mix phx.gen.presence task to generate a presence module, like this:

```
$ mix phx.gen.presence
* creating lib/rumbl_web/channels/presence.ex
...
```

The generated lib/rumbl_web/channels/presence.ex file sets up the module for presence, defining the functions we require for tracking presence on a channel. Next we need to add this module to our supervisor tree in lib/rumbl/application.ex, like this:

```
children = [
  ...
  RumblWeb.Presence
]
```

You've seen this code before. Presence is an OTP application so we need to add it to our supervision tree. That's all of the setup work we need to do.

Tracking Presence in Channels

Let's see how easy it is to track which users are online in our VideoChannel. Open up your lib/rumbl_web/channels/video_channel.ex file and make the following changes:

```
channels/listings/rumbl/lib/rumbl_web/channels/video_channel.change6.ex
Line 1  def join("videos:" <> video_id, params, socket) do
   -      send(self(), :after_join)
   -      last_seen_id = params["last_seen_id"] || 0
   -      video_id = String.to_integer(video_id)
   5      video = Multimedia.get_video!(video_id)

   -      annotations =
   -        video
   -        |> Multimedia.list_annotations(last_seen_id)
   10       |> Phoenix.View.render_many(AnnotationView, "annotation.json")

   -      {:ok, %{annotations: annotations}, assign(socket, :video_id, video_id)}
   -    end

   15  def handle_info(:after_join, socket) do
   -      push(socket, "presence_state", RumblWeb.Presence.list(socket))
   -      {:ok, _} = RumblWeb.Presence.track(
   -        socket,
   -        socket.assigns.user_id,
```

```
20      %{device: "browser"})
     {:noreply, socket}
   end
```

This code makes an important distinction between the *user* and a *session*. A user is a unique entity within the presence. A user can have multiple sessions, such as a single user with open browser tabs or multiple devices.

On line 2, we send ourself a user-defined message called :after_join. We'll process that message in a handle_info callback that will be invoked after join successfully returns.

On line 15, we call a single presence function that does the lion's share of the work, RumblWeb.Presence.track. This function accepts our socket, a key to track, and a map of metadata. The key is a *unique user identity*. We'll pass user_id because it's unique per Rumbl user. The metadata is any arbitrary data we want to associate with a session. We want to restrict this data to the essentials. Presence will maintain this data for the life of the user. Here, we hardcode a device as "browser" since we only support web clients today, but later a native mobile app speaking to our phoenix channel could be written, and we could show an icon next to our user list indicating the kind of device each user connected with.

To finish, we simply return our unchanged socket. When we track presence, we're asking Phoenix to track broadcast messages to our socket's topic about users coming and going. These messages will automatically make it down the client like any other channel broadcast. In just a few lines of code, we've done all we need to do in our channel, so we can move on to our client.

Adding Presence to Templates

The JavaScript Presence API takes care of all the housekeeping of synchronizing user info as users come and go. It also synchronizes data on reconnect. Before we display users on our web page, we need a place to show them. Open up your lib/rumbl_web/templates/watch/show.html.eex and add a new div container to the bottom of the file:

```
channels/listings/rumbl/lib/rumbl_web/templates/watch/show.html.eex
<hr/>
<div class="row">
  <div class="column">
    <h3>Users</h3>
    <ul id="user-list">
    </ul>
  </div>
</div>
```

There's no magic here. It's just an empty li with an id of user-list. We'll lean on JavaScript to populate it.

Using Channel Presence in JavaScript

Next, add this line to the top of assets/js/video.js:

```
import {Presence} from "phoenix"
```

We're importing the library we'll need to handle Channel Presence. With our HTML and import in place, make the following additions to your onReady function in the same file:

```
channels/listings/rumbl/assets/js/video.change8.js
onReady(videoId, socket){
  let msgContainer = document.getElementById("msg-container")
  let msgInput     = document.getElementById("msg-input")
  let postButton   = document.getElementById("msg-submit")
  let userList     = document.getElementById("user-list")
  let lastSeenId   = 0
  let vidChannel   = socket.channel("videos:" + videoId, () => {
    return {last_seen_id: lastSeenId}
  })

  let presence = new Presence(vidChannel)

  presence.onSync(() => {
    userList.innerHTML = presence.list((id, {metas: [first, ...rest]}) => {
      let count = rest.length + 1
      return `<li>${id}: (${count})</li>`
    }).join("")
  })
```

On line 5, we create a new userList reference to our HTML container. Next, we instantiate a new Presence object on line 11, passing in our vidChannel. Then, on line 13, we call the onSync callback to render our users as list items when users join or leave the application.

Here, we make use of the presence.list function that takes care of grouping any given user's multiple presences into a single object. Remember, a single user in the system can be present on any number of browser tabs and devices. That means each user_id might have multiple pieces of session metadata. Your list function's job is to determine which information to display about each user, given a session metadata list.

In our callback, we simply render each user's ID, and how many tabs or devices they are connected from. We get the count by referencing the size of their presence metadata list. Later, as Phoenix improves, we'll show a browser icon for browser tabs and a mobile icon for mobile devices. Save the file so we can try it out. rumbl now has a list of users:

Though the output is a bit primitive, it works. We can see the users with ID 3 and 4 are online with a single tab open. Open and close additional tabs and check user's session counts. They update instantly!

Decorating Entries with Application Data

Showing the user ID isn't very friendly, but we can do better. Since our goal is to display a list of users online, we'll need to add a username. While we could place the user's name in the metadata for the client, this approach is frought with future misery. We'd be placing stale user data in our cluster and Channel Presence would diligently replicate that stale information across our cluster! There's a better way.

Phoenix.Presence provides a fetch callback to solve this problem. As users join and leave the application across your cluster, Phoenix batches these events together to optimize performance and network chatter. Our fetch callback will fetch the data for *a batch of presences*, not just a single presence. Let's build a context function to fetch the usernames for a list of ids in lib/rumbl/accounts.ex, like this:

```
channels/listings/rumbl/lib/rumbl/accounts.change1.ex
import Ecto.Query

def list_users_with_ids(ids) do
  Repo.all(from(u in User, where: u.id in ^ids))
end
```

In list_users_with_ids, we use Ecto to fetch users in the list of the IDs we provide and return users.

Now, we need to decorate our presence information in lib/rumbl_web/channels/presence.ex, like this:

```
channels/listings/rumbl/lib/rumbl_web/channels/presence.change1.ex
def fetch(_topic, entries) do
  users =
    entries
    |> Map.keys()
    |> Rumbl.Accounts.list_users_with_ids()
    |> Enum.into(%{}, fn user ->
      {to_string(user.id), %{username: user.username}}
    end)

  for {key, %{metas: metas}} <- entries, into: %{} do
    {key, %{metas: metas, user: users[key]}}
  end
end
```

We implement the optional fetch callback in our presence module. We take the presence entries which is a map of user_id - session_metadata pairs. We pipe those keys into our new context function and then pipe those users through an anonymous function to build our metadata map with the usernames for each user_id.

When we're done building that users map, in a for comprehension we decorate our original presence entries with usernames. We could decorate the entry map with any data you please. Our only obligation is to carry over the original :metas information as it has the data necessary for tracking presence data over a client.

All that remains is to wire the new information into the client. Head back over to assets/js/video.js and make the following change to the presence.onSync callback:

```
channels/listings/rumbl/assets/js/video.change9.js
presence.onSync(() => {
  userList.innerHTML = presence.list((id,
    {user: user, metas: [first, ...rest]}) => {
      let count = rest.length + 1
      return `<li>${user.username}: (${count})</li>`
    }).join("")
})
```

We modified our presence.onSync callback to destruct the new user key from our presence information. Then, we modified our HTML string snippet to use the user.username instead of our ID. Let's try it out!

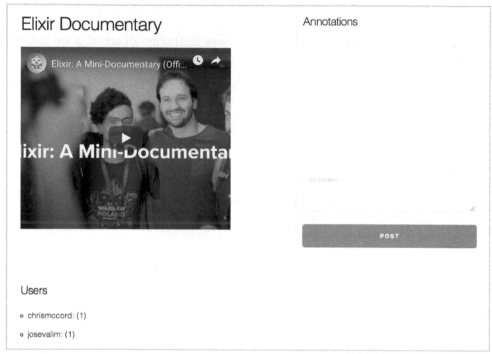

And it works! Our presence data now has friendly usernames. In a remarkably few lines of code, we've implemented a distributed Channel Presence implementation that will allow our server to reliably track presence across a distributed cluster. We've done a lot of work in this chapter. It's time to review.

Wrapping Up

In this chapter, you learned to build simple client/server APIs with Phoenix channels. Though the problem had many layers, it was easy to understand the flow because clients connected to servers, and both sides maintained the connection until the conversation was over. Along the way:

- You learned to connect to a server-side channel through an ES6 client.

- We built a server-side channel with both long-polling and WebSocket support.

- We built a simple API to let users join a channel.

- We processed inbound messages from OTP with handle_info and channels with handle_in.

- We sent broadcast messages with broadcast!.

- We authenticated users with Phoenix.Token.

- We persisted annotations with Ecto, and exposed those new features through our Multimedia context.

- We used Channel Presence to track the list of users on a video channel.

Though channels are by far the most exciting feature of Phoenix, it was far easier to build this code than it was to build the request/response counterparts for our users. In the next chapter, we'll focus on code organization using umbrellas. Along the way, we'll use a visualization tool called Observer and address how to manage configuration with subprojects. Stay tuned!

## CHAPTER 11

Observer and Umbrellas

As we add sophistication to our rumbl application, you should begin to notice that the web pieces of the system aren't like some of the other parts of the application. Both the channels and the MVC components support user interfaces and communicate directly with the business backend. It would be nice to be able to deal with the web and backend pieces of our system independently.

Most successful projects reach a point where it makes sense to break the main piece into smaller units. In this chapter, we are going to take you through the messy but necessary details of such a refactoring exercise. We'll extract the web-centered and backend pieces of our application into their own projects called child applications. When we're done, we'll be able to test, develop and deploy each child app independently. Even so, our Rumbl project has features like user authentication, multimedia management, and persistence so we want conveniences for configuring and building them only once. We need some notion of a project that is a loose confederation of parts. In Elixir, that notion is called the *umbrella project*. Each application under an umbrella is called a *child application*.

It would have been easy to build our application from scratch as an umbrella. It's much harder to refactor existing applications into child apps under an umbrella, but we know many of our readers have the need to break down their growing monoliths. We'll show you the refactoring process, but we'll also show you how to start a project from scratch should you be so inclined.

Before we get started, let's build a deeper intuition of precisely what "application" means in the context of an Elixir project. We will use a tool called Observer that ships with Erlang to offer a visualization of exactly what's happening.

Introspecting Applications with Observer

Every time we start our Rumbl application, we have multiple applications running side by side. Each of our dependencies is in fact its own application. Phoenix and Elixir itself are applications too! An Application in Elixir is a runtime concern with these responsibilities:

- Applications package our code. Every time we compile our rumbl project, Mix prints "Generated rumbl app". Open the file _build/dev/lib/rumbl/ebin/rumbl.app. It mostly contains metadata about the application, such as its modules, processes, a description and more.

- Supervisors can start and stop applications as a unit. An application may have a supervision tree, which defines exactly which services to start when the application starts, and which services to shutdown when the application shuts down.

- Applications provide unified configuration. Each application has its own environment, which is a key-value store to host application configuration.

All of those responsibilities may feel a bit abstract. Let's open up the fantastic Observer, a tool shipping with Erlang, to see how Applications look in practice. To take it for spin, start a new iex -S mix session and run this command:

```
iex> :observer.start()
:ok
```

That command opens up an graphical user interface that looks like the screenshot on page 231.

Observer is a great tool for understanding all running processes for your application. When you open it up, the initial tab gives you general information about Erlang and also statistics about your system and your application. The tabs let you access charts to visualize different aspects of your system, check out memory allocation, look at running processes, and the like.

You Might Not Have Observer Installed

 Some package managers like to break the Erlang standard library into multiple packages. If :observer.start doesn't work, you might be missing the erlang-observer (or similar) package.

Consider the Processes tab. You can see a list of all running processes in your system, providing a tremendous amount of visibility into the system. Remember that in Elixir, almost all state exists in your processes. With Observer, we can see the state of our entire system and who's responsible for each piece. The process tab also includes the Message Queue (MsgQ) for each process. If a process has a very large message queue, it is likely that it is a bottleneck in your system. Therefore, ordering the processes by the Message Queue size can be a great way to spot bottlenecks, and that's exactly what the Phoenix team did when optimizing their channels implementation to support more than 2 million connections on a single node.[1]

You won't explore all tabs now, but let's look at one more in particular: Applications. There, you can see all of the applications that run on your system as well as each application's supervision tree. Click the Applications tab and explore some of the applications on the left-side panel. When you are ready, click the Rumbl entry. You can see something like the figure on page 232.

That's the rumbl supervision tree, more or less. Because we started iex -S mix and not iex -S mix phx.server, the server is missing from the tree. Still, there is a lot for us to explore. We can see the database connection pool, the PubSub system, and more. Inspecting our supervision trees is a great way to analyze how complex our systems are. If a supervision tree is growing too big or too wide, you can use Observer as a tool to help break the system apart.

---

1. https://phoenixframework.org/blog/the-road-to-2-million-websocket-connections

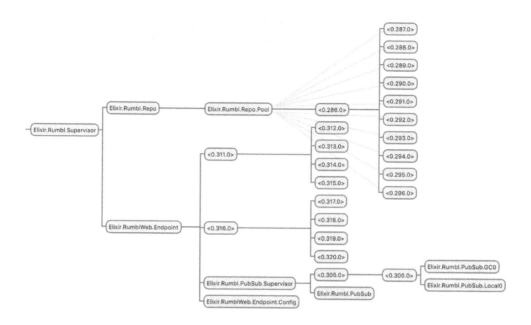

You May Have a Different Supervision Tree

 By the time we finished this book, the Phoenix team was already working on new features and enhancements to provide a more granular supervision tree. So if you are running on a Phoenix version later than Phoenix v1.4, you may see a slightly different tree than the one we showed here. We will talk about what's coming in Chapter 14, What's Next?, on page 297. Regardless of the shape of the tree, all of the points made in this discussion still apply.

Observer also allows us to trigger failures. You can right-click a process in the tree, such as Rumbl.Repo and send it a kill signal, which will cause it to terminate. You'll find a crash report in the terminal. However, since our services are supervised, the supervisor will notice the failure and start a new instance of the same service in its place.

With a more solid understanding of what constitutes each application, let's consider whether we might break our existing application into two smaller ones. Let's be clear here: the main benefit is better boundaries. If all of the code belongs to a single application, then it gets harder to visualize how all of the modules in the same application depend on each other as the application grows.

For instance, while we expect our RumblWeb modules to call into our backend, we have an implicit understanding that it would be highly unexpected for Rumbl to call into RumblWeb. After all, one of the intents behind Phoenix contexts is to allow us to write our business rules without strongly coupling them to our web frontend, be it HTML, JSON, or channels. However, those rules are implicit in our Rumbl app today. By moving to an umbrella with two separate applications underneath, we can keep the web and the backend as two distinct applications which can only use each other if they have explicit dependencies between them. For example, the web appplication will have to explicitly declare that it depends on the backend. For some teams, this may be a small benefit, but for others that enjoy strong boundaries, it makes a drastic difference.

You may have tried doing something similar to this in your previous work. You had a large application, you broke it apart into different Git repositories, and versioned them separately. Initially you were proud of the boundaries you were able to define but after working for a couple months under this new schema, you noticed you got less productive. A lot of time was spent navigating and reviewing code between the different repositories. While each project had their own version, their features were often developed together, and that required you and your team to constantly match and upgrade many packages whenever a new version of any given package was out. Umbrella projects provide an alternative to this. Instead of breaking applications into multiple distinct source-code repositories, which would add too much overhead to our development workflow, the applications in an umbrella are managed and versioned together, under the same repository.

Let's work on separating rumbl from rumbl_web now. We're going to extract all of the web functionality to its own application. When we're done, we'll effectively have two isolated applications, :rumbl and :rumbl_web, in the same umbrella project. That approach will let us deploy, build, test, and package Rumbl as a whole.

Using Umbrellas

In this section, we're going to split our application into rumbl_web, containing the web components, and rumbl, containing all backend logic in our contexts. Each umbrella project has a parent directory that defines:

- The shared configuration of the project
- The dependencies for that project
- The apps directory with child applications

Let's pick an approach that addresses each of these points. We need to choose between using generators and adjusting our existing app.

Choosing an Approach

The main goal for umbrella applications is to give us the freedom to work with distinct pieces of the application independently, while still allowing convenient common overarching tasks. Now that we've identified the logical pieces to separate, let's take a peek into the different approaches we might take.

We could decide to roll all of this common structure and configuration by hand. We'd need to create an apps directory. Then we'd put the code for each child project into it's own directory under apps. In each one, we'd create the common configuration and the individual configuration for each child app. Then we'd adjust the paths and application names where necessary within the child apps.

It's a process that works, but it's also one that's error prone. When possible, it's best to *let Phoenix generators automate as much configuration as possible*. To prevent potential configuration errors, we're not going to take this approach.

Now that we've ruled out refactoring by hand, we have two contenders to choose from. We could use mix new with an --umbrella flag, or mix phx.new with an --umbrella flag. We'll choose the Phoenix generator since it will automate some of the web-based paths and configuration we need.

Creating a Skeleton

Let's create an umbrella project alongside the same directory of our existing rumbl application. Be sure to run the command outside of the existing rumbl application, like this:

```
[/rumbl]$ cd ..
[~]$ mix phx.new rumbl --umbrella
* creating rumbl_umbrella/config/config.exs
* creating rumbl_umbrella/config/dev.exs
* creating rumbl_umbrella/config/test.exs
* creating rumbl_umbrella/config/prod.exs
* creating rumbl_umbrella/config/prod.secret.exs
* creating rumbl_umbrella/mix.exs
* creating rumbl_umbrella/apps/rumbl_web/lib/rumbl_web.ex
* creating rumbl_umbrella/apps/rumbl_web/lib/rumbl_web/application.ex
...
* creating rumbl_umbrella/apps/rumbl_web/mix.exs
* creating rumbl_umbrella/apps/rumbl_web/README.md
```

```
* creating rumbl_umbrella/apps/rumbl_web/.gitignore
* creating rumbl_umbrella/apps/rumbl_web/test/test_helper.exs
* creating rumbl_umbrella/apps/rumbl_web/test/support/channel_case.ex
* creating rumbl_umbrella/apps/rumbl_web/test/support/conn_case.ex
...

Fetch and install dependencies? [Yn] n

...
```

Make sure to answer n to "Fetch and install dependencies?". This project will not be a new application. Instead, we plan to use it as a skeleton for our existing application. We will need to copy our Elixir code and JavaScript assets from rumbl into this new project.

You can see from the console output that Phoenix generated the rumbl_application with a top-level configuration and mix file. In addition, you can see the new apps directory that has two child applications, rumbl and rumbl_web. The generated rumbl application is a stock Elixir application with Ecto, and the rumbl_web application is a standard Phoenix project. Now you will see the method to our madness. Both projects are configured properly for an umbrella so we can copy over our code from the rumbl application we've been building and touch up some configuration code.

Understanding Umbrella Configuration

It's a great time to look at the various pieces of configuration in the old rumbl directory and our new project side by side as we go through this process. Before we copy our applications, let's get the lay of the land, starting with the generated mix file for rumbl_web. Let's look at the project and deps functions in the new rumbl_umbrella/apps/rumbl_web/mix.exs:

```
def project do
  [
    app: :rumbl_web,
    version: "0.1.0",
    build_path: "../../_build",
    config_path: "../../config/config.exs",
    deps_path: "../../deps",
    lockfile: "../../mix.lock",
    elixir: "~> 1.5",
    elixirc_paths: elixirc_paths(Mix.env()),
    compilers: [:phoenix, :gettext] ++ Mix.compilers(),
    start_permanent: Mix.env() == :prod,
    aliases: aliases(),
    deps: deps()
  ]
end
```

```elixir
defp deps do
  [
    {:phoenix, "~> 1.4.6"},
    ...
    {:rumbl, in_umbrella: true},
    ...
  ]
end
```

Notice the in_umbrella flag in the dependency tuple for :rumbl. Now we can use the :rumbl application as a dependency of :rumbl_web and Elixir will automatically start it *before* starting the :rumbl_web server.

You can see the configurations for :build_path, :config_path, :deps_path, and :lockfile. They point back to the umbrella application's directory. That's *all* it takes to make something an umbrella child. At the end of the day, Elixir simply configures the project to use the configuration, dependencies, and build paths from the parent application.

This configuration also tells us something very important about umbrella projects: *all children applications share the same configuration and the same dependencies.* Therefore, you can't have two different applications in the same umbrella that depend on two different Phoenix versions. They all have to be the same. Similarly, if you have 10 applications that use Phoenix and there is a new Phoenix version, you can't update the Phoenix version for each app individually, you will have to update all 10 at the same time. So, while umbrella projects do provide some isolation between children, all children still run on the same VM instance, sharing configuration and dependencies.

Extracting Rumbl and RumblWeb

With our tentative skeleton in place, we can start to put some meat on the bones. We have the code we need and it's already organized as we want; we just need to move it from one application to the other.

Let's copy the critical pieces of rumbl to the right child application of rumbl_umbrella/apps. We want to take advantage of the correct configuration that the phx.new --umbrella command generated. After we've extracted our app and web, and verified everything works, we'll be in a good spot to build our information system in a separate apps directory later.

You're Moving Code Without the Help of Corresponding Listings

If you're following along but mostly paying attention to the code listings, it'll be easy for you to miss these next few changes, because the listings for the code you'll be moving aren't shown. Make sure you follow the directions in the following paragraph and numbered sequence.

Copying the rumbl Source Tree

The first step is to move the source code in lib from the old app to the new. Copy the lib files from rumbl/lib/rumbl/ to rumbl_umbrella/apps/rumbl/lib, like this:

```
$ cp -R rumbl/lib/rumbl rumbl_umbrella/apps/rumbl/lib
$ cp rumbl/lib/rumbl.ex rumbl_umbrella/apps/rumbl/lib
$ cp -R rumbl/test/rumbl rumbl_umbrella/apps/rumbl/test
$ cp -R rumbl/priv/repo rumbl_umbrella/apps/rumbl/priv
$ cp rumbl/test/support/data_case.ex rumbl_umbrella/apps/rumbl/test/support
$ cp rumbl/test/support/test_helpers.ex \
    rumbl_umbrella/apps/rumbl/test/support
```

These commands just copy our code from the old structure to the new. We copy the lib files, then the rumbl.ex file, the tests, the repo, and specific test support files from one structure to the other. Keep in mind we're using the Unix cp command and / directory navigation. If you're using Windows, you will want to use xcopy for directories, copy for files, and \ to separate directories. Make sure you copy folders recursively!

Next, we need to establish our dependencies. Let's add :pbkdf2_elixir for authentication to the rumbl_umbrella/apps/rumbl/mix.exs deps function, like this:

```
defp deps do
  [
    {:ecto_sql, "~> 3.1"},
    {:postgrex, ">= 0.0.0"},
    {:pbkdf2_elixir, "~> 1.0"}
  ]
end
```

The new rumbl child app does not have a web component so it doesn't need an endpoint. We need to remove the Endpoint supervisor from the rumbl application's supervision tree. Update the children list in rumbl_umbrella/apps/rumbl/lib/rumbl/application.ex, keeping only the repository, like this:

```
children = [
  Rumbl.Repo,
]
```

Then remove the config_change function, as the endpoint is no longer a part of this application. That should do it for the application cleanup.

Let's move on to the web apps.

Copying the Web Source Files

The web source tree in lib includes our templates, views, controllers, and channels. We also need to move the top-level rumbl_web.ex and tests over as well. Let's do that now. Copy the files in rumbl/lib/rumbl_web to the new apps/rumbl_web directory:

```
$ cp -R rumbl/lib/rumbl_web rumbl_umbrella/apps/rumbl_web/lib
$ cp rumbl/lib/rumbl_web.ex rumbl_umbrella/apps/rumbl_web/lib
$ cp -R rumbl/test/rumbl_web rumbl_umbrella/apps/rumbl_web/test
$ cp rumbl/test/support/conn_case.ex \
    rumbl_umbrella/apps/rumbl_web/test/support
```

Next, we need to update the use macro in endpoint.ex to point to the right otp_app. Change the second line in rumbl_umbrella/apps/rumbl_web/lib/rumbl_web/endpoint.ex from :rumbl to :rumbl_web, like this:

```
use Phoenix.Endpoint, otp_app: :rumbl_web
```

Make a similar change in Plug.Static's :from option from :rumbl to :rumbl_web:

```
plug Plug.Static,
  at: "/", from: :rumbl_web, gzip: false,
  only: ~w(css fonts images js favicon.ico robots.txt)
```

That does it for endpoint.ex. We need to make similar changes in apps/rumbl_web/lib/rumbl_web/channels/presence.ex. Let's provide the OTP app and the PubSub name. Make them look like this:

```
use Phoenix.Presence,
  otp_app: :rumbl_web,
  pubsub_server: RumblWeb.PubSub
```

Finally, we need to list Presence as a child in apps/rumbl_web/lib/rumbl_web/application.ex, like this:

```
children = [
  RumblWeb.Endpoint,
  RumblWeb.Presence
]
```

We can move on to static assets.

Moving Assets

We've moved our Elixir code, so it is time to work on the web assets. Copy your JavaScript and CSS assets from the rumbl project to the umbrella rumbl_web project, like so:

```
$ cp -R rumbl/assets/js rumbl_umbrella/apps/rumbl_web/assets/
$ cp -R rumbl/assets/css rumbl_umbrella/apps/rumbl_web/assets/
```

With all of the assets in a single folder, we can update the dependencies paths in the apps/rumbl_web/assets/package.json to point to our new path structure, like this:

```
"dependencies": {
  "phoenix": "file:../../../deps/phoenix",
  "phoenix_html": "file:../../../deps/phoenix_html"
},
```

Now we're ready to give it all a try.

Running Tests

Let's see if it all works. Fetch dependencies from the root of rumbl_umbrella, like so:

```
(change to rumbl_umbrella)
$ mix deps.get
...
```

Now we can finally run the following npm install command inside the rumbl_umbrella/apps/rumb_web/assets directory, like this:

```
$ cd apps/rumbl_web/assets
$ npm install
$ cd ../../..
```

Now we can run tests, like this:

```
$ mix test

==> rumbl
.................

Finished in 6.2 seconds
17 tests, 0 failures

Randomized with seed 1527
==> rumbl_web
.................

Finished in 4.2 seconds
```

```
19 tests, 0 failures
Randomized with seed 1527
```

Excellent! All of our tests pass.

We still have a little bit of touching up to do. You may notice our tests are too slow. If you recall, we added configuration to config/test.exs so we could reduce the hash rounds of the Comeonin library, to make password hashing faster within tests. We have extracted the applications, but we did not copy that configuration over. Remember, configuration in umbrella projects are shared across all children, so all configuration exists at the top level. Open up rumbl_umbrella/config/test.exs and configure :pbkdf2_elixir once again:

```
config :pbkdf2_elixir, :rounds, 1
```

If you have done any other configuration while working on your application, make sure to mirror it in the relevant config files.

Now when we run tests, the password hashes will happen much more quickly. Let's try them out:

```
==> rumbl
................
Finished in 0.2 seconds
17 tests, 0 failures

Randomized with seed 823165
==> rumbl_web
.................
Finished in 0.2 seconds
19 tests, 0 failures
```

Ah, that's much better. We are back to the speedy run times for each application, so we're done! We've successfully extracted our business logic and web layers from rumbl, so we can fire up our server:

```
$ mix phx.server
[info] Running RumblWeb.Endpoint with cowboy 2.6.1 at http://localhost:4000
webpack is watching the files…
```

Here, we fired up rumbl_umbrella, but we can work with the pieces in isolation. You can also fire up any of your child apps individually!

Notice we can successfully work with the application as a whole umbrella, just as we did before. Now, we can also develop features in isolation by switching to one of the applications inside rumbl_umbrella/apps.

Whew. Let's review what we did. We physically split our application into two parts by copying files over to our rumbl_umbrella project, under the apps directory. We now have isolated our business logic from the web concerns of our application.

Take note of the big win here. When you develop code for the project, you can now focus on each application individually. If you pay attention to clean, logical interfaces, as your project grows, you can continue to extract child services to their own projects. If by the end of the book, you believe umbrella projects give you a better workflow and boundaries, you can start your next Phoenix project with umbrellas from the beginning by calling mix phx.new with the --umbrella flag.

The next candidate for an umbrella child app will be the information system. We'll build that one from scratch so you'll see both the refactoring workflow and creating a child application from scratch in the next chapter.

Wrapping Up

In this chapter, we took some time to break our growing project into bite-sized pieces. We used umbrellas, an Elixir construct that allows us to develop and test projects in isolation but integrate them into a whole. Along the way:

- We used Observer to understand the importance behind applications.
- We extracted rumbl and rumbl_web into their own child umbrella project.
- We learned to identify configuration changes, including dependencies, supervision trees, and application configuration.

Next, we'll see how to build an independent, self-healing piece of infrastructure with OTP. When we're done, you'll be able to develop and test the pieces in isolation.

## CHAPTER 12

OTP

You've now had your first Phoenix Channels experience and should be developing a good intuition for the strength of Phoenix for highly interactive applications. You've also lightly sampled OTP concepts including applications and supervision trees. You have everything you need to create beautiful code and then run it reliably at breakneck speeds.

Phoenix isn't just about user interfaces, though. You also have the experience and elegance of Erlang's OTP framework. In general, OTP is a way to think about fault-tolerance, concurrency, and distribution. It uses a few patterns that allow you to use concurrency to build state without language features that rely on mutability. OTP also has rich abstractions for supervision and monitoring. In this chapter, we'll use OTP to build an information system.

Rather than read a wave of dry prose that tells you what OTP does, you'll start with the basics by building a simple service. We'll build a counter that runs in a separate process. Then, we'll supervise it, restarting on failure. You'll see how you can hold state in an immutable world.

On its own, that knowledge will help you understand Phoenix, which is itself an OTP application. We'll use these principles to build an information service under our umbrella project, which we will develop, manage, and test in isolation.

Managing State with Processes

Functional programs are stateless, but we still need to be able to manage state. In Elixir, we use concurrent processes and recursion to handle this task. That may sound counterintuitive, but let's take a look at how it works with a simple program.

To start with, let's create a child application. From the rumbl_umbrella root directory, change to apps and create a new mix project, like this:

```
$ → cd apps
$ → mix new info_sys --sup
* creating README.md
...
$ → cd info_sys
```

We create a brand new mix project under the apps directory. Later it will evolve into our full service, but for now let's create a Counter server that counts up or down. Create a apps/info_sys/lib/info_sys/counter.ex file and key this in:

otp/listings/rumbl_umbrella/apps/info_sys/lib/info_sys/counter.ex

```
Line 1  defmodule InfoSys.Counter do
          def inc(pid), do: send(pid, :inc)

          def dec(pid), do: send(pid, :dec)
5
          def val(pid, timeout \\ 5000) do
            ref = make_ref()
            send(pid, {:val, self(), ref})

10          receive do
              {^ref, val} -> val
            after
              timeout -> exit(:timeout)
            end
15        end

          def start_link(initial_val) do
            {:ok, spawn_link(fn -> listen(initial_val) end)}
          end
20
          defp listen(val) do
            receive do
              :inc ->
                listen(val + 1)
25
              :dec ->
                listen(val - 1)

              {:val, sender, ref} ->
30              send(sender, {ref, val})
                listen(val)
            end
          end
        end
```

Our module implements a Counter server as well as functions for interacting with it as a client. The *client* serves as the API and exists only to send messages to the process that does the work. It's the *interface* for our counter. The *server* is a process that recursively loops, processing a message and sending updated state to itself. Our server is the *implementation.*

Building the Counter API

Our API sends messages to increment (:inc) and decrement (:dec) the counter, and another message called :val to get the counter's value. Let's look at each one of these in turn.

:inc and :dec take only the process ID for the server process—called pid for process ID—and a single atom command. These skinny functions exist only to send :inc and :dec messages to our server process. These are asynchronous, meaning we send a message without awaiting any reply.

The val function on line 6 is a bit different. It must send a request for the value of the counter and await the response. Since we need to associate a response with this particular request, we create a unique reference with make_ref(). This unique reference is just a value that's guaranteed to be globally unique. Then, we send a message to our counter with the send function. Our message payload is a 3-tuple with an atom designating the command we want to do, :val, followed by our process ID called pid and the globally unique reference.

Then, we await a response, matching on the reference. The ^ operator means that rather than rebinding the value of ref, we match only tuples having that exact ref. That way, we can make sure to match only responses related to our explicit request. If there's no match in a given period, we exit the current process with the :timeout reason code.

We start by defining the client API to interact with our counter. First, we create inc and dec functions to increment and decrement our counter. These functions fire off an async message to the counter process without waiting for a response. Our val function sends a message to the counter but then blocks the caller process while waiting for a response.

Let's take a look at our server.

As you'll see later, OTP requires a start_link function. Ours, on line 17, accepts the initial state of our counter. Its only job is to spawn a process and return {:ok, pid}, where pid identifies the spawned process. The spawned process calls the private function named listen, which listens for messages and processes them.

Let's look at that listen function on line 21, the engine for our counter. You don't see any global variables that hold state, but our listener has a trick up its sleeve. We can exploit recursion to manage state. For each call to listen, the tiny function blocks to wait for a message. Then, we process the trivial :inc, :dec, and :val messages. The last thing any receive clause does is call listen again with the updated state.

Said another way, the state of the server is wrapped up in the execution of the recursive function. We can use Elixir's message passing to listen in on the process to find the value of the state at any time. When the last thing you do in a function is to call the function itself, the function is *tail recursive*, meaning it optimizes to a loop instead of a function call. That means this loop can run indefinitely! In many languages, burning a thread for such a trivial task can be expensive, but in Elixir processes are incredibly cheap, so this strategy is a great way to manage state.

Taking Our Counter for a Spin

This code is pretty simple, so you already know what'll happen. Still, let's try it out in IEx with iex -S mix:

```
iex> alias InfoSys.Counter
InfoSys.Counter

iex> {:ok, counter} = Counter.start_link(0)
{:ok, #PID<0.253.0>}

iex> Counter.inc(counter)
:inc
iex> Counter.inc(counter)
:inc
iex> Counter.val(counter)
2

iex> Counter.dec(counter)
:dec
iex> Counter.val(counter)
1
```

It works perfectly, just as you expected. Think about the techniques used:

- We used concurrency and recursion to maintain state.
- We separated the interface from the implementation.
- We used different abstractions for asynchronous and synchronous communication with our server.

As you might imagine, this approach is common and important enough for us to package it for reuse. In fact, this approach has been around a while in the form of the Erlang OTP library. Let's take a look.

Building GenServers for OTP

Though our counter is an oversimplification, the basic approach has been used for over thirty years to manage both concurrent state and behavior for most important Erlang applications. The library encapsulating that approach is called OTP, and the abstraction is called a *generic server*, or GenServer. Let's modify our counter to use OTP to create our counter, instead.

We don't need to change too much. Instead of creating specific functions to handle inc, dec, and val, we use specific OTP abstractions instead. Update your counter.ex file with these contents:

```
otp/listings/rumbl_umbrella/apps/info_sys/lib/info_sys/counter.change1.ex
Line 1  defmodule InfoSys.Counter do
   -      use GenServer
   -
   -      def inc(pid), do: GenServer.cast(pid, :inc)
   5
   -      def dec(pid), do: GenServer.cast(pid, :dec)
   -
   -      def val(pid) do
   -        GenServer.call(pid, :val)
  10      end
   -
   -      def start_link(initial_val) do
   -        GenServer.start_link(__MODULE__, initial_val)
   -      end
  15
   -      def init(initial_val) do
   -        {:ok, initial_val}
   -      end
   -
  20      def handle_cast(:inc, val) do
   -        {:noreply, val + 1}
   -      end
   -
   -      def handle_cast(:dec, val) do
  25        {:noreply, val - 1}
   -      end
   -
   -      def handle_call(:val, _from, val) do
   -        {:reply, val, val}
  30      end
   -    end
```

We've changed the terminology some, but not the implementation. When we want to send asynchronous messages such as our inc and dec messages, we use GenServer.cast, as you can see on line 4. Notice that these functions don't send a return reply. When we want to send synchronous messages that return the state of the server, we use GenServer.call as we do on line 8. Notice the _from in the function head. You can use an argument leading with an underscore, just as you'd use a _ as wildcard match. With this feature, we can explicitly describe the argument while ignoring the contents.

On the server side, the implementation is much the same: we use a handle_cast line for :inc and one for :dec, each returning a noreply alongside the new state, and we also use handle_call to handle :val, and specify the return value. We explicitly tell OTP when to send a reply and when not to send one. We also have to tweak the start_link to start a GenServer, giving it the current module name and the counter. This function spawns a new process and invokes the InfoSys.Counter.init function inside this new process to set up its initial state.

Let's take that much for a spin:

```
iex> alias InfoSys.Counter
InfoSys.Counter
iex> {:ok, counter} = Counter.start_link(10)
{:ok, #PID<0.96.0>}
iex> Counter.dec(counter)
:ok
iex> Counter.dec(counter)
:ok
iex> Counter.val(counter)
8
```

Our first counter was split into client and server code. This segregation remains when we write our GenServer. init, handle_call, and handle_cast run in the server. All other functions are part of the client.

Our OTP counter server works exactly as before, but we've gained much by moving it to a GenServer. On the surface, we no longer need to worry about setting up references for synchronous messages. Those are taken care of for us by GenServer.call. Second, the GenServer module is now in control of the receive loop, allowing it to provide great features like code upgrading and handling of system messages, which will be useful when we introspect our system with Observer later on. A GenServer is one of many OTP behaviours. We'll continue exploring them as we build our information system.

Adding Failover

The benefits of OTP go beyond simply managing concurrent state and behavior. It also handles the linking and supervision of processes. Now let's explore how process supervision works. We'll supervise our new counter.

Though our counter is a trivial service, we'll play with supervision strategies. Our supervisor needs to be able to restart each service the right way, according to the policies that are best for the application. For example, if a database dies, you might want to automatically kill and restart the associated connection pool. *This policy decision should not impact code that uses the database.* If we replace a simple supervisor process with a supervisor tree, we can build much more robust fault-tolerance and recovery software.

In Phoenix, you didn't see too much code attempting to deal with the fallout for every possible exception. Instead, we trust the error reporting to log the errors so that we can fix what's broken, and in the meantime, we can automatically restart services in the last good state. The beauty of OTP is that it captures these clean abstractions in a coherent library, allowing us to declare the supervision properties that most interest us without bogging down the meaning of each individual application. With a supervision tree having a configurable policy, you can build *robust self-healing software* without building *complex self-healing software.*

We'll manage the configuration of the supervision policies in a single location. Since we're under an umbrella, we'll use the application.ex file for our info_sys. Let's add our Counter server to our application's supervision tree. In lib/info_sys/application.ex, add your new server as a child of your supervisor, like this:

```
otp/listings/rumbl_umbrella/apps/info_sys/lib/info_sys/application.change1.ex
children = [
  {InfoSys.Counter, 5}, # new counter worker
]
```

To specify the children an Elixir application will start, we define a *child spec.* In this case, we add our new counter to the existing list of children that our application already defined. You'll specify a single element containing a two-tuple having the module you want to start and the value that will be received on start_link by the GenServer. Alternatively, passing in only a module name uses a default value of [].

For our Counter, we pass a tuple, which takes the module, and the argument for the child's start_link/1. In our case, we pass the initial state, as the number 5.

In opts, you can see the policy that our application will use if something goes wrong. OTP calls this policy the *supervision strategy*. In this case, we're using the :one_for_one strategy. This strategy means that if the child dies, only that child will be restarted. If all resources depended on some common service, we could have specified :one_for_all to kill and restart all child process if any child dies. We'll explore those strategies later on.

Now if we fire up our application with iex -S mix, we don't see anything particular, since our counter is running but we aren't interacting with it.

Let's add a periodic tick to our counter to see it work in action in our supervision tree.

Modify your Counter's init function and add a new handle_info callback, like this:

```
otp/listings/rumbl_umbrella/apps/info_sys/lib/info_sys/counter.change2.ex
def init(initial_val) do
  Process.send_after(self(), :tick, 1000)
  {:ok, initial_val}
end

def handle_info(:tick, val) do
  IO.puts("tick #{val}")
  Process.send_after(self(), :tick, 1000)
  {:noreply, val - 1}
end
```

We tweak init in the counter process to send itself a :tick message every 1,000 milliseconds, and then we add a function to process those ticks, simulating a countdown. As with channels, out-of-band messages are handled inside the handle_info callback, which sets up a new tick and decrements the state.

Now you can fire our application back up with iex -S mix and see our counter worker in action:

```
iex> tick 5
tick 4
tick 3
tick 2
tick 1
^C
```

This isn't terribly exciting, but it gets interesting when we deal with our workers crashing.

Let's crash our counter if it ticks below a certain value:

```
otp/listings/rumbl_umbrella/apps/info_sys/lib/info_sys/counter.change3.ex
def handle_info(:tick, val) when val <= 0, do: raise "boom!"

def handle_info(:tick, val) do
  IO.puts("tick #{val}")
  Process.send_after(self(), :tick, 1000)
  {:noreply, val - 1}
end
```

We add a :tick clause for cases when the value is less than zero, and we raise an error that crashes our process. Let's fire up iex -S mix again and see what happens:

```
iex> tick 5
tick 4
tick 3
tick 2
tick 1
[error] GenServer #PID<0.119.0> terminating
** (RuntimeError) boom!
    (info_sys) lib/info_sys/counter.ex:22: InfoSys.Counter.handle_info/2
    (stdlib) gen_server.erl:616: :gen_server.try_dispatch/4
    (stdlib) gen_server.erl:686: :gen_server.handle_msg/6
    (stdlib) proc_lib.erl:247: :proc_lib.init_p_do_apply/3
Last message: :tick
State: 0
tick 5
tick 4
tick 3
tick 2
tick 1
^C
```

As expected, our server crashed—but then it restarted! That's the magic of supervision. When our counter crashed, it was restarted with its initial state of 5. In short, our program crashed, the supervisor identified the crash, and then it restarted the process in a known good state. We don't have to add any extra code to fully supervise every process. We need only configure a policy to tell OTP how to handle each crash.

The basic building blocks of isolated application processes and a supervision structure to manage them have been the cornerstone of Erlang reliability—whether you're running a trivial counter, a server with a million processes, or a worldwide distributed application with tens of millions of processes. The principles are the same, and they've been proven to work.

To apply these principles, you need to know how to tell Elixir what supervision behavior you expect. Here are the basics.

Restart Strategies

The first decision you need to make is to tell OTP what should happen if your process crashes. Think of these details as a software policy for dealing with failure. If we decide to use anything beyond the module to start and the initial value for the OTP server, we'll need a way to specify those options. That's called a *child spec* which configures the policy for an OTP restart.

You have a couple of options for defining those options. First, you can do it within the children definition in application.ex. To do so, you can use the Supervisor.child_spec function. For example, if we wanted to explicitly specify a :permanent restart strategy, you'd do so like this:

```
children = [
  Supervisor.child_spec({InfoSys.Counter, 5}, restart: :permanent)
]
```

That's fine for a single child spec, but having to specify the supervision values every time we list our server would be repetitive and error prone. Fortunately, Elixir allows us to also define those values directly in the Counter module, like this:

```
defmodule InfoSys.Counter do
  use GenServer, restart: :permanent
  ...
end
```

Behind the scenes, this code works because use GenServer defines a child_spec(arg) function, which returns the child specification. Most of the time this high-level using option is enough. When you need more, you can always define your own child_spec(arg) function, like this:

```
defmodule InfoSys.Counter do
  ...
  def child_spec(arg) do
    %{
      id: __MODULE__,
      start: { __MODULE__, :start_link, [arg]},
      restart: :temporary,
      shutdown: 5000,
      type: :worker
    }
  end
  ...
end
```

The keys listed here are the module, the function, and arguments to call for starting and restarting the server, the restart configuration, a shutdown value in milliseconds, and the type of child. We'll go into some of these options in more detail throughout the chapter. See the Elixir documentation for child_spec[1] for a complete list of options and more details. For now, let's focus on the restart option configuration. Child specifications support the following restart values:

:permanent

> The child is always restarted (default).

:temporary

> The child is never restarted.

:transient

> The child is restarted only if it terminates abnormally, with an exit reason other than :normal, :shutdown, or {:shutdown, term}.

:permanent is the default restart strategy and the trailing options are fully optional, so to specify a :permanent counter with an initial value of 5, we can use worker(InfoSys.Counter, [5]).

Let's say we have a situation in which *mostly dead* isn't good enough. When a counter dies, we want it to really *die*. Perhaps restarting the server would cause harm. Let's try changing our restart strategy to :temporary and observe the crash:

```
children = [
  Supervisor.child_spec({InfoSys.Counter, 5}, restart: :temporary)
]
```

Now let's fire our project back up with iex -S mix:

```
iex> tick 5
tick 4
tick 3
tick 2
tick 1
[error] GenServer #PID<0.306.0> terminating
[error] GenServer #PID<0.119.0> terminating
** (RuntimeError) boom!
    (info_sys) lib/info_sys/counter.ex:22: InfoSys.Counter.handle_info/2
    (stdlib) gen_server.erl:616: :gen_server.try_dispatch/4
    (stdlib) gen_server.erl:686: :gen_server.handle_msg/6
    (stdlib) proc_lib.erl:247: :proc_lib.init_p_do_apply/3
Last message: :tick
State: 0
```

---

1.   https://hexdocs.pm/elixir/Supervisor.html#module-child_spec-1

As you'd expect, when our counter dies it stays dead. The :temporary strategy is useful when a restart is unlikely to resolve the problem, or when restarting doesn't make sense based on the flow of the application.

Sometimes, you may want OTP to retry an operation a few times before failing. You can do exactly that with a pair of child spec options called max_restarts and max_seconds. OTP will only restart an application max_restarts times in max_seconds before failing and reporting the error up the supervision tree. By default, Elixir will allow 3 restarts in 5 seconds, but you can configure these values to whatever you want. In general, you'll use the restart strategies your specific application requires.

Supervision Strategies

Just as child workers have different restart strategies, supervisors have configurable supervision strategies. The most basic and the default for new Phoenix applications is :one_for_one. When a :one_for_one supervisor detects a crash, it restarts a worker of the same type without any other consideration. Most of the time, :one_for_one is enough but sometimes, processes depend on one another. When such a process dies, more than one process must restart. That's why Elixir supports more than one restart strategy.

Let's look at the ones that are available:

:one_for_one

> If a child terminates, a supervisor restarts only that process.

:one_for_all

> If a child terminates, a supervisor terminates all children and then restarts all children.

:rest_for_one

> If a child terminates, a supervisor terminates all child processes defined after the one that dies. Then the supervisor restarts all terminated processes.

These strategies are all relatively straightforward. To get a taste of them, let's start multiple counters and see how the termination of one of them affects the others. Back in lib/info_sys/application.ex, change the start function to this:

```
children = [
  {InfoSys.Counter, 15},
  {InfoSys.Counter, 5},
  {InfoSys.Counter, 10},
]
```

```
opts = [strategy: :one_for_all, name: InfoSys.Supervisor] # new strategy
Supervisor.start_link(children, opts)
```

Now when you boot your application via $ iex -S mix, you will notice it won't even start, with this reason:

```
** (Mix) Could not start application info_sys:
  InfoSys.Application.start(:normal, []) returned an error: bad child spec,
  more than one child specification has the id: InfoSys.Counter.
```

```
If using maps as child specifications, make sure the :id keys are unique.
If using a module or {module, arg} as child, use Supervisor.child_spec/2
to change the :id, for example:

    children = [
      Supervisor.child_spec({MyWorker, arg}, id: :my_worker_1),
      Supervisor.child_spec({MyWorker, arg}, id: :my_worker_2)
    ]
```

The error message shows us exactly what we need to do. We are starting multiple counters but they all have the same ID. We need to pass distinct IDs in each child_spec call, so let's do that:

```
children = [
  Supervisor.child_spec({InfoSys.Counter, 15}, id: :long),
  Supervisor.child_spec({InfoSys.Counter, 5}, id: :short),
  Supervisor.child_spec({InfoSys.Counter, 10}, id: :medium)
]
```

Restart the application with $ iex -S mix once more and you should see all servers counting down at the same time. As soon as the "short" counter reaches 0, it terminates, and then we can see all counters restarting from scratch. Feel free to play with the other supervision strategies and see how the system will behave.

Once the counter experiments are over, change our lib/rumbl/application.ex back to the original supervision tree and restart strategy:

```
otp/listings/rumbl_umbrella/apps/info_sys/lib/info_sys/application.ex
def start(_type, _args) do
  children = [
  ]

  opts = [strategy: :one_for_one, name: InfoSys.Supervisor]
  Supervisor.start_link(children, opts)
end
```

The GenServer is the foundation of many different abstractions throughout Elixir and Phoenix. Knowing these small details will make you a much better programmer. Let's see a couple more examples.

Using Agents

It turns out that a still simpler abstraction has many of the benefits of a GenServer. It's called an *agent*. With an agent, you have only five main functions: start_link initializes the agent, stop stops the agent, update changes the state of the agent, get retrieves the agent's current value, and get_and_update performs the last two operations simultaneously. Here's what our counter would look like with an agent:

```
iex> import Agent
nil
iex> {:ok, agent} = start_link(fn -> 5 end)
{:ok, #PID<0.57.0>}
iex> update(agent, &(&1 + 1))
:ok
iex> get(agent, &(&1))
6
iex> stop(agent)
:ok
```

To initialize an agent, you pass a function returning the state you want. To update the agent, you pass a function taking the current state and returning the new state. That's all there is to it. Behind the scenes, this agent is an OTP GenServer, and plenty of options are available to customize it as needed. One such option is called :name.

Registering Processes

With OTP, we can register a process by name with the :name option in start_link. After we register a process by name, we can send messages to it using the registered name instead of the pid.

Let's rewrite the previous example using a named agent:

```
iex> import Agent
nil
iex> {:ok, agent} = start_link(fn -> 5 end, name: MyAgent)
{:ok, #PID<0.57.0>}
iex> update(MyAgent, &(&1 + 1))
:ok
iex> get(MyAgent, &(&1))
6
iex> stop(MyAgent)
:ok
```

If a process already exists with the registered name, we can't start the agent:

```
iex> import Agent
nil
```

```
iex> {:ok, agent} = start_link(fn -> 5 end, name: MyAgent)
{:ok, #PID<0.57.0>}
iex> {:ok, agent} = start_link fn -> 5 end, name: MyAgent
** (MatchError) no match of right hand side value:
  {:error, {:already_started, #PID<0.57.0>}}
```

Agents are one of the many constructs built on top of OTP. You've already seen another, the Phoenix.Channel. Let's take a look.

OTP and Channels

If we were building a supervisor for a couple of application components, the simple default :one_for_one strategy might be enough. The goal for Phoenix Channels is bigger, though. To us, supervisors aren't just tiny isolated services. Channels are core infrastructure. We intentionally build all of our infrastructure with a tree of supervisors, where each node of the tree knows how to restart any major service if it fails.

When you coded your channels in the previous chapter, you might not have known it, but you were building an OTP application. Each new channel was a process built to serve a single user in the context of a single conversation on a topic. Though Phoenix is new, we're standing on the shoulders of giants. Erlang's OTP has been around as long as Erlang has been popular—we know that it works. Much of the world's text-messaging traffic runs on OTP infrastructure. WhatsApp runs on Erlang to process more than tens of billions messages every day. You can count on this infrastructure always being up and available because it's built on a reliable foundation.

Designing an Information System with OTP

With these high-level basics demystified, let's use another OTP abstraction to enhance our application. Let's take our video annotations to another level with some OTP-backed information services. We're going to use some common web APIs to enhance our application.

For any request, we're going to ask our information system for highly relevant facts that we can inject. We'll be providing enhanced question/answer–style annotations as the video is playing. This'll give our live viewers and replayed visits alike an enhanced experience about the video that's showing.

The goal for our application is to have multiple information systems. We might pull from an API like WolframAlpha while at the same time referencing a local database. WolframAlpha is a service that allows users to ask natural-language questions and get rich responses. We'd like our design to start multiple information system queries in parallel and accumulate the results. Then, we can take the best matching responses.

Planning our Supervision Strategy

Think about our information system requirements. We want to fetch the most relevant information for a user in real time, across different backends. Since we're fetching results in parallel, a failure likely means the network or one of our third-party services failed. That's out of our control. It doesn't make sense for us to retry the computation because this operation is time sensitive—a video is playing. Instead, we want to spawn processes in parallel and let them do their work, and we'll take as many results as we can get within some limited block of time. Say we spawn requests from Google, WolframAlpha, and Bing. If one of those three information system backends crashes, it's not a problem, or at least not a problem we can solve. Let's think about how we might code those services.

If you find yourself in the position of spinning off some concurrent process without the need to supervise that process, you can usually use a *task* without having to specify any supervision at all. For the sake of performance, you'll often start several tasks to do high-latency jobs and then wait for them to finish, like this:

```
task1 = Task.async(fn -> access_some_api() end)
task2 = Task.async(fn -> access_another_api() end)
Task.await(task1)
Task.await(task2)
```

Here's what's happening. The parent process is starting two asynchronous tasks, which are linked processes. If either of them fails, they are linked so our parent will also fail. This model is generally fine because of the linking. When a child or parent dies, cleanup will happen exactly as it should.

But think about our InfoSys requirements. We *don't want to link those processes* because we can't address a failure in, say, Bing, but we still want the parent to continue. That means we can't use Task.async and Task.await. You might think it makes perfect sense to start a one-off fire-and-forget process for each service.

That would be a mistake. We always want to start processes inside supervision trees for cleanup and discoverability. Each process we start should obey its explicit start and shutdown rules, so we'll clean up effectively and be able to view those supervised processes through tools like Observer. Therefore, we'll start our tasks through Task.Supervisor.async_nolink instead of the typical Task.async.

Upon deeper inspection, we will also need another process in the supervisor tree. Most external systems are rate-limited, or at the very least, resource constrained so we must limit our requests wherever possible. We will implement the cache system in a module yet to be created called InfoSys.Cache.

Both the InfoSys.Cache and Task.Supervisor will be part of our InfoSys supervision tree, like this:

```
otp/listings/rumbl_umbrella/apps/info_sys/lib/info_sys/application.change2.ex
defmodule InfoSys.Application do
  @moduledoc false

  use Application

  def start(_type, _args) do
    children = [
      InfoSys.Cache,
      {Task.Supervisor, name: InfoSys.TaskSupervisor},
    ]

    opts = [strategy: :one_for_one, name: InfoSys.Supervisor]
    Supervisor.start_link(children, opts)
  end
end
```

With that accomplished, we're ready to code our service. Since we don't have to worry about managing error conditions, we're free to focus on the main task of the information system, and we can let the error cases crash. The real work gets simpler.

Building a Cache Server Without Bottlenecks

Now that we've sketched a supervision tree that allows us to start tasks dynamically under their own supervisor, we'll need to create our information retrievers. First, we need to consider one final detail. We need to decide how our main interface will work with our Information System. We'd like to be able to choose from several different backends—say one for Google, one for WolframAlpha, and so on—as shown in the figure on page 260.

That seems right. When a user makes a query, our information system will start up as many different task queries as we have backends. Then, we'll collect the results from each and choose the best one to send to the user, caching the results of each request for better performance. We have an open question, though. We may have multiple requests coming at the same time. If all requests depend on a single process for caching, said process will become a bottleneck and hurt the user experience.

The answer is surprisingly simple. We will use a shared service to write things to memory. It turns out that Erlang already has such a service called :ets, which stands for Erlang Term Storage (ETS). ETS is an in-memory storage

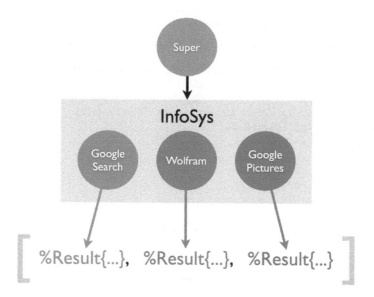

solution included with OTP that allows you to store and retrieve any valid Erlang or Elixir data, and it's super fast. That's perfect for our caching service. Using ETS with our cache will let us use a single cache server to handle the cache expiration, while allowing concurrent reads and writes from every possible client to happen directly in ETS. However, since the cache is in-memory, it is not shared between different Phoenix nodes so every time the node starts — during deployments, for example — the cache starts empty.

Create a new file in lib/info_sys/cache.ex and key this in:

```
otp/listings/rumbl_umbrella/apps/info_sys/lib/info_sys/cache.ex
defmodule InfoSys.Cache do
  use GenServer

  def put(name \\ __MODULE__, key, value) do
    true = :ets.insert(tab_name(name), {key, value})
    :ok
  end

  def fetch(name \\ __MODULE__, key) do
    {:ok, :ets.lookup_element(tab_name(name), key, 2)}
  rescue
    ArgumentError -> :error
  end

  def start_link(opts) do
    opts = Keyword.put_new(opts, :name, __MODULE__)
    GenServer.start_link(__MODULE__, opts, name: opts[:name])
  end
```

```
20  def init(opts) do
      new_table(opts[:name])
      {:ok, %{}}
    end

25  defp new_table(name) do
      name
      |> tab_name()
      |> :ets.new([
        :set,
30        :named_table,
        :public,
        read_concurrency: true,
        write_concurrency: true])
    end
35
    defp tab_name(name), do: :"#{name}_cache"
  end
```

Our server isn't doing any stateful work yet, but for now we can focus on the interface and ETS usage. We start by defining start_link on line 15, where we ensure a :name option is present, which is used to name the GenServer. Skipping put and fetch for a second, we default the server name to that of our module, which will allow us to use a generic single cache for now, but start other independent caches as needed. This approach will also come in handy later when it comes to testing OTP services. Both functions make use of a private tab_name function, which we defined on line 36. This function simply returns an atom of the table name to use for our ETS table.

Now, let's get back to our client cache interface. Any cache needs a read and write. Ours are fetch and put on lines 4 and 9. In our put function, we call :ets.insert, converting our GenServer's name to a table name, and passing a key and value pair to store in the table as a tuple. We match on the true result to ensure it was successful, then return :ok to the caller. Our fetch function wraps the somewhat clumsy API of ETS. We used :ets.lookup_element to fetch a value out of our table for a given key, passing the one-based index of the value—2 in our case. ETS unfortunately throws an ArgumentError if we try to look up a key which does not exist, so we use rescue to translate the result into an :error value.

Next, we begin the stateful work of our server by defining the init function. We create and name our ETS table with new_table and return {:ok, %{}}, where the empty map is the server state. ETS tables are owned by a single process, and the table's existence lives and dies with that of its owner. This is great because we don't have to worry about state values or cleanup when a process stops, either naturally or via a crash.

Let's break down new_table on line 25. We call :ets.new, passing our table name, as well as a list of options. The options are important. :set is a type of ETS table that acts as a key-value store. The :named_table option allow us to locate this table by its name. Critically, :public lets processes other than the owner read and write values. Finally, we enable read and write concurrency to maximize the performance of our cache for concurrent workloads.

Our Cache isn't quite complete, but let's take what we have so far for a spin in iex:

```
iex> alias InfoSys.Cache
iex> Cache.put("one plus one?", "two")
:ok
iex> Cache.fetch("one plus one?")
{:ok, "two"}
iex> Cache.fetch("not here")
:error
```

We have nothing too fancy yet, but it all works just fine, almost. We have a problem, though. Our cache doesn't yet expire old values. If we don't remove old values from our cache, our memory footprint will just continue to grow. In our case, we only require a short-lived cache for remotely fetched data, so let's change that.

Here's our strategy for sweeping the cache. We'll change the shape of the state data for our supervisor. We'll have a map with these keys. :interval will define the amount of time between sweeps, :timer will hold the pid for a timer, and table will hold our ETS table. We will start a timer process after our interval to schedule a sweep. Then the sweep will purge all of the values in our cache. It's not a sophisticated sweep strategy, but it should be enough for our purposes to take some load off of the server for oft-used information requests. Crack open cache.ex, add the schedule_clear function and call it from the handle_info, like this:

```
otp/listings/rumbl_umbrella/apps/info_sys/lib/info_sys/cache.change1.ex
Line 1  @clear_interval :timer.seconds(60)
    -
    -   def init(opts) do
    -     state = %{
    5       interval: opts[:clear_interval] || @clear_interval,
    -       timer: nil,
    -       table: new_table(opts[:name])
    -     }
    -
   10     {:ok, schedule_clear(state)}
    -   end
```

```
   def handle_info(:clear, state) do
     :ets.delete_all_objects(state.table)
15   {:noreply, schedule_clear(state)}
   end

   defp schedule_clear(state) do
     %{state | timer: Process.send_after(self(), :clear, state.interval)}
20 end
```

We rewrote our init function to build a map of state containing our :table, along with new values for a :timer, as well as millisecond :interval for clearing the cache, which we've defaulted to sixty seconds. Before returning from init, we call to a new private schedule_clear function on line 18, which simply uses Process.send_after to send our process a message in the future, after state.interval milliseconds have passed. We then pick up the :clear messages inside a handle_info callback, defined on line 13. This callback has two jobs. First, it purges the cache of all values by calling :ets.delete_all_objects. Second, it reschedules the next purge with schedule_clear.

Our cache expiration is a very basic sweep for now, but it will be perfect for our use case. We can always update our cache sweeper if it proves to be necessary, and our API will not need to change, only the supervisor implementation. Let's try it out in iex:

```
iex> alias InfoSys.Cache
InfoSys.Cache

iex> Cache.put("one plus one?", "two")
:ok

iex> Cache.fetch("one plus one?")
{:ok, "two"}

iex> Process.sleep(60_000)
:ok

iex> Cache.fetch("one plus one?")
:error
```

We can see our cache expiration in action by inserting a cached query, waiting for a minute, and fetching again. Our next query shows a cache miss, indicating our cache has been pruned. It works!

Using Tasks to Fetch Data

With our cache in place and our Task supervisor up and running, we can build our generic information system. We want an interface that knows about available backends. We'll spawn tasks to concurrently query each available backend service, fetch the response from each and cache the result. Then we can pick the best result from all possible candidates. It sounds complicated, but our layering will make building each service surprisingly simple. We'll lean on Elixir and OTP to handle the details.

Let's create our interface in apps/info_sys/lib/info_sys.ex, like this:

```
otp/listings/rumbl_umbrella/apps/info_sys/lib/info_sys.ex
Line 1  defmodule InfoSys do

          @backends [InfoSys.Wolfram]

   5      defmodule Result do
            defstruct score: 0, text: nil, backend: nil
          end

          def compute(query, opts \\ []) do
  10        opts = Keyword.put_new(opts, :limit, 10)
            backends = opts[:backends] || @backends

            backends
            |> Enum.map(&async_query(&1, query, opts))
  15      end

          defp async_query(backend, query, opts) do
            Task.Supervisor.async_nolink(InfoSys.TaskSupervisor,
              backend, :compute, [query, opts], shutdown: :brutal_kill
  20        )
          end
        end
```

Of the three hypothetical backends, we're going to focus on WolframAlpha. Building each of the others should be the same. Let's break it down. Our InfoSys is a generic module to spawn computations for queries. These backends are their own processes, but InfoSys isn't. We put all of the results into a single list, wait for each response from each spawned task, and finally pick the best one to return to the user.

At the top of our module, we use a module attribute called @backends to build a list of all the backends we support, which is initially only InfoSys.Wolfram. We'll leave this API open so we can add other backends over time.

Next, we define a Result struct to hold each search result. Our struct has :score for storing relevance, :text to describe the result, and the :backend to use for the computation. With the preliminary supporting ceremony out of the way, we move on to define a simple basic API. We'll use compute as the main entry point for our service and async_query to actually spawn off a task to do the actual work.

On line 9, we define compute. That function maps over all backends, calling a async_query function for each one. We start with only one of them, but the implementation for multiple backends is exactly the same. This is the basic API function. The magic all happens in async_query.

On line 17, you can see our Task Supervisor in action. There's a lot going on, so let's break it down. We are invoking a task, so we need to provide the module, function and arguments for our new task. We call Task.Supervisor.async_nolink to spawn off the new task. That function spawns off a task in a new process, calling the function we specify, complete with our query and limit attributes. We use async_nolink to spawn the task isolated from our caller, allowing our clients to query backends and not be worried about a crash or unexpected error. This strategy makes sense for our application because we have real end-users waiting on results. If a result doesn't come back from one of our services, we'll just discard the result and the supervisor will kill it. The function returns the Task struct, which we'll await later on. When you consider how much this code is doing, this listing is remarkably compact.

Now it's time to build the actual Wolfram backend.

Building the Wolfram Info System

Now that we have our generic InfoSys module in place, we can work on specific backends. We'll start with only one, our Wolfram backend. This module will call WolframAlpha to retrieve relevant information about our users' annotations.

Our first step is to define our backend interface. Since all our backends will have the same contract, this is a perfect use case for a backend *behaviour*. A behaviour is a contract, a common API across modules. We have seen OTP behaviours, such as GenServer and Supervisor, as well as behaviours from libraries like Plug. Remember, each plug implements two functions, init/1 and call/2. Our behaviour will be a tiny contract between the information system and each backend, consisting of just two callbacks, name and compute. Create a file in lib/info_sys/backend.ex, and key this in:

otp/listings/rumbl_umbrella/apps/info_sys/lib/info_sys/backend.ex
```
defmodule InfoSys.Backend do
  @callback name() :: String.t()
  @callback compute(query :: String.t(), opts :: Keyword.t()) ::
    [%InfoSys.Result{}]
end
```

We define two functions. We don't actually declare a function. Instead, we use *typespecs*, which specify not just the name of our functions but also the types of arguments and return values. In our case, the name function takes no arguments but returns a String type, so you can see the String.t in the type-spec. The compute function takes a String.t query, a Keyword.t list of options, and returns a list of %InfoSys.Result{} structs.

With our behaviour in place, we can write our first backend. To do so, we'll need to establish our dependencies. Wolfram Alpha returns XML responses, and we'll use an XML parser to avoid processing those by hand. Let's add :sweet_xml to our deps list in mix.exs. We want to add the dependencies to info_sys since umbrellas manage dependencies at the child applications:

otp/listings/rumbl_umbrella/apps/info_sys/mix.change1.exs
```
{:sweet_xml, "~> 0.6.5"},
```

Next, run $ mix deps.get to grab the dependency from Hex. With our XML library in place, we're ready to sign up as a WolframAlpha API developer and retrieve our application ID. Visit the WolframAlpha developer portal,[2] sign up for a new account, and follow the instructions to get your AppID.

Now that you have a developer API key, you could place it directly in config/dev.exs, but there's a better way. You shouldn't check in private credentials under version control. In fact, Phoenix points you in the right direction with the generated config/prod.secret.exs file. That file references environment variables that are securely set on the production server, meaning you can establish sensitive configuration in your local development environment without checking secret values into version control. That way you can include sensitive credentials properly. Let's add our API key lookup to our development and prod environments. Since tests will not hit the Wolfram API directly, we don't need to set a key for that environment. Add the following entry to your config/dev.exs and config/prod.secret.exs like this:

```
wolfram_app_id =
  System.get_env("WOLFRAM_APP_ID") ||
    raise """
    environment variable WOLFRAM_APP_ID is missing.
    """

config :info_sys, :wolfram, app_id: wolfram_app_id
```

With setup out of the way, we can now implement our Wolfram backend in lib/info_sys/wolfram.ex, like this:

otp/listings/rumbl_umbrella/apps/info_sys/lib/info_sys/wolfram.ex
```
Line 1  defmodule InfoSys.Wolfram do
   -      import SweetXml
   -      alias InfoSys.Result
```

---

2.   https://developer.wolframalpha.com/portal/signup.html

```
 5   @behaviour InfoSys.Backend

     @base "http://api.wolframalpha.com/v2/query"

     @impl true
10   def name, do: "wolfram"

     @impl true
     def compute(query_str, _opts) do
       query_str
15     |> fetch_xml()
       |> xpath(~x"/queryresult/pod[contains(@title, 'Result') or
                                    contains(@title, 'Definitions')]
                          /subpod/plaintext/text()")
       |> build_results()
20   end

     defp build_results(nil), do: []

     defp build_results(answer) do
25     [%Result{backend: __MODULE__, score: 95, text: to_string(answer)}]
     end

     defp fetch_xml(query) do
       {:ok, {_, _, body}} = :httpc.request(String.to_charlist(url(query)))
30
       body
     end

     defp url(input) do
35     "#{@base}?" <>
       URI.encode_query(appid: id(), input: input, format: "plaintext")
     end

     defp id, do: Application.fetch_env!(:info_sys, :wolfram)[:app_id]
40 end
```

To start our module, we import the functions we'll need and set up a single alias. SweetXml will help us parse the XML we receive, and Result has the struct for the results we'll use.

Next, we establish our module as a implementation of the InfoSys.Backend behaviour on line 5. In compute on line 13, we build a pipe to take our query, fetch the XML we'll need, extract the results using the xpath function from SweetXml, and then build the results. We specify our compute function as an implementation of a behaviour with the @impl true notation. That module attribute is not required but it makes our intentions clear. Users of our module can immediately tell which functions implement our behaviour and which ones don't. Next, we'll look at the functions that do each one of these tasks.

In fetch_xml on line 28, we contact WolframAlpha with the query string that interests us. We use :httpc, which ships within Erlang's standard library, to do the straight HTTP request, matching against :ok and the body that we return to the calling client. We use private functions to extract our API key from our application configuration and build the full URL of our API request.

In build_results on line 22, we build a list of result structs. build_results has two different forms, depending on whether we get results back or not. We match on the first argument in our function head. On nil, we need only return an empty list. Otherwise, we build a list of result structs with our expected results and score, and return them to the caller.

Let's try it out with iex -S mix. First, start a query. We've designed our backend to return results to the calling process, which we've wrapped in Tasks inside our InfoSys.compute. We don't yet await the task completion inside compute, but we can issue compute requests and await the tasks inside iex. Remember, each backend will return a spawned Task, like this:

```
iex> InfoSys.compute("what is elixir?")
[
  %Task{
    owner: #PID<0.320.0>,
    pid: #PID<0.340.0>,
    ref: #Reference<0.4138658672.566755329.204828>
  }
]
```

That query fires off a single Wolfram backend query and then the task sends results to the calling process. We can call Task.await on our task, but the result should be waiting for us in our current process when the task completes.

Let's use the flush helper from IEx to see any messages we've received:

```
iex(13)> InfoSys.compute("what is elixir")
iex(14)> flush()
[
  %InfoSys.Result{
    backend: InfoSys.Wolfram,
    score: 95,
    text: "1 | noun | a sweet flavored liquid (usually containing a small ..."
  }
]
...
```

```
iex(15)> InfoSys.compute("what is firebird?")
iex(16)> flush()
[
  %InfoSys.Result{
    backend: InfoSys.Wolfram,
    score: 95,
    text: "1 | noun | the male is bright red with black wings and tail\n2..."
  }
]
...
```

Brilliant. Our Wolfram service is working exactly as we expect. Once the task is complete, we receive the results in our mailbox. We can wait for each task to complete with Task.await. Your results may not be the same, but for every result you see in the list, you get our hardcoded score of 95 percent. Remember, flush() can just return :ok if the message isn't yet in your inbox. If that happens to you, wait a few seconds and try again.

Monitoring Processes

If you watched closely, you may have also noticed the {:DOWN, ...} message we received, in addition to the task results. Internally, the Task library sets up a monitor from the caller process to the Task. If we wanted to, we could use Process.monitor to detect backend crashes while we're waiting on results. Once a monitor is set, we'll get a message when the monitored process dies. For example, you can see this concept at work in IEx:

```
iex> pid = spawn(fn -> :ok end)
iex> Process.monitor(pid)
#Reference<0.0.2.2850>
```

We spawn a pid with a trivial function. We set up a monitor with Process.monitor. We get a reference back to identify this monitor. Meanwhile, the pid process dies immediately because it has no work to do. Let's use flush to check out our IEx mailbox, like this:

```
iex> flush()
{:DOWN, #Reference<0.0.2.2850>, :process, #PID<0.405.0>, :normal} :ok
```

Nice! We receive a regular Elixir message as a {:DOWN, ...} tuple, informing us that our process died. We won't be monitoring our backends directly with Process.monitor because the Task module calls it for us, but it's nice to know how the monitoring primitives work as they power much of the high-level OTP tools you are used to using, such as supervisors and monitors.

To make our backends more friendly to our clients, we need to make a few modifications. We'll need to detect when a backend crashes so we don't wait for results that might never arrive. In addition, we need to order the results we get from all the backends by our relevance score so it will be easier to pick the best one. Finally, we need to specify a reasonable timeout so the information systems that take too long won't hold up other results. Let's get started.

Working with Task Tools

Elixir's Task module has a perfect feature for our requirements: task *yielding*. While Task.await would crash the caller should a given task time out, Task.yield blocks the caller, returning the result, an error, or nil, depending on whether a reply is received. We also need the ability to wait on *all tasks*, taking no more than a given time for total execution. Fortunately, Elixir provides Task.yield_many, which gives us exactly that.

Let's apply this feature to our InfoSys client. We'll automatically collect results and ignore responses from crashed or tardy backends, making our services predictable and safe. Extend your apps/info_sys/lib/info_sys.ex, like this:

```
otp/listings/rumbl_umbrella/apps/info_sys/lib/info_sys.change1.ex
def compute(query, opts \\ []) do
  timeout = opts[:timeout] || 10_000
  opts = Keyword.put_new(opts, :limit, 10)
  backends = opts[:backends] || @backends

  backends
  |> Enum.map(&async_query(&1, query, opts))
  |> Task.yield_many(timeout)
  |> Enum.map(fn {task, res} -> res || Task.shutdown(task, :brutal_kill) end)
  |> Enum.flat_map(fn
    {:ok, results} -> results
    _ -> []
  end)
  |> Enum.sort(&(&1.score >= &2.score))
  |> Enum.take(opts[:limit])
end
```

The compute function now automatically waits for results. When we receive results, we sort them by score and report the top ones. The pipeline is interesting. We start with our backends, and map over them with the queries we fire to our backends. Starting on line 8, we take all spawned backend tasks and call Task.yield_many with our timeout.

Now, things get interesting. Let's study the pipeline starting on line 9 through the end of the function. It's an extremely dense chunk of code, but it's all important.

First we need to walk through each of the task results. We map over each result, which comes in the form of a task-result tuple. In the function head, we match both to task and res for later use. For each one, we execute the expression res || Task.shutdown(task, :brutal_kill). That little snippet is the lynchpin of this block of code.

If we get a result back in res we simply return it, and the other half of the || operator never fires. If we get a nil back, we'll process the right side. We shut down the task with a :brutal_kill option, meaning it's an immediate shutdown, without waiting for completion. Note that this snippet also protects us from a race condition. Theoretically, a task could complete between when we ask for the yield_many and when we actually process the results. In this case, we still want to make sure to kill the task.

The result of this map is tuples with either {:ok, result} or {:error, reason}, and we're ready to process those results. We grab successful results, ignore :error results by returning a []. We sort by score, and then use Enum.take to return up to the limit our client specifies.

And that's a wrap. Whew.

Now that our code is yielding to our tasks, we're left with only results that complete successfully within the specified timeout. That's the beauty of tasks. They allow us a tidy way to handle resources that could otherwise leak.

Let's give it a try:

```
iex> InfoSys.compute("what is the meaning of life?")
[
  %InfoSys.Result{
    backend: "wolfram",
    score: 95,
    text: "42\n(according to the book The Hitchhiker's Guide...",
  }
]
```

Our information system now handles failures exactly as we desire. We were able to add complexity such as isolated failures and timeouts to the combined information system service without changing the policies for individual backends.

Because each backend is simply synchronous code running inside a new task process, we can leverage everything in OTP to make our system resilient without changing the business code.

Caching Results

With our asynchronous backend in place, we're ready to integrate our Cache server. Open up apps/info_sys/lib/info_sys.ex and add the compute function just below the defstruct, like this:

```
otp/listings/rumbl_umbrella/apps/info_sys/lib/info_sys.change2.ex
Line 1  alias InfoSys.Cache

     -  def compute(query, opts \\ []) do
     -    timeout = opts[:timeout] || 10_000
     5    opts = Keyword.put_new(opts, :limit, 10)
     -    backends = opts[:backends] || @backends
     -
     -    {uncached_backends, cached_results} =
     -      fetch_cached_results(backends, query, opts)
    10
     -    uncached_backends
     -    |> Enum.map(&async_query(&1, query, opts))
     -    |> Task.yield_many(timeout)
     -    |> Enum.map(fn {task, res} ->
    15        res || Task.shutdown(task, :brutal_kill)
     -      end)
     -    |> Enum.flat_map(fn
     -      {:ok, results} -> results
     -      _ -> []
    20    end)
     -    |> write_results_to_cache(query, opts)
     -    |> Kernel.++(cached_results)
     -    |> Enum.sort(&(&1.score >= &2.score))
     -    |> Enum.take(opts[:limit])
    25  end
```

We modified our compute function to read from the cache for each backend given a query, join those values to the fetched results, and write new values to the cache. First, we added a lookup to return results from uncached backend queries, and merged those with existing cached results, on line 9. Then we piped the filtered backends to our original pipeline, performing our async task work as before. Next, we added a new pipe operation, where we write the new results to the cache, then append the cached results before sorting by score, on lines 21 and 22.

To support our new pipe operations, we wrote two private functions. Let's add the first of them now, below our new compute function:

```
otp/listings/rumbl_umbrella/apps/info_sys/lib/info_sys.change2.ex
Line 1  defp fetch_cached_results(backends, query, opts) do
   -      {uncached_backends, results} =
   -        Enum.reduce(
   -          backends,
   5          {[], []},
   -          fn backend, {uncached_backends, acc_results} ->
   -            case Cache.fetch({backend.name(), query, opts[:limit]}) do
   -              {:ok, results} -> {uncached_backends, [results | acc_results]}
   -              :error -> {[backend | uncached_backends], acc_results}
   10           end
   -          end)
   -
   -      {uncached_backends, List.flatten(results)}
   -    end
```

On line 1, we defined a fetch_cached_results function to take all backends and accumulate the cached results for the given query, as well as the backends which contain no cached information. This way we can return both the cached result set, as well as the remaining backends that need fresh queries. Now, we can write the results, like this:

```
otp/listings/rumbl_umbrella/apps/info_sys/lib/info_sys.change2.ex
Line 1  defp write_results_to_cache(results, query, opts) do
   2      Enum.map(results, fn %Result{backend: backend} = result ->
   3        :ok = Cache.put({backend.name(), query, opts[:limit]}, result)
   4
   5        result
   6      end)
   7    end
```

On line 1, we defined a write_results_to_cache function which uses Cache.put to write our uncached results to our cache using the backend, query, and relevant options as our cache key. These previous three listings hold a moderately large amount of code, but just about all of it is fulfilling the goal of organizing, writing, and reading responses from the cache. Very little of the code is related to the ceremony of managing our cache server. That code lives elsewhere, in our supervisor. Let's try it out in IEx:

```
iex> :timer.tc(InfoSys, :compute, ["how old is the universe?"])

{1306573,
 [
   %InfoSys.Result{
     backend: InfoSys.Wolfram,
     score: 95,
     text: "1.4×10^10 a (Julian years)\n(time elapsed since the Big Bang)",
   }
 ]}
```

```
iex> :timer.tc(InfoSys, :compute, ["how old is the universe?"])
{53,
 [
   %InfoSys.Result{
     backend: InfoSys.Wolfram,
     score: 95,
     text: "1.4×10^10 a (Julian years)\n(time elapsed since the Big Bang)",
   }
 ]}
iex> :timer.tc(InfoSys, :compute, ["1 + 1"])
{1121249,
 [
   %InfoSys.Result{
     backend: InfoSys.Wolfram,
     score: 95,
     text: "2",
   }
 ]}
iex> :timer.tc(InfoSys, :compute, ["1 + 1"])
{47,
 [
   %InfoSys.Result{
     backend: InfoSys.Wolfram,
     score: 95,
     text: "2",
   }
 ]}
```

We used :timer.tc to measure the execution time in microseconds to run the given module, function and arguments. We can see our first call returned in 1.3s, while our second identical query returned in 53 microseconds. Issuing a new query of "1 + 1", yielded a similar result. The first query was uncached, and had to make the remote hop to WolframAlpha, taking just over one second. The next call hit the cache and returned in 47 microseconds. Not bad!

If you want to see the cache sweeping in action, wait 60 seconds, and re-issue one of our cached queries. You'll see higher latency since our Cache clear operation is doing what it should. That wraps up our service. All that remains is to tie it into our channels.

Integrating OTP Services with Channels

Now that we have a complete information system, let's integrate it with our web frontend. Our goal is to call into our information system any time a user adds an annotation to a video, to see if we have relevant results to add to that user's conversation.

First let's make sure rumbl_web depends on info_sys. Open up apps/rumbl_web/mix.exs and add this entry under deps:

```
{:info_sys, in_umbrella: true},
```

Note how we were able to build and test info_sys in complete isolation and now we can introduce it as a dependency to any of the sibling applications that need it. If an application doesn't need info_sys, then it doesn't have to depend on it either.

Next let's integrate InfoSys with the VideoChannel. Whenever we receive a new annotation in handle_in, we want to invoke the compute function. Since the compute function is a blocking call, we want to make it asynchronous in our channel so our user gets the annotation broadcast right away. Let's first use a task to spawn a function call for our InfoSys computation by making the following changes to your lib/rumbl_web/channels/video_channel.ex:

```
otp/listings/rumbl_umbrella/apps/rumbl_web/lib/rumbl_web/channels/video_channel.change1.ex
Line 1  def handle_in("new_annotation", params, user, socket) do
          case Multimedia.annotate_video(user, socket.assigns.video_id, params) do
            {:ok, annotation} ->
              broadcast_annotation(socket, user, annotation)
    5         Task.start(fn -> compute_additional_info(annotation, socket) end)
              {:reply, :ok, socket}

            {:error, changeset} ->
              {:reply, {:error, %{errors: changeset}}, socket}
   10     end
        end

        defp broadcast_annotation(socket, user, annotation) do
          broadcast!(socket, "new_annotation", %{
   15       id: annotation.id,
            user: RumblWeb.UserView.render("user.json", %{user: user}),
            body: annotation.body,
            at: annotation.at
          })
   20   end
```

On line 4, we extract our broadcast to a shared broadcast_annotation function so our information system can make use of it when it has relevant results to share. Next, we spawn a task on line 5 to asynchronously call a new compute_additional_info function, which we'll write in a moment. We use Task.start because we don't care about the task result nor if it fails. It's important that we use a task here so we don't block on any particular messages arriving to the channel.

Now, let's write compute_additional_info to ask our InfoSys for relevant results:

`otp/listings/rumbl_umbrella/apps/rumbl_web/lib/rumbl_web/channels/video_channel.change1.ex`
```elixir
defp compute_additional_info(annotation, socket) do
  for result <-
    InfoSys.compute(annotation.body, limit: 1, timeout: 10_000) do

    backend_user = Accounts.get_user_by(username: result.backend.name())
    attrs = %{body: result.text, at: annotation.at}

    case Multimedia.annotate_video(
      backend_user, annotation.video_id, attrs) do

      {:ok, info_ann} ->
        broadcast_annotation(socket, backend_user, info_ann)
      {:error, _changeset} -> :ignore
    end
  end
end
```

First, we call into our information system, asking for only one result. Our service returns the best information it has, given our query. We tell it we are willing to wait ten seconds for an answer. Next, we use a comprehension to grab the backend user from our Accounts context, get the relevant attributes and annotate our video with that information. Finally we call broadcast_annotation on line 13 to report the new annotation to all subscribers on this topic. The integration is tight and smooth, and it's done. Our code is extremely efficient with our caching layer. Imagine an active chat of users watching a sports game or chanting the same message. Our service won't waste any cycles recomputing values.

We need to seed our database with a wolfram user to post annotations along with our real user conversations. Create a priv/repo/backend_seeds.exs, like this:

`otp/listings/rumbl_umbrella/apps/rumbl/priv/repo/backend_seeds.exs`
```elixir
{:ok, _} = Rumbl.Accounts.create_user(%{name: "Wolfram", username: "wolfram"})
```

Now, you can run these seeds with mix run, like this:

```
$ cd apps/rumbl
$ mix run priv/repo/backend_seeds.exs
[debug] QUERY OK db=0.8ms
begin []
[debug] QUERY OK db=80.9ms
INSERT INTO "users" ("name","username","inserted_at", ...
[debug] QUERY OK db=7.5ms
commit []
```

Note we're using our internal create_user function instead of the user-facing register_user function. The context function perfectly fits this scenario and allows us to not mix up end-user code paths with the path for internal users. Let's try it out on the frontend:

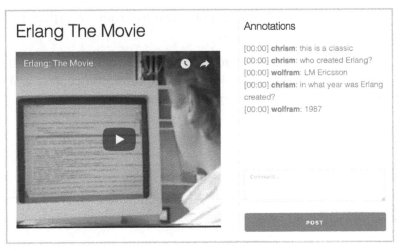

It works!

At this point, you can use this template to add services to our information system. Bing has an API that you might use to retrieve search results for linking. You could also build your own service. The important thing is that you have a framework to add services to.

We're at a convenient breaking point. It's time to wrap up.

Wrapping Up

In this chapter dedicated to OTP services, we first took our time so you could build a solid understanding of how OTP uses concurrency and message passing to safely encapsulate state without implicit state, or instance or global variables. Then, we built an information system for our annotations. Along the way:

- We created a new child app under our umbrella.

- We built a counter that demonstrates how some OTP behaviours work.

- You looked at several OTP supervision and restart strategies.

- You saw examples of a full OTP service as GenServer.

- You learned how tasks wrap behavior and agents encapsulate state.

- You implemented an ETS backed cache, with GenServer powered cache expiration.

- We implemented an information system abstract frontend with concrete backends.

- You learned to fetch WolframAlpha results from an HTTP service and share them with our channels.

In the next chapter, we'll look at how to test your applications. You'll see how to test channels and OTP, and also how our umbrella project will help us manage all of it. Don't stop now—you're almost done!

## CHAPTER 13

Testing Channels and OTP

The last few chapters were packed with new features. We've spent quite a bit of time and effort establishing new features that are interactive, compelling, and fast. Our information system uses an external API with flexible backends. Our channels-based API offers real-time web support for a rich user interface, one extremely sensitive to good server performance. Our channels allow peer-to-peer messaging. We're missing only one thing. Tests.

In this chapter, you'll see how to test OTP processes in isolation. You'll learn to use the Phoenix helpers to simplify channels testing. Before we dive in, let's briefly talk about what you can expect.

Recall that in Part I, the test cases for our controllers used Phoenix test helpers in ConnCase. We tested our HTTP-backed features, the router, controller, and views. Our integrated tests also hit the database. We used helpers such as html_response to remove some of the boilerplate from our typical tests.

In Part II, our code stack is fundamentally different. The MVC code gave way to channels and OTP. Still, the basic approach will be the same. We'll build tests that hit a single channel call, one that integrates everything down to the database.

We'll draw the line at the external requests. Since we want to run our integration tests within our sphere of control, we'll want our usual test stack to focus on everything we've built *except our external HTTP request to WolframAlpha*. We'll want to isolate our tests from that piece of code.

Let's start our testing process with our information system.

Testing the Information System

To warm up, we're going to start our tests with our independent caching layer. Since our cache is made up of a standalone genserver, we can test it in isolation. It's a good place to start because our cache can do two things: fetch and put.

Testing Our Cache

For the most part, testing our cache will work like testing any other service. We'll create a cache and try some fetches and puts. Then we'll use asserts to check what actually happened against our expectations. Let's begin with a few basic tests and then we can handle corner cases for timeouts and shutdown. Shift into the apps/info_sys directory and then make tests/cache_test.exs look like this:

```
testing_otp/listings/rumbl_umbrella/apps/info_sys/test/cache_test.exs
defmodule InfoSysTest.CacheTest do
  use ExUnit.Case, async: true
  alias InfoSys.Cache
  @moduletag clear_interval: 100

  setup %{test: name, clear_interval: clear_interval} do
    {:ok, pid} = Cache.start_link(name: name, clear_interval: clear_interval)
    {:ok, name: name, pid: pid}
  end
```

We're creating a test, and including the usual ceremony. We have a module tag to specify the interval for clearing a cache. We'll use that feature to customize the cache expiration during our tests.

We also set up the tests by creating a simple GenServer by calling the start_link for our cache, passing in the shortened interval. Then we return the pid in the test context.

Now, we're ready to run a couple of tests. One will check puts and fetches, and the other will check nonexistent keys:

```
testing_otp/listings/rumbl_umbrella/apps/info_sys/test/cache_test.exs
  test "key value pairs can be put and fetched from cache", %{name: name} do
    assert :ok = Cache.put(name, :key1, :value1)
    assert :ok = Cache.put(name, :key2, :value2)

    assert Cache.fetch(name, :key1) == {:ok, :value1}
    assert Cache.fetch(name, :key2) == {:ok, :value2}
  end

  test "unfound entry returns error", %{name: name} do
    assert Cache.fetch(name, :notexists) == :error
  end
end
```

The first test puts a couple of keys and verifies an :ok result, and then verifies both with fetches. The next test checks a simple fetch of a nonexistent key, and verifies an :error.

If you'd like, you can run the test. You'll find it clean and green:

```
$ mix test test/cache_test.exs
.

Finished in 0.02 seconds
1 test, 0 failures
```

The tests are dead simple so far, but we should check out a couple of corner cases. We must make sure the GenServer shuts down cleanly and also make sure we handle error conditions like timeouts. We're going to need a couple of test helper functions to assist us for each one. Above the test setup function, key this in:

```
testing_otp/listings/rumbl_umbrella/apps/info_sys/test/cache_test.change1.exs
defp assert_shutdown(pid) do
  ref = Process.monitor(pid)
  Process.unlink(pid)
  Process.exit(pid, :kill)

  assert_receive {:DOWN, ^ref, :process, ^pid, :killed}
end
defp eventually(func) do
  if func.() do
    true
  else
    Process.sleep(10)
    eventually(func)
  end
end
```

That's a bit more meaty. Let's talk through those helpers. The first one will serve as a custom set of assertions to verify a server shuts down cleanly. We start a monitor and then unlink the process. We remove the link, otherwise killing the server would make our test process also crash. Next we kill the process and make sure we get a :DOWN message on the monitor. We break this code into its own function because we'll use it twice in the tests that follow.

The second helper is a small helper, to prevent tests from having to sleep for long periods while the test waits on an expected result. Ideally, we want to have our tests react only to messages. But when that's not enough, we will execute some function until it eventually returns true. Let's see how these two helpers work in the context of our tests. Add these tests to the bottom of cache_test.exs:

```
testing_otp/listings/rumbl_umbrella/apps/info_sys/test/cache_test.change1.exs
test "clears all entries after clear interval", %{name: name} do
  assert :ok = Cache.put(name, :key1, :value1)
  assert Cache.fetch(name, :key1) == {:ok, :value1}
  assert eventually(fn -> Cache.fetch(name, :key1) == :error end)
end

@tag clear_interval: 60_000
test "values are cleaned up on exit", %{name: name, pid: pid} do
  assert :ok = Cache.put(name, :key1, :value1)
  assert_shutdown(pid)
  {:ok, _cache} = Cache.start_link(name: name)
  assert Cache.fetch(name, :key1) == :error
end
```

Nice! The first test puts a key into the cache and then uses the eventually function to check whether the values eventually clear. Recall that the @moduletag at the top of the test module sets the clear_interval to 100 milliseconds. After that waiting period, the cache should be cleared and our test will pass. If all is well, the test runs as quickly as it can. If not, ExUnit will time out the test after 60 seconds and we can fix the problem.

In the second test we verify that shutting down the cache actually erases all cached entries. To do so, we use @tag to set the clear_interval to a high value, overriding the value set in @moduletag. We do this to ensure clear_interval won't interfere with our tests since we want to check that the shutdown of the cache erases all values, and not clear_interval. We do so by writing a key and shutting down the server. The test awaits for the :DOWN message, which is only delivered once the cache process exits. The test then checks to make sure the key is not present.

You can see that testing GenServers is a bit trickier than testing pure functions, but it's not too bad. Our InfoSys has a new set of challenges, though, since it's pulling data from an external source. It's time to attack that challenge.

Testing the InfoSys

We'll move on to perhaps our most significant testing challenge, the InfoSys. Since this information system interacts with an external interface, we have some decisions to make. We also have quite a bit of behavior to cover, such as timeouts and forced backend termination. You'll be surprised at how quickly we can cover all this functionality with a few short and sweet test cases. Let's get started.

A natural first step for testing our InfoSys is to simply look for successful results. Create a new rumbl_umbrella/apps/info_sys/test/info_sys_test.exs with the following code:

```
testing_otp/listings/rumbl_umbrella/apps/info_sys/test/info_sys_test.exs
Line 1  defmodule InfoSysTest do
   -      use ExUnit.Case
   -      alias InfoSys.Result
   -
   5      defmodule TestBackend do
   -        def name(), do: "Wolfram"
   -
   -        def compute("result", _opts) do
   -          [%Result{backend: __MODULE__, text: "result"}]
  10        end
   -        def compute("none", _opts) do
   -          []
   -        end
   -        def compute("timeout", _opts) do
  15          Process.sleep(:infinity)
   -        end
   -        def compute("boom", _opts) do
   -          raise "boom!"
   -        end
  20      end
```

The top of the file has the typical module declaration and aliases. Then we move to our first problem, how to isolate our test code from the internet requests.

We solve this isolation problem by defining a stub called TestBackend on line 5. This module will act like our Wolfram backend, returning a response in the format that we expect. Since we don't use the URL query string to do actual work, we can use this string to identify specific types of results we want our test backend to fetch:

```
testing_otp/listings/rumbl_umbrella/apps/info_sys/test/info_sys_test.exs
Line 1  test "compute/2 with backend results" do
   2      assert [%Result{backend: TestBackend, text: "result"}] =
   3             InfoSys.compute("result", backends: [TestBackend])
   4    end
   5
   6    test "compute/2 with no backend results" do
   7      assert [] = InfoSys.compute("none", backends: [TestBackend])
   8    end
```

With our stub in place, the tests will be remarkably simple. We define a test case for computing successful results. We pass a query string of "result", signaling our backend to send fake results. Then we assert that the result set is what we expect. Next, we use the same approach to handle empty datasets.

That takes care of the cases in which backends properly report results. Next, we need to cover the edge cases, like backend timeouts.

Chris says:
What's the Difference Between a Stub and a Mock?

Stubs and mocks are both testing fixtures that replace real-world implementations. A *stub* replaces real-world libraries with simpler, predictable behavior. With a stub, a programmer can bypass code that would otherwise be difficult to test. Other than that, the stub has nothing to say about whether a test passes or fails. For example, a http_send stub might always return a fixed JSON response. In other words, a stub is just a simple scaffold implementation standing in for a more complex real-world implementation.

A *mock* is similar, but it has a greater role. It replaces real-world behavior just as a stub does, but it does so by allowing a programmer to specify expectations and results, playing back those results at runtime. A mock will fail a test if the test code doesn't receive the expected function calls. For example, a programmer might create a mock for http_send that expects the test argument, returning the value :ok, followed by the test2 argument, returning :ok. If the test code doesn't call the mock first with the value test and next with the value test2, it'll fail. In other words, a mock is an implementation that records expected behavior at definition time and plays it back at runtime, enforcing those expectations.

Incorporating Timeouts in Our Tests

A backend might time out. To test timeouts, we need a way to simulate a backend taking longer than expected. We also need to be able to make sure that the information system terminates the backend in such cases, as we expect it to. We want to do all of this in a fast test. Fortunately, with our testing structure, it's a simple job:

```
testing_otp/listings/rumbl_umbrella/apps/info_sys/test/info_sys_test.exs
Line 1  test "compute/2 with timeout returns no results" do
     2    results = InfoSys.compute("timeout", backends: [TestBackend], timeout: 10)
     3    assert results == []
     4  end
     5  end
```

We want our test to be fast, so we shorten the timeout interval to 10 milliseconds. We simply call the correct stub and it sleeps forever. We assert that we get an empty result. Mission accomplished.

Now we can shift to our last corner case. We need to check exceptions. It's a relatively easy job but we'll need one tiny trick. To keep our tests from printing out a bunch of noisy log messages when the exception fires we need to capture the log. With that in mind, key this last test in:

```
testing_otp/listings/rumbl_umbrella/apps/info_sys/test/info_sys_test.exs
@tag :capture_log
test "compute/2 discards backend errors" do
  assert InfoSys.compute("boom", backends: [TestBackend]) == []
end
```

The test is short and, um, suite. We capture the log in a test tag. Then we assert that no results are returned. Believe it or not, that's all the testing we need to do at this level. We are ready to fire our test up:

```
$ mix test test/info_sys_test.exs
....

Finished in 0.06 seconds
4 tests, 0 failures
```

Nice. It all works perfectly. Our new tests are nice and tidy, just like we want them. We've done pretty well with our generic information system, but there's still some supporting Wolfram code that we'd like to test. Since that code has an external interface, it's better to test that part in isolation.

Isolating Wolfram

We'd like to keep our Wolfram tests isolated, but we have a problem. Our code makes an HTTP request to the WolframAlpha API, which isn't something we want to perform within our test suite. You might be thinking, "Let's write a bunch of mocks!"

Within the Elixir community, we want to avoid mocking whenever possible. Most mocking libraries, including dynamic stubbing libraries, end up changing global behavior—for example, by replacing a function in the HTTP client library to return some particular result. *These function replacements are global*, so a change in one place would change all code running at the same time. That means *tests written in this way can no longer run concurrently*. These kinds of strategies can snowball, requiring more and more mocking until the dependencies among components are completely hidden.

The better strategy is to identify code that's difficult to test live, and to build a configurable, replaceable testing implementation rather than a dynamic mock. We'll make our HTTP service pluggable. Our development and production code will use our simple :httpc client, and our testing code can instead use a stub that we'll call as part of our tests. Let's update our Wolfram backend to accept an HTTP client from the application configuration, or a default of :httpc. Update rumbl_umbrella/apps/info_sys/lib/info_sys/wolfram.ex with this code:

```
testing_otp/listings/rumbl_umbrella/apps/info_sys/lib/info_sys/wolfram.ex
Line 1  @http Application.get_env(:info_sys, :wolfram)[:http_client] || :httpc
     2  defp fetch_xml(query) do
     3    {:ok, {_, _, body}} = @http.request(String.to_charlist(url(query)))
     4
     5    body
     6  end
```

We have made only a minor change to this file. First, we look up an :http_client module from our mix configuration and default it to the :httpc module. We bake that module into an @http module attribute at compile time for speedy runtime use. Next, we replace our :httpc.request call with an @http.request invocation.

The result is simple and elegant. We simply call the function as before, using our environment's HTTP client instead of hardcoding the HTTP client. This way, our behavior remains unchanged from before, but we can now stub our HTTP client as desired.

Now let's update our test configuration to use our stubbed client. Update the config/test.exs file at the umbrella root, like this:

```
testing_otp/listings/rumbl_umbrella/config/test.exs
config :info_sys, :wolfram,
  app_id: "1234",
  http_client: InfoSys.Test.HTTPClient
```

This bit of configuration sets two configuration keys for Wolfram. One key is the as-yet unwritten module for our test backend. The other is a fake configuration key that we can replace if we need to do some direct testing—for example, as we're creating data for our stub.

Now on to the tests. To test our stubbed WolframAlpha API results, we need an example XML payload. Wolfram conveniently includes an API explorer[1] that accepts a search query and displays the XML response. We've grabbed a result for you for a query of "1 + 1". Keep in mind that this file is incomplete. You will need to use the Wolfram service to build your own or copy our version from the sample code for our book. Either way, place the entire XML response into a new rumbl_umbrella/apps/info_sys/test/fixtures/ directory and save it as wolfram.xml:

```
<?xml version='1.0' encoding='UTF-8'?>
<queryresult success='true'
    error='false'
    numpods='6'
    ...
```

---

1.   http://products.wolframalpha.com/api/explorer.html

With our fixture in place, now we need a stubbed HTTP client, one that returns fake XML results using our fixture. Create a new rumbl_umbrella/apps/info_sys/test/backends/ directory and add the following module to a new rumbl_umbrella/apps/info_sys/test/backends/http_client.exs file:

```
testing_otp/listings/rumbl_umbrella/apps/info_sys/test/backends/http_client.exs
defmodule InfoSys.Test.HTTPClient do
  @wolfram_xml File.read!("test/fixtures/wolfram.xml")
  def request(url) do
    url = to_string(url)
    cond do
      String.contains?(url, "1+%2B+1") -> {:ok, {[], [], @wolfram_xml}}
      true -> {:ok, {[], [], "<queryresult></queryresult>"}}
    end
  end
end
```

We define an InfoSys.Test.HTTPClient module that stubs our request function and returns fake Wolfram results. We cheat as we did before. We check the fetched url for the URI-encoded "1 + 1" string. If it matches, we simply return the XML contents of our wolfram.xml fixture. For any other case, we return a fake request for empty XML results.

Our goal isn't to test the Wolfram service, but make sure we can parse the data Wolfram provides. This code elegantly lets us write tests at any time that return a result. To confirm our HTTPClient module is loaded before our tests, add the following line to the top of your rumbl_umbrella/apps/info_sys/test/test_helper.exs:

```
testing_otp/listings/rumbl_umbrella/apps/info_sys/test/test_helper.exs
Code.require_file "../../info_sys/test/backends/http_client.exs", __DIR__
ExUnit.start()
```

With our HTTP client in place, create a new rumbl_umbrella/apps/info_sys/test/backends/wolfram_test.exs file with the following contents:

```
testing_otp/listings/rumbl_umbrella/apps/info_sys/test/backends/wolfram_test.exs
defmodule InfoSys.Backends.WolframTest do
  use ExUnit.Case, async: true

  test "makes request, reports results, then terminates" do
    actual = hd InfoSys.compute("1 + 1", [])
    assert actual.text == "2"
  end

  test "no query results reports an empty list" do
    assert InfoSys.compute("none", [])
  end
end
```

Since we've put in the hard work for testing the cache and generic InfoSys this test will be light, and that's exactly how we want tests that must consider external interfaces. Using our stubbed HTTP client, we add test cases to handle requests with and without results.

Now let's run the test:

```
$ mix test
..

Finished in 0.2 seconds (0.1s on load, 0.09s on tests)
5 tests, 0 failures
```

And they pass. Since we're handling the rest of the edge cases in our base info_sys tests, that should wrap up the Wolfram tests!

 José says:
At What Level Should We Apply Our Stubs/Mocks?

For the WolframAlpha API case, we chose to create a stub that replaces the :httpc module. However, you might not be comfortable with skipping the whole HTTP stack during the test. You'll have to decide the best place to stub the HTTP layer. No single strategy works for every case. It depends on your team's confidence and the code being tested. For example, if the communication with the endpoint requires passing headers and handling different responses, you might want to make sure that all of those parameters are sent correctly.

One possible solution is the Bypass[a] project. Bypass allows us to create a mock HTTP server that our code can access during tests without resorting to dynamic mocking techniques that introduce global changes and complicate the testing stack.

---

a.   https://github.com/PSPDFKit-labs/bypass

Our tests are all green, and they'll be consistently green because we make sure that our measurements await the completion of our tests.

You may have noticed that these tests are more involved than the typical single-process tests you might be used to. But by using the specific helpers that ExUnit provides and thinking through possible outcomes and orderings, you'll quickly get the hang of writing tests that aren't too much more difficult than synchronous ones. When you're done, you'll have one major advantage. Your tests will run concurrently, meaning they'll finish much more quickly than their synchronous counterparts.

With our Wolfram backend covered, it's time to move on to the last part of our application: the channels. We're ready to use the testing tools from Phoenix.ChannelTest to set up your tests and finish out the rest of our tests.

Adding Tests to Channels

We started this chapter by testing our information system, including unit-testing our supporting code for the Wolfram backend. Now it's time to test our channels code. Remember that underneath, channels are also OTP servers. Phoenix includes the Phoenix.ChannelTest module, which will simplify your testing experience. With it, you can make several types of common assertions. For example, you can assert that your application pushes messages to a client, replies to a message, or sends broadcasts. Let's look at some code.

The rumbl_umbrella/apps/rumbl_web/test/support/channel_case.ex is a file that was generated by Mix when we generated the rumbl application. You've already seen a couple of similar test cases with data_case and conn_case in Chapter 8, Testing MVC, on page 145.

Let's take a deeper look at how those files work. Crack it open now:

```
testing_otp/rumbl_umbrella/apps/rumbl_web/test/support/channel_case.ex
defmodule RumblWeb.ChannelCase do
  @moduledoc """
  This module defines the test case to be used by
  channel tests.

  Such tests rely on `Phoenix.ChannelTest` and also
  import other functionality to make it easier
  to build common data structures and query the data layer.

  Finally, if the test case interacts with the database,
  it cannot be async. For this reason, every test runs
  inside a transaction which is reset at the beginning
  of the test unless the test case is marked as async.
  """

  use ExUnit.CaseTemplate

  using do
    quote do
      # Import conveniences for testing with channels
      use Phoenix.ChannelTest

      # The default endpoint for testing
      @endpoint RumblWeb.Endpoint
    end
  end
```

```
setup tags do
  :ok = Ecto.Adapters.SQL.Sandbox.checkout(Rumbl.Repo)

  unless tags[:async] do
    Ecto.Adapters.SQL.Sandbox.mode(Rumbl.Repo, {:shared, self()})
  end

  :ok
  end
end
```

Knowing what's happening here in basic broad strokes is enough. First you see use ExUnit.CaseTemplate, which establishes this file as a test case. Next is a using block to start an inline macro, and a quote to specify the template for the code that we want to inject. The use Phoenix.ChannelTest statement establishes Phoenix.ChannelTest as the foundation for our test file. Then, we do a few imports and aliases for convenience, and so on.

The result is a file that prepares your tests for the features you're most likely to use in your channel tests. Our application has just one channel: the VideoChannel, which supports features like real-time annotations and integration with our InfoSys layer. All of our tests go through a single endpoint.

Before we test the VideoChannel, let's start where the channel process begins by testing the UserSocket module.

Authenticating a Test Socket

Most of our channels code relies on an authenticated user. We'll start our tests with the socket authentication. Let's do that now.

Create a rumbl_umbrella/apps/rumbl_web/test/channels/user_socket_test.exs file containing:

```
testing_otp/listings/rumbl_umbrella/apps/rumbl_web/test/rumbl_web/channels/user_socket_test.exs
Line 1  defmodule RumblWeb.Channels.UserSocketTest do
   -      use RumblWeb.ChannelCase, async: true
   -      alias RumblWeb.UserSocket
   -
   5      test "socket authentication with valid token" do
   -        token = Phoenix.Token.sign(@endpoint, "user socket", "123")
   -
   -        assert {:ok, socket} = connect(UserSocket, %{"token" => token})
   -        assert socket.assigns.user_id == "123"
  10      end
   -
   -      test "socket authentication with invalid token" do
   -        assert :error = connect(UserSocket, %{"token" => "1313"})
   -        assert :error = connect(UserSocket, %{})
  15      end
   -    end
```

On line 5, we make sure that a user with a valid token can open a new socket connection. The test is pretty simple. We generate a valid token, use the connect helper to simulate a UserSocket connection, and ensure that the connection succeeds. That's not enough. We also make sure that the socket's user_id is placed into the socket. With the happy path tested, we can move on to the negative condition.

On line 12, we test the opposite case. We first try to log in with a nonexistent token. Next, we test a simple edge condition, attempting to connect with no token at all. Since these tests don't require side effects such as database calls, they can run independently and concurrently. In the use line, we set :async to true, and we can feel a little happier inside. Our tiny test saves milliseconds, but when we aggregate thousands of tests, we'll be saving full minutes or more. Thcsc tiny savings can add up to hours every day.

We can see the finish line. It's finally time to test our video channel.

Communicating with a Test Channel

Let's see how easy it is to test our VideoChannel features. Our plan is simple. We're going to set up some data to share across our tests and then sign the user in within our setup block. Then, we can write some independent tests against that live connection.

First we'll need a few helper functions to make it easicr to create users and videos. Make the file test/support/test_helpers.ex look like this:

```
testing_otp/listings/rumbl_umbrella/apps/rumbl_web/test/support/test_helpers.ex
defmodule RumblWeb.TestHelpers do

  defp default_user() do
    %{
      name: "Some User",
      username: "user#{System.unique_integer([:positive])}",
      password: "supersecret"
    }
  end

  def insert_user(attrs \\ %{}) do
    {:ok, user} =
      attrs
      |> Enum.into(default_user())
      |> Rumbl.Accounts.register_user

    user
  end
```

The first part creates users. For convenience, we start with a default user and then merge in keywords so a user can specify as many or few users as they want. The context work we did earlier makes this easy. Next, we need to do the same for videos.

```
testing_otp/listings/rumbl_umbrella/apps/rumbl_web/test/support/test_helpers.ex
defp default_video() do
  %{
    url: "test@example.com",
    description: "a video",
    body: "body"
  }
end

def insert_video(user, attrs \\ %{}) do
  video_fields = Enum.into(attrs, default_video())
  {:ok, video} = Rumbl.Multimedia.create_video(user, video_fields)
  video
end
```

Easy enough. We do the same thing. We start by creating a default video, then merge in defaults, create a video, pattern match it out and finally return the video to the user. Now all that remains is a quick helper to log a user in:

```
testing_otp/listings/rumbl_umbrella/apps/rumbl_web/test/support/test_helpers.ex
  def login(%{conn: conn, login_as: username}) do
    user = insert_user(username: username)
    {Plug.Conn.assign(conn, :current_user, user), user}
  end
  def login(%{conn: conn}), do: {conn, :logged_out}
end
```

We insert a user and then merge the user into the conn. If there's no user, we just log the user out. Now we can put these functions to use.

Create a new rumbl_umbrella/apps/rumbl_web/test/channels/video_channel_test.exs file that looks like this:

```
testing_otp/listings/rumbl_umbrella/apps/rumbl_web/test/rumbl_web/channels/video_channel_test.exs
Line 1  defmodule RumblWeb.Channels.VideoChannelTest do
   -      use RumblWeb.ChannelCase
   -      import RumblWeb.TestHelpers
   -
   5      setup do
   -        user = insert_user(name: "Gary")
   -        video = insert_video(user, title: "Testing")
   -        token = Phoenix.Token.sign(@endpoint, "user socket", user.id)
   -        {:ok, socket} = connect(RumblWeb.UserSocket, %{"token" => token})
  10
   -        {:ok, socket: socket, user: user, video: video}
   -      end
```

```
   test "join replies with video annotations",
15       %{socket: socket, video: vid, user: user} do
     for body <- ~w(one two) do
       Rumbl.Multimedia.annotate_video(user, vid.id, %{body: body, at: 0})
     end
     {:ok, reply, socket} = subscribe_and_join(socket, "videos:#{vid.id}", %{})
20
     assert socket.assigns.video_id == vid.id
     assert %{annotations: [%{body: "one"}, %{body: "two"}]} = reply
   end
 end
```

On line 5, we add a setup block to prepare our tests with a user and video. Next, we use connect to start a simulated socket connection. We can use that connection for each of our tests. We put the user, the video, and the connected socket into our test context, one that we'll be able to match for individual tests.

Note we haven't passed the async: true flag to the ChannelCase as we did to other cases. Here's why. In Ecto's Sandbox mode, every process has its own connection. That's not a problem in applications that limit database access to a single process. The test case starts a transaction, modifies the database, asserts results and then rolls back the transaction when the test completes.

This application is different. It has two or more processes talking to the database at the same time, in the same test. Because processes might need to acces *the same data*, the only way for them to share data in the sandbox mode is to share the same connection. To maintain isolation for each test, we can't run tests concurrently. That means we can't set async. It's not ideal, but since the rest of the tests run in async mode, we won't fret too much.

In the test, the function head matches the connected socket and video, so our test can take advantage of the setup work we've done. We then proceed to create two annotations that we expect to be sent as a reply on join. We call the subscribe_and_join test helper to attempt to join the channel responsible for the "videos:#{vid.id}" topic. If the join is successful, this helper function returns {:ok, reply, socket}. An unsuccessful join fails the match and forces an error for our test. Then we assert the socket has a user_id assigned and the join reply contains the previously creatrd annotations.

Let's try this much:

```
$ mix test test/rumbl_web/channels/video_channel_test.exs
...

Finished in 0.2 seconds (0.1s on load, 0.09s on tests)
3 tests, 0 failures
```

No problem! Our tests pass, and we know the following:

- Our user can successfully connect.
- Our user successfully joined a topic.
- The topic is the correct one.
- The reply has all of the annotations in the video.

That's a good start. Now that we've tested that we can join the VideoChannel, we can test a conversation with the client. Let's test the incoming new_annotation event. We want to simulate the creation of a new annotation, and we want to make sure we correctly augment the state in the socket.

Code the new test in rumbl_umbrella/apps/rumbl_web/test/channels/video_channel_test.exs, like this:

```
testing_otp/listings/rumbl_umbrella/apps/rumbl_ ... umbl_web/channels/video_channel_test.change1.exs
test "inserting new annotations", %{socket: socket, video: vid} do
  {:ok, _, socket} = subscribe_and_join(socket, "videos:#{vid.id}", %{})
  ref = push socket, "new_annotation", %{body: "the body", at: 0}
  assert_reply ref, :ok, %{}
  assert_broadcast "new_annotation", %{}
end
```

As before, our function head matches the video and socket we created in setup. Like last time, we subscribe and join with our helper. This time, we use the push helper function to push a new event to the channel. We use assert_reply to make sure we get a :ok response. We could also pass in additional key/value pairs to assert on specific parts of the reply, but we don't need to do so in this case, so we pass an empty map.

Finally, we use the assert_broadcast function to make sure that our annotation were broadcast to subscribers. The assert_reply and assert_broadcast functions are provided by Phoenix and built on top of the assert_receive function that we used in the previous section.

Notice how our test process works as a client of the channel, because we were able to establish a test connection using subscribe_and_join. In the same way, the browser is a channel client. That's why we can assert that we've received some particular reply. The test process also subscribes to the same topic as its channel, explaining why we can assert that something was broadcast.

Let's test the integration with our information system. Crack your test open once again, and add this test to the end:

testing_otp/listings/rumbl_umbrella/apps/rumbl_ ... umbl_web/channels/video_channel_test.change1.exs

```
test "new annotations triggers InfoSys", %{socket: socket, video: vid} do
  insert_user(
    username: "wolfram",
    password: "supersecret"
  )

  {:ok, _, socket} = subscribe_and_join(socket, "videos:#{vid.id}", %{})
  ref = push socket, "new_annotation", %{body: "1 + 1", at: 123}
  assert_reply ref, :ok, %{}
  assert_broadcast "new_annotation", %{body: "1 + 1", at: 123}
  assert_broadcast "new_annotation", %{body: "2", at: 123}
end
```

We first need to insert the Wolfram user into the database because our compute_additional_info needs to have a user named wolfram to post the additional info.

Then our function head picks off the things our test needs, just as we did in the previous test. We subscribe and join, push a new annotation, and check the response. This time, use the special stubbed "1 + 1" query to return fake answers. We verify that the original response and the InfoSys annotation are both broadcast successfully.

Let's switch to the top-level directory and try our tests.

```
$ → cd ../..
$ mix test
==> rumbl_web
Compiling 1 file (.ex)
==> info_sys
..........

Finished in 0.2 seconds
10 tests, 0 failures

Randomized with seed 292879
==> rumbl

................

Finished in 0.1 seconds
17 tests, 0 failures

Randomized with seed 292879
==> rumbl_web

......................

Finished in 0.1 seconds
24 tests, 0 failures

Randomized with seed 292879
```

Everything passes!

As you can see, Phoenix provides plenty of support for testing your channels code. These testing features are first-class features for our ecosystem. It's a good time to see how far we've come.

Wrapping Up

Amazingly, this is the last chapter dealing with our Rumbl application! In this chapter, we tested the most sophisticated features in our entire application stack. You probably noticed that the functional nature of Phoenix made testing the application much easier than you might have expected. Our tests run quickly, and they're compact, thanks to the helpers that abstract concepts like assert_reply, assert_broadcast, and assert_receive. Here's what we accomplished:

- We tested our OTP layer for our InfoSys OTP application.

- We split out an independent caching layer for performance.

- We built a specific backend rather than a dynamic stub or mock to keep our tests isolated, as our unit and integration tests should be.

- We tested our sockets authentication code.

- We used the Phoenix testing support to test our channels.

By no means is this testing story complete. We didn't cover user acceptance testing. Nor did we cover performance testing. We did accomplish quite a bit in a short time. These kinds of concurrent, interactive applications can be notoriously difficult to test.

In the next chapter, we'll wrap up. We'll cover some features that didn't make it into our application such as internationalization. We will also cover the newest Phoenix library, LiveView, and learn how you can build whole pages without MVC-style controllers or JavaScript. Then, we'll take a brief look at what's next for the Phoenix team.

We're not quite done. Let's go!

## CHAPTER 14

What's Next?

We hope you've enjoyed reading this book as much as we've enjoyed putting it together for you. The Phoenix story is an incredible one, and the telling is nowhere near done. If you've coded along with us, you should have a better handle on how the bits of your code fit together to form interactive, scalable, reliable applications. Let's review what we've done so far.

First, we built a toy application so you could learn where to put each piece of code. You worked with the Phoenix router. You learned how connections flowed through plugs to controllers and views. You built a trivial controller and a simple view that rendered a template.

Next, we started working on our rumbl application, one that you used throughout the rest of the book. We created a controller, and rather than integrating a full database right away, we defined the context as the API to our business domain so we could focus on the controller. We then created a couple of actions, and some views and templates to render our results.

With that out of the way, we dove into Ecto to integrate our context with a full database-backed repository. Initially, we focused on the initial schema for users. We built a migration and a changeset to help us manage change. In the next few chapters, we improved our context to support iterations on the frontend. We created a plug to help integrate authentication in our application, and then we built some more sophisticated schemas and contexts with relationships. Then, we tested the work we'd done so far.

Next, we moved into Part II. We built a channel to handle the real-time features of our application. We learned that the Phoenix Channels allows us to build applications with state, but without the performance penalties you generally see with similar frameworks. We used these features to deliver real-time features, allowing users to comment on a playing video in real time. We worked on the server in Elixir and paired it with an ES6 JavaScript client. We used channels to let users post messages, and then broadcast those messages to all other interested users. Then, we extended our authentication system, adopting token-based authentication. We also built in Channel Presence to detect when users come and go.

We then started to get more familiar with the underlying principles of building applications in Elixir and converted our rumbl app into an umbrella project. Along the way, we used Observer to get a full picture of what was happening with our application in real time. The umbrella project let us isolate the development and testing of individual applications.

Once our umbrella project was ready, we crafted an information system service as a brand new application. We learned how to add state to our applications with concurrency, message passing, and recursive functions. We also learned to use supervisors to keep our system reliable and take action when things break.

We tried to build a broad and exciting application, but it was impossible to cover all of the useful projects happening in the language, the Phoenix project, or the community. Here are some of the things you can explore.

Other Interesting Features

In any successful development ecosystem, a tension always exists between currency and stability. We've tried to walk as closely to currency as we could without stepping over. Still, exciting things are happening, many of which weren't ready to include in this text. These are some exciting features you may want to use in your next project.

Supporting Internationalization with Gettext

In version v1.1, Phoenix added integration with Gettext, an internationalization (i18n) and localization (l10n) system commonly used for writing multilingual programs. Gettext can automatically extract translations from your source code, reducing the burden on the developer. Furthermore, since the Gettext standard is used by so many communities, you can take advantage of a rich set of tooling for both developers and translators.

When you ran mix phx.new rumbl, Phoenix generated a RumblWeb.Gettext module at lib/rumbl_web/gettext.ex. You can see it in use in the lib/rumbl_web/views/error_helpers.ex file, used to translate the error messages coming from Ecto. Since programmers often organize translations into namespaces called domains, Phoenix places Ecto messages in the errors domain by default.

The translations for different languages are in the priv/gettext directory. There you'll find a default template for Ecto messages called errors.pot. A translation for each language is placed in directories such as priv/gettext/en/LC_MESSAGES.

To learn more about the integration between Phoenix and Gettext, we recommend this fantastic article by Rebecca Skinner entitled "Internationalization using Gettext in the Phoenix framework."[1] For general information, check out the Gettext documentation.[2]

Next, we'll move from internationalization to intercept and handle, a couple of functions that make it easier to manage channel messages.

Intercepting on Phoenix Channels

When you broadcast a message, Phoenix sends it to the Publish and Subscribe (PubSub) system, which then broadcasts it directly to all user sockets. We call this approach *fastlaning* because it completely bypasses the channel, allowing us to encode the message once. Phoenix Channels also provide a feature called intercept, which allows channels to intercept a broadcast message before it's sent to the user.

For example, maybe we'd like to let the video's creator edit all of its annotations. For such a feature, we could append an is_editable field to the annotation map when we broadcast it so the frontend can adapt accordingly. Using intercept, we could build this feature like this:

```
intercept ["new_annotation"]

# For every new_annotation broadcast,
# append an is_editable value for client metadata.
def handle_out("new_annotation", msg, socket) do
  %{video: video, user_id: user_id} = socket.assigns
  push socket, "new_annotation",
      Map.merge(msg, %{is_editable: video.user_id == user_id})
  {:noreply, socket}
end
```

For each event that we specify in intercept, we must define a handle_out clause to handle the intercepted event. You can also intercept an event and choose not to push it at all, in case you want to make sure that some clients don't receive specific events.

intercept is a nice feature, but you need to be careful. Imagine that you have 10,000 users watching a video at the same time. Instead of using intercept,

---

1. http://sevenseacat.net/2015/12/20/i18n-in-phoenix-apps.html
2. http://hexdocs.pm/gettext

you could write a few extra lines of code to include a :video_user_id field in the message, letting the client decide whether the message is editable. For that implementation, Phoenix would encode the broadcast once and send the message to all sockets.

With the intercept implementation, Phoenix would send the message to the first 10,000 channel processes, one for each client. While processing the intercept, each channel would independently modify the intercepted message and push it to the socket to be encoded and sent. The cost of intercept is 10,000 extra messages, one per channel, as well as encoding those messages 9,999 times—again, once per channel—compared to the one-time encoding of the implementation without intercept. For those reasons, we recommend using intercept with care.

On the other hand, intercept can be tremendously useful when we're evolving code. Imagine building a new version of the annotations feature in the future, with new frontend and backend code, including a different payload when new annotations are broadcast. However, imagine that you also have old clients that can take a while to migrate. You could use the new annotation-broadcast format throughout the new code and use intercept to retrofit the new_annotation broadcast into the old one. For these cases, intercept would be an ideal solution. You'd pay a temporary performance price to make your code easier to build and understand.

For more information on intercept and handle, check the Phoenix documentation on channels.[3] Next, we'll move on to live code reload.

Understanding Phoenix Live Reload

One of the features we used throughout the entire book was Phoenix Live Reload, which allows us to see changes propagated to the browser as soon as we save them to the filesystem. Phoenix Live Reload is composed of:

- A dependency called file_system that watches the filesystem for changes

- A channel that receives events from the file_system application and converts them into broadcasts

- A plug that injects the live-reload iframe on every request and serves the iframe content for web requests

There isn't much to Live Reload, and that's exactly why we recommend that you to study its source code to learn more about how simple it is to extend

---

3.   http://hexdocs.pm/phoenix/Phoenix.Channel.html

Phoenix. If the feature is something you might want to customize, consider reading more or even following the project. You can find the source code in our Phoenix Live Reload GitHub project.[4]

While we're on the subject of customization, let's see how you might customize the Phoenix PubSub adapter.

Phoenix PubSub Adapter

By default, Phoenix PubSub uses distributed Erlang to ensure that broadcasts work across multiple nodes. This requires all machines to be connected together according to the Erlang Distribution Protocol. Setting up distributed Erlang is straightforward, but it might not be directly supported in some deployment platforms.

You needn't worry, though. Phoenix PubSub is extensible—it supports multiple adapters. One is the Redis adapter,[5] maintained by the Phoenix team, which empowers the PubSub system by using Redis as its message-distribution mechanism. You can use one of these options or even write your own.

You've seen how to customize Phoenix messaging on the server side. Some interesting things are happening on the client side too.

Phoenix Clients for Other Platforms

In our channels chapter, you saw how we customized the Phoenix transport to work with our ES6 code. Phoenix Channels support the nearly ubiquitous JavaScript and also a wide range of other clients and platforms, including C#, Java, Objective-C, and Swift.[6]

All these clients use WebSockets, but don't forget that Phoenix Channels are transport agnostic. If you have special requirements, as in embedded software or working on special platforms, you can always use a custom protocol to talk to Phoenix.

The Phoenix project has surpassed our expectations in its first few years, but we're even more excited about what's coming next. In the next few sections, we offer a preview, listing those we expect the soonest first. Be careful, though. We offer no guarantees!

By far the most anticipated change is Phoenix Liveview. Let's take a peek.

---

4.   http://github.com/phoenixframework/phoenix_live_reload

5.   https://github.com/phoenixframework/phoenix_pubsub_redis

6.   https://github.com/livehelpnow/CSharpPhoenixClient, https://github.com/eoinsha/JavaPhoenixChannels, https://github.com/livehelpnow/ObjCPhoenixClient, and https://github.com/davidstump/SwiftPhoenixClient.

Phoenix LiveView

As the base infrastructure for channels matures, we're seeing an acceleration of higher level libraries that take advantage of them. LiveView is the perfect example. In essence, it's a library for building interactive, rich applications, that are bi-directional. That much is not new. Throughout the second half of this book, we've done very much the same thing with channels.

Here's the best part, though. What if you could do the same thing without writing custom JavaScript? In this short section, we'll walk you through how you can do exactly that. Don't get us wrong. We love working with the Phoenix toolchain including JavaScript, but juggling fewer frameworks means more brainpower is available to attack the business problem.

Let's look at how it all works. Conceptually, LiveView:

- Represents a web page as a function over web state
- Establishes messages and callbacks to change that state
- Allows browser events such as mouse clicks, form submits, and key presses to send events

Though it's a young library, LiveView users are already pushing the boundaries of what can be done without writing JavaScript. It is excellent for a wide variety of scenarios from form validation and autocompletion to handling communication triggered by links and keystrokes. We're not going to show you an exhaustive list of LiveView use cases, but we'd love to show you how some of the most important ones work.

To show the interplay of routes and events, we'll walk you through a couple of simple examples and then show progressively more complex scenarios.

We'll start with a static page and progressively move to more advanced examples. So that we can start with a foundation that's going to stay up to date, we'll walk you through the Phoenix LiveView Example.[7]

Establishing a Static LiveView

To get things started, let's build our own LiveView. For the simplest of examples, all of our code can live in two places: the router and the live view. First, let's start with the router.

---

7. https://github.com/chrismccord/phoenix_live_view_example

We've set up LiveView according to the project instructions. It takes about fifteen minutes or so the first few times. Once we're done, we can add routes to router.ex, like this:

```
import Phoenix.LiveView.Router

...

live "/welcome", WelcomeLive
```

We import the LiveView router code and use one of the imports, the live function, to create a new route that points the /welcome route to a module holding a live view. Now we're ready to create the live view. We'll put it in lib/demo_web/live/welcome_live.ex, and make it look like this:

```
defmodule DemoWeb.WelcomeLive do
  use Phoenix.LiveView

  def render(assigns) do
    ~L"""
    <div>
      <h2>Welcome to LiveView, from Chris, José and Bruce</h2>
    </div>
    """
  end

  def mount(_session, socket) do
    {:ok, socket}
  end
end
```

In every case, render/1 is a pure function that takes socket.assigns as its lone argument. This structure is functional programming at its finest. Because every LiveView page is a simple pure function, debugging is much easier than you might find in alternatives. We'll unlock some complexity over time. For now, point your browser to our route, http://localhost:4000/welcome. You'll see the message "Welcome to LiveView, from Chris, José and Bruce."

Let's shed some light on what's happening after Phoenix calls the route. LiveView is a Phoenix Channels implementation so the live view for each end user will run in its own process. When router.ex has a live route, it will call the mount/2 function on that live view. The mount function's job is to establish the initial state of the live view. Dutifully, our function returns an :ok tuple with an empty socket.

That's not all, though. This function is analogous to an init function in an OTP GenServer. When that's done, LiveView will render the initial view. We'll simply render the HTML directly inline using the ~L""" sigil. As you might expect, this sigil does everything necessary to render a LiveView.

What we've built is not a one-time render. It actually starts a process and will loop over messages, calling render/1 each time there's a new event.

Since pure HTML is not too interesting, let's spice things up a little bit. Let's set some state in the socket within our mount, like this:

```
defmodule DemoWeb.WelcomeLive do
  use Phoenix.LiveView

  def render(assigns) do
    ~L"""
    <div>
      <h2><%= @salutation %></h2>
    </div>
    """
  end

  def mount(_session, socket) do
    salutation = "Welcome to LiveView, from the Programming Phoenix team!"
    {:ok, assign(socket, salutation: salutation)}
  end
end
```

We moved the changing text to the socket, and added a substitution to the LiveView. Now, you can get a better look at how we'll encorporate changing state in the LiveView. We can simply define fields in socket.assigns, and access those directly to do substitutions in LiveView. Whenever that state changes, Phoenix LiveView will use channels to make sure that the changes (and only the changes) to our state make it down to the client.

So the initial lifecycle for a LiveView before we consider events looks like this:

```
live(url, LiveView)
|> mount
|> render
```

You've already seen the basics so it's time to add some interaction. Let's take a look at an example with some interaction, a clock.

Processing Events in a Clock

Now that you know how to handle an inbound route with the live macro, let's go to the ClockLive view within the Phoenix LiveView example project for help with the next example. We'll look at a clock. To keep things simple, we'll strip out a few of the bells and whistles.

In this case, we'll use the Erlang :timer module to send periodic messages to the end user's live view process. Here's how it works.

First, establish a route in lib/demo_web/router.ex, like this:

```
live "/clock", ClockLive
```

We create a route that will go to our live view. Now, let's take a look at a live view. For reference, if you are looking at the example, the file is in lib/demo_web/live/clock_live.ex. It won't look exactly like this one, but it will be close:

```
defmodule DemoWeb.ClockLive do
  use Phoenix.LiveView
  import Calendar.Strftime

  def render(assigns) do
    ~L"""
    <div>
      <h2>It's <%= strftime!(@date, "%r") %></h2>
    </div>
    """
  end
```

That's easy enough. We render a view, with just a little bit of dynamic data, a @date field in assigns. We'll initialize that value when we mount, and also trigger a periodic message to our process like this:

```
def mount(_session, socket) do
  if connected?(socket), do: :timer.send_interval(1000, self(), :tick)

  {:ok, put_date(socket)}
end
defp put_date(socket) do
  assign(socket, date: :calendar.local_time())
end
```

In the mount function, we call :timer.send_interval to send a simple :tick message every 1000 milliseconds to the self() PID, the id for our process. Then, we call a private function called put_date that uses assign to initialize the @date field in socket.assigns to the current date and time,so LiveView can render it after we mount.

We still have one more job to do. We need to handle the :tick message, like this:

```
  def handle_info(:tick, socket) do
    {:noreply, put_date(socket)}
  end
end
```

Marvelous! Handling the :tick message is a simple handle_info. That's because under the hood, this LiveView is a GenServer! Straight process messages come in through handle_info.

The only thing we need to do is to call our existing put_date(socket) to update the socket with the current timestamp.

Browse on over to http://localhost:4000/clock and you'll see the counting date! Keep in mind that we didn't have to create any custom JavaScript. Phoenix is sending down only the parts of the page that need to change.

Let's see how LiveView handles incoming events from the web page. Let's build a simple counter.

Handling Links in a Counter

Let's say you had a web page and a few links on it for interacting with some server side content. We could build a Phoenix MVC application. We'd have to establish a separate route for each link and form. We'd then need to add in a controller, a view, and we'd need to render HTML, either with functions or via a template. We'd also possibly need some backend logic, fronted by a context.

Alternatively, we could build a channel and make all communication flow over a channel. We'd segregate all backend code in the context, just as we do for MVC apps. That's a drastic improvement in user experience, and the only cost is that we have to commit to working in two languages, JavaScript and Elixir. Still, we can do better.

With LiveView, for the simplest of scenarios, all of our code can live in two files, the live view and the route. Once we get to the point where we need to segregate code, we are still free to break backend code into a context, and frontend code into functions or templates. Let's take a look.

In lib/demo_web/router.ex, you'll see the familiar live route, like this:

```
live "/counter", CounterLive
```

Next, let's look at the live view. First, here's the counter code we're rendering from the example in lib/demo_web/live/counter.ex:

```
defmodule DemoWeb.CounterLive do
  use Phoenix.LiveView

  def render(assigns) do
    ~L"""
    <div>
      <h1>The count is: <%= @val %></h1>
      <button phx-click="boom" class="alert-danger">BOOM</button>
      <button phx-click="dec">-</button>
      <button phx-click="inc">+</button>
    </div>
    """
  end
```

This render function is starting to have some real meat on the bones. After the initial ceremony that defines the module and the use LiveView directive to announce our intention to use LiveView directives, we do the work to render our page. First we have a heading with our count, @val.

After the initial heading, we have three buttons. One calls an unsupported message called boom. The other two operate our counter. The only difference from pure HTML is that they support data attributes called phx-click. This attribute signals the JavaScript code on the client to send a Phoenix Channels message to the client!

You can already imagine what the rest of the app looks like. Here's the initial mount:

```
def mount(_session, socket) do
  {:ok, assign(socket, :val, 0)}
end
```

We must initialize every assigns field so our mount function establishes the initial value of our counter, a :val of 0. Then, we build the functions to handle our events and update the server, like this:

```
  def handle_event("inc", _, socket) do
    {:noreply, update(socket, :val, &(&1 + 1))}
  end

  def handle_event("dec", _, socket) do
    {:noreply, update(socket, :val, &(&1 - 1))}
  end
end
```

These are custom LiveView events, but they work just like messages. The channel process for a given user will get a handle_event message each time that user clicks on an element with a phx-click data attribute. In this case, we have events for inc and dec. They both work the same, so let's look at just the inc message.

We send a :noreply tuple, updating the :val field in socket with an anonymous function to increment a counter, and...

we're done! There's no additional route for each action, no custom JavaScript to parse the result, no work to determine which pieces of the page change and which stay the same. LiveView *handles it all.*

Typically, the handle_event will update the state in some way, but it doesn't have to. Let's take a look at a third use case, command-line completion.

Here's what the pipeline looks like for an arbitrary event:

```
handle_event(event, data, socket)
|> render
```

While we're here, open up your browser and navigate to the counter page. Increment the counter a couple of times and you'll see the count update. Notice that it's extremely snappy! It will usually remain so once you deploy it live.

Let's try one more thing. Remember, channels is built on OTP, and it wouldn't be an OTP demo without some kind of a crash. Click the boom button. We haven't implemented boom yet, so when you flip over to your Phoenix server tab, you'll see a stack trace like this one:

```
[error] GenServer #PID<0.568.0> terminating
** (FunctionClauseError) no function clause matching in
   DemoWeb.CounterLive.handle_event/3
   (demo) lib/demo_web/live/counter_live.ex:24:
      DemoWeb.CounterLive.handle_event("boom", "",
      %Phoenix.LiveView.Socket{assigns: %{val: 2},
      changed: nil, connected?: true, ...})
...
```

Since we're on OTP, our supervisor will start again! You'll see a brief reloading indicator. Then, you can go back to your browser to see the counter, restarted to zero. Click it a few times. It still works:

The count is: 3

Now that we can process links, we are ready to take the next step. Let's take an interactive use case for forms, autocomplete.

Implementing Autocomplete Forms

Command-line completion is typically a tedious use case that is a headache to implement but also tremendously useful for users. This is what it looks like with LiveView.

Rather than show you *all* of the example, let's look at the bits that do the most work.

First, here's the view:

```
def render(assigns) do
  ~L"""
  <form phx-change="suggest" phx-submit="search">
    <input type="text" name="q" value="<%= @query %>" list="matches"
           placeholder="Search..." <%= if @loading, do: "readonly" %>/>
```

As you might expect, the form is a pure HTML form. We tag the form with two attributes. phx-change triggers an event when anything on the form changes and phx-submit triggers an event whenever a user submits a form.

Note that we also introduce a @loading field so we can disable the text field when we're loading results.

Next, let's look at the real HTML work, the rendering of the results.

```
    <datalist id="matches">
      <%= for match <- @matches do %>
        <option value="<%= match %>"><%= match %></option>
      <% end %>
    </datalist>
    <%= if @result do %><pre><%= @result %></pre><% end %>
  </form>
  """
end
```

We present the results in two pieces: the @matches that we return on phx-change and the @result we return on phx-submit.

We use for to produce an option for each of the @matches. We then conditionally display a @result if one exists.

Here's the cool part. LiveView will only send down the parts of the page that need to change! If any typing triggers no change, the user's browser will not get an update command!

Here's the handle_event that processes the suggest message that we asked for with the phx-change data attribute:

```
def handle_event("suggest", %{"q" => query}, socket)
  when byte_size(query) <= 100 do

  {words, _} =
    System.cmd("grep", ["^#{query}.*", "-m", "5", "/usr/share/dict/words"])
  {:noreply, assign(socket, matches: String.split(words, "\n"))}
end
```

Note that this command is specific to Unix! This code simply calls an OS shell command to look for results in a system dictionary and sets the state based on the results.

Now, let's look at a form submit:

```
def handle_event("search", %{"q" => query}, socket)
    when byte_size(query) <= 100 do

  send(self(), {:search, query})
  {
    :noreply,
    assign( socket,
      query: query,
      result: "Searching...",
      loading: true,
      matches: [])
  }
end

def handle_info({:search, query}, socket) do
  ... do search ...
end
```

We send an asynchronous message to ourselves so that we can report back to the user while the system loads the results. As this application gets more robust, we can break out the search and autocomplete business logic into its own context.

If you'd like, you can open up the developer's tools for your browser. In Chrome, you can do so by inspecting an element on the page and then clicking on the network tab. Type a few characters and you'll see that LiveView is sending down only the precise parts of the page that change!

We've touched on a basic form submission. Let's take on a more complex problem, form validation.

Validating Forms

You have seen the main two LiveView events. phx-change fires on each form change and phx-submit fires on submit. Form validation is an especially tedious use case for most web applications, but they are tremendously useful to users.

When a user's head space can stay in one place, a live view, the problem gets much easier to solve. Once again, we'll go to the LiveView examples to find the user_live demonstration.

In this file, you'll find a more practical production code organization. In lib/demo/context, you'll find an accounts context much like the one we built for Rumbl. We'll use a few of these throughout the demo.

In lib/demo_web/live/user_live, you'll find live views for various use cases. We're going to focus on new.ex.

First, let's look at the mount function:

```
def mount(_session, socket) do
  {:ok, assign(socket, changeset: Accounts.change_user(%User{}))}
end
```

Notice that we're calling into our Accounts context to get a changeset for a User. Otherwise, the mount looks exactly like the other examples you've seen.

Next, let's look at the render. It may surprise you:

```
def render(assigns) do
  Phoenix.View.render(DemoWeb.UserView, "new.html", assigns)
end
```

For the first time in one of these examples, you see us render a template directly. We can also render other live views, but this one is similar to the simple template Phoenix generates for a new generated resource. It's a skinny wrapper that in turn renders a form with fields that look like this:

```
<%= f = form_for @changeset,
                 "#",
                 [phx_change: :validate, phx_submit: :save] %>
...
<%= label f, :username %>
<%= text_input f, :username %>
<%= error_tag f, :username %>
...
```

There are no surprises here. We simply add the data attributes for phx_change and phx_submit. The main thing to note for the rest of the form is that we have the error_tag fields that will show messages for a changeset when errors are present. Again, this code is not LiveView specific. These look exactly as they would for any other MVC style template.

Let's see what happens when a user submits a form:

```
def handle_event("save", %{"user" => user_params}, socket) do
  case Accounts.create_user(user_params) do
    {:ok, user} ->
      {:stop,
       socket
       |> put_flash(:info, "user created")
       |> redirect(to: Routes.live_path(socket, UserLive.Show, user))}

    {:error, %Ecto.Changeset{} = changeset} ->
      {:noreply, assign(socket, changeset: changeset)}
  end
end
```

This code is remarkably simple. We use our context to create the user. Based on the results, we either redirect directly to another live view, or we assign the :changeset with errors to our existing socket.

That's *all we need to do* to get full validation! If you type a partial email address, you'll get an error code until the email you type is valid, like this:

Create Your Account

Username

Email

incomplete@

must be a valid email address

Phone number

SAVE

We've just coded validation with a full interactive experience, but with less effort than we would put into an old school MVC application. The end result is snappy, highly interactive, and easy to code.

Learning More

We've just scratched the surface. LiveView can process other kinds of events too, including keystrokes. It's not built for games but it's fluid and efficient enough to build them easily. Let's briefly highlight some of the LiveView features you have not seen yet.

- Live views can render other live views like this: live_render(@socket, DemoWeb.ImageLive)

- When LiveView sends down new content for a page, it sends down *only changes since the last render*. If there are no changes, nothing is sent.

- LiveView can handle other kinds of events too, including keystroke events for both key up and key down.

- It works seamlessly with Phoenix PubSub. Therefore, you can push changes down to the page at any time, like we did with channels.

You can see how LiveView might reshape how we write many of the web applications that we develop every day. With it, you get three huge wins. You'll write much less code to solve a given problem; you won't have to become a JavaScript expert to build a nice interactive application; and you don't need to think about sending data between the client and the server. Removing those burdens will represent tremendous gains for the typical Phoenix developer.

Now that you've seen what's happening in LiveView, it's time to move on to one of the foundational libraries that makes Phoenix click, the PubSub layer.

Phoenix PubSub 2.0

Phoenix PubSub is the heart of real-time Phoenix. It powers both Phoenix Channels, via the `Phoenix.PubSub` module, and Channel Presence, via `Phoenix.Tracker`. Originally, Phoenix PubSub was written as part of Phoenix, and then extracted as its own project. Since then, many companies have contributed to the project, especially to ensure that its implementation scales to potentially millions of users.

For the upcoming Phoenix PubSub version, the Phoenix team is working mostly on simplifying the implementation, streamlining the code and making custom adapters easier to implement. On the Phoenix side of things, one important change is also coming: Phoenix will no longer start the Phoenix PubSub as part of the endpoint. Instead, you will need to explicitly start Phoenix PubSub in your supervision tree.

In other words, the supervision tree that Phoenix generates in lib/rumbl/application.ex will probably look something like this:

```
children = [
  # Start the Ecto repository
  Rumbl.Repo,
  # Start the PubSub system
  {Phoenix.PubSub, name: Rumbl.PubSub, adapter: Phoenix.PubSub.PG2},
  # Start the Endpoint when the application starts
  RumblWeb.Endpoint,
  # Starts a Worker by calling: Rumbl.Worker.start_link(arg)
  # {Rumbl.Worker, arg},
]
```

This change is particularly important for umbrella projects, which probably want to start Rumbl.PubSub as part of their non-web applications. (e.g. rumbl), while consuming from Rumbl.PubSub in the web application (e.g. rumbl_web). With this small tweak, you'll be able to do exactly that.

Phoenix and Telemetry Integration

As companies started using Phoenix production, there was a growing need to get data out of their Phoenix applications. Because the Erlang VM provides a huge amount of insight about the running system, developers had to reimplement the infrastructure that collects metrics over and over again, and write the integration with their preferred metrics platforms.

Other teams would choose Application Performance Monitoring tools, such as AppSignal,[8] Scout App,[9] New Relic,[10] and others. However, when it came to tracking app specific data, each of those tools would have distinct APIs which you would need to learn.

The Elixir community decided to tackle this challenge by implementing the Telemetry toolset. With Telemetry, developers have a unified API for dispatching metrics and instrumentation.[11] Telemetry also provides a mechanism for collecting built-in VM metrics[12] and a shared vocabulary for consuming and reporting those metrics.[13]

You might wonder what all of this means for Phoenix developers. In future Phoenix versions, we will probably have a new lib/rumbl_web/telemetry.ex file that outlines all the metrics you may want to extract from your system and how they should be reported. At the moment, we don't have all details in place, but the file may look like this:

```
Line 1  defmodule RumblWeb.Telemetry do
          use Supervisor
          import Telemetry.Metrics

     5    def start_link(arg) do
            Supervisor.start_link(__MODULE__, arg, name: __MODULE__)
          end

          def init(_arg) do
    10      children = [
              {:telemetry_poller,
               measurements: periodic_measurements(),
               period: 10_000},
              {Telemetry.StatsD, metrics: metrics()}
    15      ]
```

---

8. https://appsignal.com/elixir
9. https://scoutapm.com/elixir-monitoring
10. https://newrelic.com/
11. https://github.com/beam-telemetry/telemetry
12. https://github.com/beam-telemetry/telemetry_poller
13. https://github.com/beam-telemetry/telemetry_metrics

```
            Supervisor.init(children, strategy: :one_for_one)
          end

20     defp metrics do
          [
            # VM Metrics
            last_value("vm.memory.total", unit: :byte),
            last_value("vm.total_run_queue_lengths.total"),
25          last_value("vm.total_run_queue_lengths.cpu"),
            last_value("vm.total_run_queue_lengths.io"),

            last_value("rumbl.worker.memory", unit: :byte),
            last_value("rumbl.worker.message_queue_len"),
30
            # Database Time Metrics
            summary("rumbl.repo.query.total_time", unit: {:native, :millisecond}),
            summary("rumbl.repo.query.decode_time", unit: {:native, :millisecond}),
            summary("rumbl.repo.query.query_time", unit: {:native, :millisecond}),
35          summary("rumbl.repo.query.queue_time", unit: {:native, :millisecond}),

            # Phoenix Time Metrics
            summary("phoenix.endpoint.stop.duration",
                    unit: {:native, :millisecond}),
40          summary(
              "phoenix.route_dispatch.stop.duration",
              unit: {:native, :millisecond},
              tags: [:plug]
            )
45        ]
        end

        defp periodic_measurements do
          [
50          {:process_info,
            event: [:rumbl, :worker],
            name: Rumbl.Worker,
            keys: [:message_queue_len, :memory]}
          ]
55      end
      end
```

The new file starts by defining a supervisor. The supervisor has two children. The first is a :telemetry_poller child that executes a list of measurements every 10 seconds. The second is a StatsD[14] reporter on line 14. In this case, StatsD is just an example for a metric aggregation tool. You may add others or you may completely replace it. As the community and more companies rely on Telemetry, we expect integration with many other reporters in the future.

---

14. https://github.com/statsd/statsd

You can also see two private functions in the module. The supervisor will invoke them when starting the supervision children as part of the init function. In the metrics function, we list all of the metrics we want the reporter to publish. These include VM metrics, such as memory usage and the run queue length—which shows how busy the machine is while performing I/O and CPU tasks. Then we list time measurements for database queries and Phoenix operations.

Finally, in the periodic_measurements function, we define all periodic measurements for a process. For example, you can collect information such as memory usage and message queue length from any process in the system. Other custom measurements, such as ets_info, may be available in the future. This can be useful to track memory usage per table, such as the ETS table used by the InfoSys system.

Though the final API may change a little or a lot, the goal of integrating Phoenix and Telemetry remains clear: help developers, teams, and companies extract the maximum amount of insight possible from their production systems.

Good Luck!

That's a brief taste of what's happening in the Phoenix ecosystem right now. With the continuous growth in this space, we hope and fully expect the community to contribute ideas faster than we can write about them. We also expect that you, our readers, will use the ideas in this book to change the way the world thinks about what's possible.

We're excited to see what you do with Phoenix. Thanks for taking this journey with us!

Index

Thank you!

How did you enjoy this book? Please let us know. Take a moment and email us at support@pragprog.com with your feedback. Tell us your story and you could win free ebooks. Please use the subject line "Book Feedback."

Ready for your next great Pragmatic Bookshelf book? Come on over to https://pragprog.com and use the coupon code BUYANOTHER2019 to save 30% on your next ebook.

Void where prohibited, restricted, or otherwise unwelcome. Do not use ebooks near water. If rash persists, see a doctor. Doesn't apply to *The Pragmatic Programmer* ebook because it's older than the Pragmatic Bookshelf itself. Side effects may include increased knowledge and skill, increased marketability, and deep satisfaction. Increase dosage regularly.

And thank you for your continued support,

Andy Hunt, Publisher

Real-Time Phoenix

Give users the real-time experience they expect, by
using Elixir and Phoenix Channels to build applications
that instantly react to changes and reflect the application's true state. Learn how Elixir and Phoenix make
it easy and enjoyable to create real-time applications
that scale to a large number of users. Apply system
design and development best practices to create applications that are easy to maintain. Gain confidence by
learning how to break your applications before your
users do. Deploy applications with minimized resource
use and maximized performance.

Stephen Bussey
(250 pages) ISBN: 9781680507195. $45.95
https://pragprog.com/book/sbsockets

Designing Elixir Systems with OTP

You know how to code in Elixir; now learn to think in
it. Learn to design libraries with intelligent layers that
shape the right data structures, flow from one function
into the next, and present the right APIs. Embrace the
same OTP that's kept our telephone systems reliable
and fast for over 30 years. Move beyond understanding
the OTP functions to knowing what's happening under
the hood, and why that matters. Using that knowledge,
instinctively know how to design systems that deliver
fast and resilient services to your users, all with an
Elixir focus.

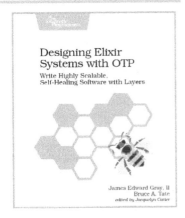

James Edward Gray, II and Bruce A. Tate
(220 pages) ISBN: 9781680506617. $41.95
https://pragprog.com/book/jgotp

Programming Ecto

Languages may come and go, but the relational database endures. Learn how to use Ecto, the premier database library for Elixir, to connect your Elixir and Phoenix apps to databases. Get a firm handle on Ecto fundamentals with a module-by-module tour of the critical parts of Ecto. Then move on to more advanced topics and advice on best practices with a series of recipes that provide clear, step-by-step instructions on scenarios commonly encountered by app developers. Co-authored by the creator of Ecto, this title provides all the essentials you need to use Ecto effectively.

Darin Wilson and Eric Meadows-Jönsson
(242 pages) ISBN: 9781680502824. $45.95
https://pragprog.com/book/wmecto

Property-Based Testing with PropEr, Erlang, and Elixir

Property-based testing helps you create better, more solid tests with little code. By using the PropEr framework in both Erlang and Elixir, this book teaches you how to automatically generate test cases, test stateful programs, and change how you design your software for more principled and reliable approaches. You will be able to better explore the problem space, validate the assumptions you make when coming up with program behavior, and expose unexpected weaknesses in your design. PropEr will even show you how to reproduce the bugs it found. With this book, you will be writing efficient property-based tests in no time.

Fred Hebert
(374 pages) ISBN: 9781680506211. $45.95
https://pragprog.com/book/fhproper

Craft GraphQL APIs in Elixir with Absinthe

Your domain is rich and interconnected, and your API should be too. Upgrade your web API to GraphQL, leveraging its flexible queries to empower your users, and its declarative structure to simplify your code. Absinthe is the GraphQL toolkit for Elixir, a functional programming language designed to enable massive concurrency atop robust application architectures. Written by the creators of Absinthe, this book will help you take full advantage of these two groundbreaking technologies. Build your own flexible, high-performance APIs using step-by-step guidance and expert advice you won't find anywhere else.

Bruce Williams and Ben Wilson
(302 pages) ISBN: 9781680502558. $47.95
https://pragprog.com/book/wwgraphql

Functional Web Development with Elixir, OTP, and Phoenix

Elixir and Phoenix are generating tremendous excitement as an unbeatable platform for building modern web applications. For decades OTP has helped developers create incredibly robust, scalable applications with unparalleled uptime. Make the most of them as you build a stateful web app with Elixir, OTP, and Phoenix. Model domain entities without an ORM or a database. Manage server state and keep your code clean with OTP Behaviours. Layer on a Phoenix web interface without coupling it to the business logic. Open doors to powerful new techniques that will get you thinking about web development in fundamentally new ways.

Lance Halvorsen
(218 pages) ISBN: 9781680502435. $45.95
https://pragprog.com/book/lhelph

The Pragmatic Bookshelf

The Pragmatic Bookshelf features books written by developers for developers. The titles continue the well-known Pragmatic Programmer style and continue to garner awards and rave reviews. As development gets more and more difficult, the Pragmatic Programmers will be there with more titles and products to help you stay on top of your game.

Visit Us Online

This Book's Home Page
https://pragprog.com/book/phoenix14
Source code from this book, errata, and other resources. Come give us feedback, too!

Keep Up to Date
https://pragprog.com
Join our announcement mailing list (low volume) or follow us on twitter @pragprog for new titles, sales, coupons, hot tips, and more.

New and Noteworthy
https://pragprog.com/news
Check out the latest pragmatic developments, new titles and other offerings.

Save on the eBook

Save on the eBook versions of this title. Owning the paper version of this book entitles you to purchase the electronic versions at a terrific discount.

PDFs are great for carrying around on your laptop—they are hyperlinked, have color, and are fully searchable. Most titles are also available for the iPhone and iPod touch, Amazon Kindle, and other popular e-book readers.

Buy now at *https://pragprog.com/coupon*

Contact Us

Online Orders:	*https://pragprog.com/catalog*
Customer Service:	*support@pragprog.com*
International Rights:	*translations@pragprog.com*
Academic Use:	*academic@pragprog.com*
Write for Us:	*http://write-for-us.pragprog.com*
Or Call:	+1 800-699-7764